RAP
ON
RAP

RAP
ON
RAP

STRAIGHT-UP TALK ON HIP-HOP CULTURE

EDITED AND WITH AN INTRODUCTION BY
ADAM SEXTON

Delta
Trade Paperbacks

A Delta Book

Published by
Dell Publishing
a division of
Bantam Doubleday Dell Publishing Group, Inc.
1540 Broadway
New York, New York 10036

Permissions appear on pp. 266–270.

Design by Jeffrey L. Ward

Library of Congress Cataloging in Publication Data
Rap on rap : straight-up talk on hip-hop culture / [compiled] by Adam Sexton.
    p.   cm.
  ISBN 0-385-31247-4
  1. Rap (Music)—History and criticism.   I. Sexton, Adam.
ML3531.R35 1995
782.42164–dc20   94-29168
                                     CIP
                                     MN

Manufactured in the United States of America
Published simultaneously in Canada

April 1995

10 9 8 7 6 5 4 3 2 1

BVG

For Kira

Shout-Outs

For getting this party started right, thanks to my editor, Betsy Bundschuh. For rapping with me about hip-hop, thanks to Kira Budoff, Paul Chrystie, Harvard's Lynne Layton, Ann Marlowe, Susan McClary of McGill University, Jeff Salamon of *The Village Voice*, Deb Schwartz, Robert Walser at Dartmouth, and Richard Weisman. Thanks to the staff of the Periodicals Room at the Main Branch of the Brooklyn Public Library, and to the libraries of Yale University. Thanks to Judy McCoy for *Rap Music in the 1980s*. For listening to the music with me from back in the day, thanks to Sly, Brian, Jules, Wayne, and Steve at the Federal Courthouse on Foley Square, to Jeff and Danny at the *Times*, and to Billy Reichbach and Michael Weisman. Thanks to Nick Malfitani, cowriter of "What It Is," for the chicken-scratch guitar and for his friendship. Thanks to the Schubert sisters for *3 Feet High and Rising*. Thanks to Campbell Whitford, for teaching me everything I know about music. Thanks to Robert Farris Thompson, for the best class I ever attended. Thanks to Liz Rosenberg, for her assistance with my Introduction. Thanks to Camille Paglia, for her encouragement. Props to Dave Marsh, as always. Thanks to Amy Pierpont, to Bantam Doubleday Dell's Suzanne Telsey for her sage legal counsel, and to Evan Boorstyn at Dell Publicity. Speaking of publicity, thank *you*, Madonna. Thanks to the creators of the works collected herein. For fa-

cilitating beyond the call of duty, thanks to Kristin Crawford *(The Recorder)*, The Indefatigable Kate Duffy *(Spin)*, Lisa Ely *(Chicago Citizen)*, Liz Haberfeld (the Cartoon Bank), Pat Kratz (University Presses of New England), Taneshia Nash Laird (Posro Komics), Linda Rath *(Vibe)*, Deirdre Robinson *(Essence)*, and Ursula Williams (40 Acres and a Mule Filmworks). For more than I can mention (quite literally), thanks to James Sexton, and thanks to my mother and especially my father.

Thanks, finally, to the Hip-hop Nation—and most of all to Kurtis Blow, Grandmaster Flash and the Furious Five, Africa Bambaataa, the Beastie Boys, Ice-T, Public Enemy, Neneh Cherry, 3rd Bass, De La Soul, Black Sheep, Queen Latifah, Digital Underground, Del the Funky Homosapien, PM Dawn, and the Goats, each of whom led me back to the fold when I strayed. It won't happen again.

Contents

"After all the history that we've been through, this is where we're at?"

—Wynton Marsalis

"It's no fad, man. And it's not just a new kind of music. It's a whole new subculture that's been invented by the disenfranchised. . . . It may be profane and abrasive, but I think it's a very powerful and positive force. And it's the freshest thing that's happened musically in thirty years."

—Quincy Jones

"So long as there's different types of music, rap will always be around. Besides, there will always be people that can't sing."

—Fresh Prince

RAP
ON
RAP

As the girl walked in she pulled off her hood.
Had a pang in my stomach, this would come to no good.
This was not *any* girl I had met in the wood—
I was trifling with Little Red Rappinghood.

Don't Believe the Hype: Why Isn't Hip-hop Criticism Better?

by Adam Sexton

Rap is not a critics' music,
it is a disciples' music.

—*Los Angeles Times*, August 28, 1990

Speak for yourself.

On the other hand, at least the "critic" quoted above admits that rap is *music*. That's more than can be said for most of the form's detractors—and, I would venture, even some of its fans.

After all, rap is music without melody. Of course, the digital samples that fuel all but the

most Spartan hip-hop tracks contain bits of melodies from scavenged songs. For that matter, the best rap, like a Pentecostal preacher's sermon or lyric poetry read aloud—like speech itself—can be truly songlike. The majority of contemporary pop is barely melodic anyhow; stripped of beat and lyrics, most rock-and-roll and rhythm-and-blues songs wilt like a balloon three days after the party, as anyone who's ever paid attention to Muzak knows.

But nobody actually *sings* rap songs, goes the argument; isn't that a contradiction in terms? Correct me if I'm wrong, but there's no singing in Glenn Miller's "In the Mood," or "Tequila," either. Godfather of Soul James Brown isn't exactly known for his golden throat, and Bob Dylan . . . You get the point.

Finally, most hip-hop music isn't even played with "real" musical instruments, though why anyone would consider a digital sampler less of an instrument than Keith Emerson's synthesizer—or Eric Clapton's electric guitar—is a mystery. (It might be worth mentioning here that Beethoven's Fifth was the first symphony to use the trombone. The saxophone wasn't invented until the 1840s. Music changes.) Try cutting and scratching on your home turntable sometime the way Grandmaster Flash does on "Wheels of Steel," and then tell me he isn't an instrumentalist just as virtuosic as Wynton Marsalis—and vastly more inventive. Are the Bomb Squad not equal as orchestrators to Rimsky-Korsakov? (Hmm, *Rimsky*, not a bad tag for a rapper, that.) You can have your *Boris Godunov*—I'll take *AmeriKKKa's Most Wanted*.

Nevertheless, it's understandable that hip-hop has been on the defensive since the moment it burst into the public consciousness a decade and a half ago. Add the fact that to this day the form is made predominantly by young black males, our society's least-trusted, least-respected element by a long shot, and you have a recipe for not just defensiveness but clinical paranoia. There is no loyalty comparable to that of the beseiged for what they defend—and rap is certainly beseiged. The image from *Do the Right Thing* of Sal's baseball bat descending upon the boom box of Radio Raheem (reproduced in this book in the form of director Spike Lee's original storyboards) sums things up pretty accurately, I'd say. Thus, "a disciples' music."

But why not "a critics' music" too? Is the charge even valid? Or is it comparable to the oft-heard assertion that white teenagers from the 'burbs comprise the majority of the genre's audience? (*Rap on Rap* con-

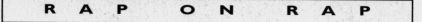

tributor Tricia Rose has convincingly argued that sales of bootleg tapes in poor urban areas combined with a high "pass-along rate" among black and Hispanic teen consumers make these statistics invalid anyway.) Is the claim made in the quote above just another means—albeit a marginally more sophisticated one—by which to question the form's very legitimacy?

My answer is that *of course* rap is "a critics' music." At the same time I would suggest that the critics themselves, for the most part, have failed to treat it as such. Straight up: most hip-hop criticism is either ill-informed rap-bashing of the it's-not-even-music! variety alluded to earlier or, at the other end of the spectrum, your basic cheerleading. If hip-hop itself wishes to be taken as seriously by the culture at large as, say, jazz and film, this must change.

Don't get me wrong. I'm delighted by every one of the critical responses to hip-hop culture collected here. And I'm honored to be the editor of a book that contains contributions by heavyweights like Henry Louis Gates, Jr., and Andrew Ross, who offer commentary on 2 Live Crew and Ice-T, respectively; personal-fave critics Greg Tate ("What Is Hip-hop?"), Danyel Smith ("Why Women Rappers Don't Sell"), and Ann Marlowe ("The Hermeneutics of Rap"); and columnists the likes of Barbara Grizzuti Harrison, Mike Royko, and William Safire (on women-hating, cop-killing, and the etymology of *dope*, respectively).

There's also a chunk of Nelson George's hip-hop novel *Urban Romance*—not to mention the words of the rappers themselves: Run-DMC, Ice Cube, Luke of 2 Live Crew, Ice-T, and Paris. This collection easily could have been twice as long as it is. And yet, I'm sorry to report that the passionate but thoughtful takes on the topic that comprise *Rap on Rap* are the exception rather than the rule. During the course of my research I looked at between nine and ten thousand pieces that mention rap in one context or another, from the most likely sources (that is, well, *The Source*, who devised this book's astonishingly difficult hip-hop quiz) to the least (*Footwear News*). And in general I'm disappointed by what I found.

The fact is, though some writing on rap entertained me, precious little beyond what you'll find collected here really taught me anything about the genre. Furthermore—and this remains the biggest letdown of all—almost nothing I read *surprised* me.

I can't say, for instance, that I ran across anything comparable to

Nelson George on R&B in *The Death of Rhythm and Blues*—the theme of which being dashed hopes, or at least dreams deferred. (The opportunity has certainly presented itself for such a response, as anyone familiar with De La Soul's second and third albums can attest.) For that matter, where's the hip-hop analogue to a review by heavy-metalologist Chuck Eddy praising Debbie Gibson to the skies? Okay: Harry Allen says in a *Village Voice* review from a few years back that he loves Jazzy Jeff and the Fresh Prince.

In spite of the widely held misapprehension that critics get into the game to slash and bash, the opposite is of course true; they're diehard devotees, followers, *fans*. And a fan's notes on the object of his/her passion can be the most satisfying criticism of all. But love must be leavened a little—in criticism, at least—with reason. Otherwise, a review becomes so imbalanced that it totters, tips, and then topples, resounding with the crash of a tree falling in a deserted forest.

The very best hip-hop criticism examines its subject from every angle. Greg Tate on Public Enemy is a model of the form: "To know PE is to love the agitprop (and artful noise) and to worry over the whack retarded philosophy they espouse," he has written;

. . . PE are obviously making it up as they go along. Since PE show sound reasoning when they focus on racism as a tool of the U.S. power structure, they should be intelligent enough to realize that dehumanizing gays, women, and Jews isn't going to set black people free. . . . For now swallowing the PE pill means taking the bitter with the sweet, and if they don't grow up, later for they asses.

In *Rap on Rap*, both Joan Morgan's "Nigga Ya Hate to Love" and "Those T.I.R.E.D. Acronyms" by Mimi Valdés manage, in very different ways, to express love for the music and frustration with it at the very same time.

Compare that with something far more typical. In a three-hundred-plus-word *Vibe* review of *Doggystyle* ("a pretty damn fine album"—and it is, in many respects), all of one sentence is devoted to Snoop Doggy Dogg's relentless misogyny: "As for the 'bitch this, ho that' rhymes that make up the bulk of *Doggystyle* (and the ghastly cover cartoon), they're mostly wearying and obnoxious."

"Mostly wearying and obnoxious"? I mean, if these rhymes "make up the bulk" of the album, doesn't that merit more than a single rote (not to mention parenthetical) allusion? What's "mostly wearying and ob-noxious" is the refusal by so many hip-hop critics to give the music a good hard listen, celebrate what succeeds with every faculty at their dis-posal—and come down on what doesn't with the same strength and smarts. As it is, claims are often made that the music (and lyrics) can't support. Plus, a critic-who-cried-wolf syndrome is in effect: when some-thing genuinely remarkable comes along, it's hard to tell.

Why such an imbalanced approach?

Hip-hop foregrounds race relentlessly, and not just in manifestations as extreme as albums by X-Clan and Brand Nubians, but every time a rapper utters the word *nigga*. (The same is not necessarily true of all black forms, or artists. Because of her deep roots in gospel and sixties soul, everything Aretha Franklin has ever recorded seems to resonate with racial implications. I would argue that the same is true of Donna Summer, because disco is a music of the disenfranchised and dispos-sessed: blacks, gays, women. But, to continue the analogy, Whitney Houston's breathtakingly bland music denies race—any race—and in its ceaseless *reaching*, both literal and metaphorical, it ironically denies her prodigious gifts, as well.)

Even white rap is about race; *à la* Living Colour's wailing, bashing exposé of just how lily-white the heavy metal genre is, Caucasian rap-pers like 3rd Bass and Snow make the basic blackness of hip-hop that much more apparent. Is race as fundamental an issue in the writing about rap as in the music itself, even if it isn't mentioned explicitly in most reviews? Is it, in a way, the unspoken topic of all hip-hop criti-cism?

Perhaps some black critics fear that they will be accused of disloyalty if they criticize freely—though this clearly isn't the case with *Rap on Rap* contributors Calvin Butts, Brent Staples, and Jesse Jackson. Such a response would be understandable; again, hip-hop has been embattled since the second it broke out. Back in the day, solidarity was a *necessity*. Rap was fighting for its life. (Nor was its success a foregone conclusion; R.I.P., graffiti and break dancing.)

In addition, there may be other, extra–hip-hop pressures on black critics of the form. African-American writer bell hooks has written (in the anthology *Black Popular Culture*) that, within her community, the work she does is frequently "resisted and resented":

As a cultural critic who writes and talks about black pop-ular culture . . . I often confront audiences that are en-

**raged by rigorous critique that does not simply celebrate
any work done by a black artist or cultural worker. This
hostility surfaces for several reasons. It is rooted both in
the general fear and suspicion of intellectuals and in the
traditional black modes of practicing the art of critique,
which make it appear solely a negative act.**

"As long as many black folks see critique solely in negative terms,"
hooks concludes, "the work of black critics will be misunderstood and
devalued."

What about white hip-hop critics, who, because of greater access to
mainstream media, are perhaps even more visible than black writers on
rap? Certainly some are afraid of being labeled racists if they question,
much less condemn, a hip-hop performance or even an aspect of one.
Too, there's a fascination with and attraction to black culture on the
part of many young whites, most famously documented in Norman
Mailer's essay "The White Negro" and James Baldwin's response to it
("The Black Boy Looks at the White Boy"), that may often mitigate a
clear-headed appraisal by whites of black cultural artifacts like rap
records. One well-known writer privately calls this trend "white boy
ass-kissing," but I think the phenomenon is more complicated than
that.

Since the release of "Rapper's Delight" in 1979, white pop performers have been "borrowing" hip-hop for a variety of purposes. Clearly,
Blondie's Deborah Harry and Chris Stein recorded "Rapture" because
in downtown New York in 1980, hip-hop equaled hip. (Remember
when the work of graffiti artists was being shown in SoHo galleries, and
dance troupes incorporated breaking and electric boogaloo into their
programs?) Blondie was admirably conscientious about giving props to
Fab 5 Freddy and Grandmaster Flash in the song's lyrics, and the band
made an excellent record that introduced rap, albeit in a diluted form,
to Middle America. Still, they were appropriating rap because of what it
signified about *them*.

Sinéad O'Connor has "used" hip-hop too: she once appeared on a
Grammy Awards telecast with a Public Enemy logo shaved into her
crew cut, she teamed up with MC Lyte on a remix of O'Connor's "Lay
Your Hands on Me," and she sampled rap's ubiquitous "Funky
Drummer" beat for her song "I Am Stretched on Your Grave." But
O'Connor appropriates the form to signify not a smug aesthetic know-
ingness but rather her brand of semiradical politics, the general resis-

tance to the status quo that is far more prevalent among young whites in Britain and her native Ireland than here.

Although there have been women rappers from the very beginning, O'Connor is also donning a mantle of "maleness"—or at least attributes like independence and potency that are stereotypically associated with maleness—when she takes on rap trappings. (Prince was after the same effect when he began adding rap to his music six or seven years ago; at first, it was not he but the women in his band that did all the rapping, with the result that they became as tantalizingly androgynous as he.)

Finally, and perhaps most obviously, what white performers are after when they incorporate hip-hop into their music—or their personae—is sheer blackness, with all that concept implies. Think of Paula Abdul's "Straight Up," which displays as many "signs" of blackness as a genuine rap record—which "Straight Up" is not, and very clearly does not aspire to be. The song's inventive arrangement combines an astonishingly supple New Jack (New Jill?) Swing beat, a call-and-response exchange between voice and what sounds like a synthesized trombone, and jittery, sampled electronic percussion behind the bridge.

Abdul's vocal performance is a virtually seamless collage of R&B singing and legitimate rap, which vary in proportion to each other with every bar of music. A high point of "Straight Up" is her stuttered "b-b-b-b-bye b-b-b-b-bye"—a clever parody of deejay scratch technique, and an allusion as well to the "human beat-box" phenomenon, which also vocally reproduces a technologically reproduced performance. (It's a little like a pre-Restoration performance of As You Like It, in which a boy played a girl playing a boy.)

The "Straight Up" video, shot not incidentally in lustrous *black-and-white* by virtuoso director David Fincher, opens with Abdul tap-dancing sans musical accompaniment; this abets the song's swing feel, as do later shots of a boogying stand-up bassist, stylistically correct though musically anomalous. (Both, of course, function as pre–hip-hop signifiers of blackness.) When Abdul, who has now reminded us subtly that she choreographed the video clips that made Janet Jackson a crossover star, slides to her knees at the conclusion of this prologue, the sound of a needle careering across vinyl segues into the tune itself, and introduces its hip-hop elements handily. A vertically split backdrop of black and white corresponds visually to "Straight Up" 's rap/singing dichotomy in addition to its theme of race. And then there's that cameo by Arsenio Hall, who, despite everything else, is after all the man who brought hip-hop to the late-night talk show. (Woof woof.)

All evidence to the contrary, by clip's end you're wondering if perhaps Paula Abdul is, well, *black*. Light skinned, maybe, like Vanessa Williams, Lonette McKee. Jennifer Beals. And that is precisely the intent of "Straight Up." For prior to the dopey duets with cartoon cats, the Bob Fosse *hommages* and *Rebel*-ripoffs, Abdul was sold to a black audience with performances on *Showtime at the Apollo* and songs like "Knocked Out." Having established a fan base among black listeners, all her record company then had to do was push Paula's (actual) whiteness (note the synthesized string quartet break in "Cold Hearted") for complete media saturation. Nothing like crossing over to where you started from in the first place.

My point? I believe that many white writers on hip-hop are using the form for their own purposes in precisely the same manner as the performers mentioned here—that is, to amass by association an aura of hip, resistance, maleness, and/or blackness. (Of course there are exceptions; *Rap on Rap*'s Jon Pareles has written adoringly about music as unhip as Argentine tangos and Celtic reels, so I trust him, and it seems unlikely to me that the eminently sensible Anna Quindlen desires to be down with the homeboys.) Whatever the legitimacy of their goals, Blondie, O'Connor, and Abdul have achieved satisfying, or at least intriguing, results through the process of appropriating rap and rap signifiers. I wish the same could be said for most white rap critics.

Announcing in the spring of 1994 that *The Source* would be presenting a Lyricist of the Year prize at its then-new annual awards ceremony, the magazine's spokesman seemed really to be talking about vocal delivery—something *entirely* different. I wondered, at the time, Does *The Source* plan to honor the rapper who writes the "best" words (because that's what lyrics basically are) or the one who declaims them most effectively, or both, or what?

Let's at least begin to draw distinctions among hip-hop music's basic components:

1. the crucial backing tracks (including, but not always limited to, samples)
2. lyrics
3. a rapper's delivery or "flow"—articulation, phrasing, and the like—and
4. everything else, more or less: "look," originality, aura of legitimacy, charisma. The hard-to-quantify stuff.

Snoop Doggy Dogg's arguably the most inventive vocalist in popular music since Sam Cooke. But that doesn't make the brutality of Snoop's "mostly wearying and obnoxious" lyrics any less abhorrent. Big Daddy Kane, too, possesses virtuosic talent as a rapper, as well as an outsize persona, but Kane's killer chops are rarely equaled by the banal music behind him.

By the same token, everybody knows that M.C. Hammer was once a dazzling performer, even if he couldn't rap for shit. (As newly hard Hammer, he doesn't seem able to do either.) Diggable Planets and De La Soul *blow* as emcees per se, yet the unique worldview of each renders that point moot—and the samples of De La often are a revelation. Public Enemy are a triumph of casting; their (if you will) good cop–bad cop act remains unequaled, even by the one-two punch of Digital Underground's Humpty Hump and Shock G. PE are profoundly musical, too, an attribute many mistake for just plain profundity. There's a difference, though. And recognizing it—recognizing all of these differences—might be the key to a more probing hip-hop criticism.

In other words, just because I'm barely aware of the lyrics on an album like Del the Funky Homosapien's *No Need For Alarm* doesn't mean the music (including the music in Del's voice) is not mesmerizing. Just because Ice-T's word choice isn't especially striking doesn't mean I'm not riveted by the content of his message. (Just check out "The Controversy" in Part 3 of this book if you disagree.) L.L. Cool J's shtick is tiresome at this point. His delivery always wakes me up.

Is it reasonable of me to submit that a rudimentary knowledge of instrumentation and notation ought to be evinced by a hip-hop review? After all, the great majority of rock and roll writing has forever been wholly ignorant of what would seem to be the essence of the form—that is, the music. (Hey—why bother when you can discuss those *heavy lyrics*, man?)

Yet the best hip-hop is vastly more complex, musically, than all but the rarest rock song; for evidence of this, see *Rap on Rap* contributor Robert Walser's essay on the sounds of Public Enemy, forthcoming in *Ethnomusicology*—perhaps the most remarkable analysis of rap music ever written. It's a shame, therefore, that hip-hop's advocates often aren't capable of making the best case for the music they love. I mean, at least know that it's a minor key making those Dr. Dre jams sound "spooky" or "foreboding," that syncopation is what's happening when Queen Latifah's words seem to be "struggling against the beat." Know what sixteenth notes are (cf. the programmed bass-drum pattern in

Herbie Hancock's "Rockit"), and swing time ("La Di Da Di" by Doug E. Fresh).

What *is* sampling, anyway? How does it work? (J.D. Considine offers an abbreviated, opinionated answer to these questions in his Part 1 essay "Larcenous Art?") Hip-hop is intensely postmodern; in fact, it exemplifies *postmodern* better than any form I know—including contemporary architecture, the discipline that gave us the term in the first place. A hip-hop critic therefore must strive to know the sources of samples, which means at least gaining familiarity with 1970s funk—and with classic disco. Houston Baker's claims to the contrary notwithstanding, rap has more in common with disco than most rappers would care to admit. Some hard-rock literacy wouldn't hurt, either, nor would having a clue or two about jazz. Not to mention those French language instruction records.

Otherwise, the allusions fundamental to a complete understanding of many hip-hop narratives will be lost on the writer. The realization that it samples from "Mothership Connection" makes Dr. Dre's "Let Me Ride" enormously less parochial than it might otherwise seem. Recognizing that P.M. Dawn's "The Beautiful" lifts a piece of "Baby You're a Rich Man" by the Beatles lends the track an ironic spin. PE sample the sung *I*—and only the *I*—from Bob Marley's "I Shot the Sheriff" and add it to the maelstrom that is "Fight the Power"—chew on *that* for a moment. Even Vanilla Ice benefits from a little thought regarding the sources of his samples: "Ice Ice Baby" recapitulates "Under Pressure" by Queen— the very band whose 1980 hit "Another One Bites the Dust" quoted the bass line from "Rapper's Delight," which in turn ripped off Chic's "Good Times." Didn't I say it all goes back to disco?

Poetry: it's a truism that Rakim is a rap poet, but *why* are his verses so compelling when, say, KRS-One's put you to sleep? Black Sheep's Mista Lawnge has said that "if people paid closer attention in English class when they were talking about literature, if they knew what a good poem or a good short story was, they'd know what a good rap song was," and that's at least partly true. Examine Kool Moe Dee's introduction to the all-star version of the jazz-fusion classic "Birdland" on Quincy Jones's *Back on the Block*—a choice I make because no album has ever been more explicit about rap's aspirations to be taken seriously as an art form. Does Kool Moe Dee make the grade?

A tribute to the Birdman,
The father of Birdland,

A masterpiece of release:
The homes's words and
The musical greats
Salute the late
Mentor, inventor
Of a sound that dates
Back from bebop to pop
And pop to hip-hop.
We fused the times
Of jazz and rhymes and got
Kool Moe Dee and Big Daddy Kane
To bring on the legends.
Kane, hit the names!

In academic terms this passage employs a genuinely sophisticated rhyme scheme (AABA-CCDC-EEFE-GHG). It contains rhymes both masculine (greats/late/dates, etc.) and feminine (birdman/birdland/words and); assonantal (birdman/birdland, hip-hop/got, Kane/names) and consonantal (salute/the late). It is rife with internal rhyme (masterpiece/release, salute/the late, mentor/inventor, pop/hip-hop, Kane/names). Finally, Kool Moe Dee's rap contains a remarkable degree of enjambment (eight lines out of fifteen)—this is no singsong nursery rhyme. In fact, it's much denser, certainly, and more sophisticated in its use of the devices of prosody than the rock and folk songs generally accepted as most "poetic."

Ditto Eric B. and Rakim's "I Ain't No Joke":

I ain't no joke. I used to let the mic smoke;
Now I slam it when I'm done and make sure it's broke.
When I'm gone, no one gets on, 'cause I won't let
Nobody press up and mess up the scene I set.
I like to stand in the crowd and watch the people wonder:
"Damn!" But think about it. Then you'll under-
Stand I'm just an addict addicted to music.
Maybe it's a habit; I gotta use it.

Now, as Tricia Rose has written,

Simply to recite or read the lyrics to a rap song is not to understand them; they are also inflected with the syn-

copated rhythms and sampled sounds of the music. The music, its rhythmic patterns, and the idiosyncratic articulation by the rapper are essential to the song's meanings.

And I couldn't agree more. But the fact is, the best of the genre stands up to traditional artistic criteria, and, more germane to this discussion, those criteria might help illuminate the work.

Of course, the argument could be made that what I'm suggesting hip-hop critics employ are Western techniques of critical scrutiny, techniques that are therefore irrelevant to hip-hop—a decidedly non-Western form, as Khephra Burns emphasizes in his *Essence* essay "Words from the Motherland," greatly expanded for use in this book. But if hip-hop is to be generally acknowledged as in every way the equal of established modes, it will have to fight those modes on their own turf.

Or will it? An obvious alternative would be to disengage from this sort of contest altogether. Fair enough. Then hip-hop critics must invent an *alternate* critical approach, one that doesn't avail itself of Western musical notation or English poetic sound-and-sense jargon—but doesn't lean on twelve-car pileups of adjectives to make its case either.

Like any great art, the best hip-hop resists easy description. That's one of the things that make it great. Performance artist Laurie Anderson once told me that if she knew precisely what her work meant, she'd just write that down on a piece of paper and call it quits. It's not easy to comprehend all the complexity and contradiction contained in a song by N.W.A., Warren G, or even an ostensibly "pop" act like Salt-N-Pepa, much less put that into words on paper.

But hip-hop demands that the effort be made. Like bebop, hip-hop deconstructs its sources (à la, as you're probably tired of hearing by now, Coltrane's "My Favorite Things"), pinching a Led Zep beat here, a James Brown yelp there, maybe a catch phrase from a TV rerun or a snippet from one of Malcolm X's speeches. Hip-hop is like punk rock, too, in that anyone can grab a mike and do it—do it him-herself. (Whether anyone can do it *well* is another question, and I think we know the answer.) And hip-hop is like doo-wop (that is, the a cappella harmonizing of the earliest doowoppers), in that it doesn't require musical instruments; arguably, it doesn't even require the traditional two-turntables-and-a-crate-of-records, just a steady beat (handclaps, anyone?) and some kind of rhyming ability.

As many have pointed out, neither instruments nor training was *available* to the inventors of the form, and the fact that rap's founders made music anyway speaks of the profound need on the part of human beings to express themselves artistically, whatever it takes. Rap shares much with its sometime hip-hop handmaidens graffiti and break dancing—plugging your system into a streetlight is a lot like painting a subway car in the train yard by night or spinning on your head on a piece of cardboard on the sidewalk. In other words, hip-hop is resourceful, audacious, perhaps even truly heroic.

That's why it deserves better than the half-assed writing so often perpetrated in its name—deserves, in fact, a criticism as innovative, and yet as rigorous, as the best rap music itself. My hope is that the material in this collection—the best of the best gleaned from the thousands of reviews, profiles, columns, editorials, comics, cartoons, poems, papers, lists, quizzes, legal documents, TV transcripts, and the like that have appeared since hip-hop happened—will serve as a model for future efforts at reacting to the music and culture.

Of course, I hope it will be fun to read, as well.

Enjoy.

(1995)

PART I

Looking for the
Perfect Beat

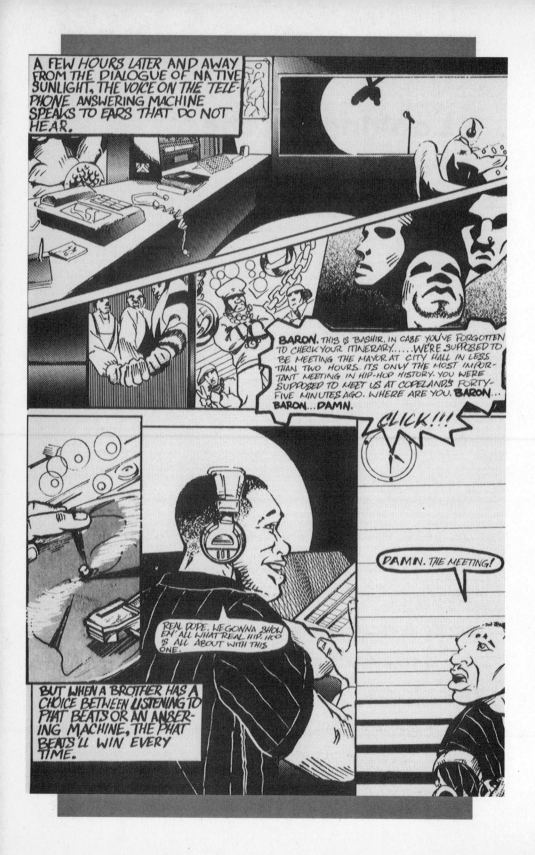

What Is Hip-hop?

by Greg Tate

To beg the question is not to seek answers but to riddle a paradox with a host of non sequiturs. This shotgun manifesto was originally conceived by dream hampton and myself as a means to end simpleminded conceptions of hip-hop that pervade the culture from within and without. I've

been reading the following piece on the lecture circuit and in Downtown New York poetry venues like Fez for the past year. dream's contribution to this encyclopedic narrative is forthcoming. On this there are more words yet to be manifested.

Buddha blessed and boo-ya blasted,
These are the words that she manifested.
A grim little tyke in a black pleather raincoat.
She stepped to the mike and said,
Repeat after me, there is no such thing as alternative hip-
    hop.
So Boo in the blue silk hoody pops up,
Hey baby you'd be a good-looking man if you worked at it
    but what the fuck you know about hip-hop?
Why he go and say that?
She said, I know hip-hop like I know your mother.
Your mother so hip-hop, I seen her laying pipe in Alaska.
Your mother so hip-hop, she yelled ho 'fo I even axed
    her.
Your mother so hip-hop, she thinks Biz Markie's cute as
    shit.
Your mother so hip-hop, she told you, time to get off your
    dick.
Next time you speak to mother, send her my best.

Buddha blessed and boo-ya blasted.
These are the words that she manifested:
Hip-hop is inverse capitalism.
Hip-hop is reverse colonialism.
Hip-hop is the world the slaveholders made, sent into
    nigga-fide future shock.
Hip-hop is the plunder from down under, mackin' all oth-
    ers for pleasure.
Hip-hop is the black aesthetic by-product of the
American dream machine, our culture of consumption,
    commodification, and subliminal seduction.
Where George Clinton warned us about Madison
Avenue urge overkill, the pimping of the pleasure princi-
    ple, hip-hop embraces the pleasures of the pimping
    principle.

Hip-hop is the first musical movement in history where black people pimped themselves before the white boy did.

Hip-hop pimped the funk before the white boy and heavy metal too.

Hip-hop is the perverse logic of capitalism pursued by an artform.

Like capitalism, hip-hop converts raw soul into store-rack commodity.

Like capitalism, hip-hop has no morals, no conscience, and no ecological concern for the scavenged earth or the scavenged American minds it will wreck in its pursuit of new markets.

Unlike Sigourney Weaver's nemesis Alien, hip-hop is not the other man's rape fantasy of the black sex machine gone berserk.

Hip-hop is James Brown's pelvis digitally grinded into technomorphine.

Hip-hop is dope-know-logy, the only known antidote for prime-time sensory deprivation.

There is no such thing as alternative hip-hop because the only alternative to hip-hop is dead silence and we all know such silence signifies a lack of breath.

There is no such thing as good hip-hop or bad hip-hop, progressive hip-hop or reactionary hip-hop, politically incorrect hip-hop or hip-hop with a message.

It's either hip-hop or it ain't. Shit.

Hip-hop is beyond good and evil, hip-hop is beyond life and death.

Hip-hop was dead but hip-hop reanimated.

Hip-hop does not live on *YO! MTV Raps*.

Hip-hop currently resides beneath the noise where all the fly girlz and boyz use hip-hop as a form of telemetry telepathy and telekinesis.

Hip-hop is how you say I love you to a hip-hop junkie.

Hip-hop is your password into the cult of hip-hop infomaniacs.

You know hip-hop when you see it.

You may not see hip-hop before it seizes you.

Hip-hop is not what it is today but what it could be to-morrow.

Hip-hop ain't shit but everything is hip-hoppable, mad flava beatable.

Hip-hop is Pumas and a hoody today but why not leather fringe and sequins tomorrow?

If hip-hop wanted to be that corny, who could argue with it but a muhfuhkuh who was faded?

What's hip-hop today could easily become passé.

Arguing with hip-hop about the nature of hip-hop is like arguing with water about the nature of wetness.

Like Bunny Wailer said, some tings come to ya, some tings come at 'cha but hip-hop flows right through ya.

Hip-hop is so far gone up its own ass you can't even speak on it unless you follow the trail of hip-hop's intestines out the lower end.

Hip-hop is the rattlesnake that bit off its own tail, then listened to the death rattle warning the head that it was swallowing up the body.

Hip-hop is what happened when the black community be-came the

Bermuda Triangle and lost track of itself on the radar screen of Reaganomics.

Hip-hop is the blip that boom-bipped then turned up to crack, black is back all in we're gonna exterminate our own next of kin.

Pink people wanna know if other pink people like hip-hop how can it still be hip-hop?

That's like asking, if black people like

Dirty Harry is he still Clint Eastwood?

Hip-hop is beyond black nationalism.

Hip-hop is not hung up on countersupremacy because it reigns supreme like all the other dope fiends.

Hip-hop is half black and half Japanese.

Hip-hop is digital chips on the shoulders of African lips.

Hip-hop is black Prozac.

Hip-hop is if you can't join 'em, beat 'em, if you can't beat 'em, blunt 'em.

Hip-hop is black sadomasochism.

Hip-hop is where the hurting ends and the feeling begins
  or is that the other way around?
Hip-hop is how we rip off the Band-Aids and pour salt-
  peter on the wounds.
Hip-hop is Ralph Ellison, who once said the blues is like
  running a razor blade along an open sore.

If it wasn't for black English and hip-hop I wouldn't have
  no blues at all.
Hip-hop is my black cat moan.
Hip-hop is my black cat scan.
Hip-hop is I need to stop.
It's time for my medicine.
Time to face the music again.
Buddha blessed and boo-ya blasted
These are the words that she manifested.

(November 1993)

Hip-hop History

from *The Source*

1. What are the four original components of hip-hop expression?

2. What was the name of Kool DJ Herc's crew?

3. Who was the original "Chief Rocker"?

4. What was Kurtis Blow's first record?

5. Name the Furious Five.

6. During what famous B-boy (break dancing) battle did the stage collapse?

7. Which DJ is widely credited with inventing "transforming"?

8. How was Run (of Run-DMC) originally billed?

9. Who was the first rapper signed to a major label?

10. What was the first record to bear the Def Jam logo?

11. What James Brown record is considered by many to be the B-boy anthem?

12. Name the first hip-hop artist to collaborate with James Brown and the record they created.

13. What was the first film to show the world B-boying (break dancing)?

14. Who directed the film *Wild Style?*

15. Who spells out his name in dollars in *Wild Style?*

16. Who compiled the seminal graffiti book *Subway Art?*

17. What was the name of the graf writer filmed in the kitchen with his mom in *Style Wars?*

18. Who were the two stars of *Breakin'?*

19. What cut did Ice-T perform on the *Breakin'* soundtrack?

20. Who produced the film *Beat Street?* Who directed it?

21. Who performed the fat cut "Santa's Rap" in the film *Beat Street?*

22. Who played Russell Simmons in *Krush Groove?*

23. What Prince protégée rapped on the *Krush Groove* theme song, along with Run-DMC, the Fat Boys and Kurtis Blow?

24. What rappers battled on the single episode of the 1984 television show "Graffiti Rock"?

25. Who was the first rap group to make a national TV appearance and on what show?

26. What was the first major network news program to document hip-hop?

27. What label released "Rockin' It" by the Fearless Four?

28. Who wrote lyrics for "Rapper's Delight" but was not credited?

29. Where was the original "writers' bench" in New York, a central gathering point for graffiti artists?

30. Who went on to success after winning a record deal in the Tin Pan Apple rap contest?

31. At what club did these famous battles take place: Cold Crush vs. Fantastic Five, Busy Bee vs. Kool Moe Dee?

32. What was the Force MD's original name?

33. Who was the first hip-hop artist to collaborate with a jazz artist on wax?

34. Who was the first real rapper to collaborate with an R&B artist?

35. What rapper opened up for the Commodores and Bob Marley at a seminal show at New York's Madison Square Garden?

36. Who was the host of the first rap radio show in New York? On what station and in what year?

37. This same station carried at least four other rap shows in the early '80s. Name one of them.

38. What was the first radio station in Los Angeles to play rap?

39. What was Ice Cube's first group, and what current producer was also in this group?

40. What was the title and label of the first Kid Frost record?

41. Name at least two of the influential DJs of the early LA crew Uncle Jam's Army?

42. Both members of the rap duo Dr. Jeckyl & Mr. Hyde went on to later success in the rap industry. What are their real names and current titles?

43. What was the first rap hit to use Billy Squier's ubiquitous "Big Beat"?

44. What was the first rap hit to use the slamming "Substitution" beat?

45. What was Oakland rapper Too Short's first label?

46. Who was the artist on the early Tommy Boy mix single known as "The Lessons"—featuring a cut-and-paste mix of G.L.O.B.E. & Whiz Kid's "Play That Beat Mr. DJ"?

47. Name the Beastie Boys' first and second DJs.

48. Name the first hip-hop record to use rock guitars, and the crew who recorded it. Hint: It wasn't Run-DMC.

49. Who were widely rumored to be the owners of the TROOP Gear clothing line, and what were the letters TROOP rumored to stand for—rumors which eventually caused the brand's death?

50. Who was TROOP Gear's most prominent celebrity endorser?

51. Name the original members of the Cold Crush Brothers. Hint: Don't go to their records. It's not the line-up that recorded under that name.

52. Now go to their records, and name all of the Cold Crush singles in order of release.

53. Which independent rap label was the first signed subsidiary of a major label, in what year did the deal begin, and with which major label?

54. Sure, the Sugar Hill Gang rapped over the bass, drums, and violins of "Good Times." However, what record was used for the *intro* of "Rapper's Delight"—the one that plays before "Good Times" starts?

55. Much is presently being made of Cypress Hill's endorsement of

marijuana. Name the seminal rapper who actually named himself after the plant.

56. Which member of the rock band Living Colour besides Vernon Reid is important to the history of recorded hip-hop, and why?

57. Name the L Brothers. Tell what the "L" stood for.

58. N.W.A. was not the first hip-hop crew to use the epithet *nigger* as part of its name. Although this first crew never recorded, their name is well known to true members of the original school. Who were they, and what did they do?

59. Speaking of expletives, upon which hip-hop recording do the words *bitch* and *pussy* both appear for the very first time?

60. What was the first case of hip-hop radio censorship, where rap lyrics had to be deleted for radio airplay? Name the censored record, and tell what was taken out.

61. Name Whitney Houston and the Human Beat Box's sole musical collaboration.

62. With which famously rotund athlete did the Fat Boys collaborate on a 12-inch single?

63. Which member of Whodini had a twin brother, and what was the brother's name?

64. The Whodini song "Magic's Wand" was a tribute to whom?

65. What record was the source of the "Oh My God!" on Doug E. Fresh's classic release "The Show"?

66. Name the record that Def Jam CEO Russell Simmons recorded as the sole vocalist.

67. Name Simmons's second recording effort.

68. Name the record upon the cover of which Tommy Boy president Monica Lynch posed dressed as the Statue of Liberty. Name the artists who recorded the record, and tell what significant ethnic first they established by recording together.

69. Name the title and artist of the only rap record to ever feature three MCs rhyming simultaneously.

70. Who did MC Shan accuse of stealing his beat on his "Beat Biter" single?

71. What is the name of hip-hop's first female solo recording artist and what was the name of her record?

72. Which well-known hip-hop artist sampled this record's intro on the intro of a popular single from his 1992 album?

73. In what year, and in a rap on what record, by whom, does what is perhaps the first reference in popular music to AIDS appear?

74. What was Bushwick Bill's original name and original role in the Geto Boys?

75. With which female rapper did MC Lyte exchange a "10% Dis"?

76. Name the MCs that rhyme on the Marley Marl posse cut "The Symphony."

77. On which record did Biz Markie make his first appearance?

78. What was Naughty by Nature's original name and label?

79. What hit from Dr. Dre's old group, the World Class Wreckin' Cru, featured Michel'le belting fat vocals?

80. Which group did Grand Puba belong to before Brand Nubian?

81. Which pioneering DJ from Philly was called "the green-eyed brother—brother with the green eyes"?

82. Before he teamed up with Hammer under the name Joey B. Ellis, what was this Philly MC known as?

83. On which independent label was Schoolly D's first single released?

84. From which record, by which artist, did the Flavor Unit get its name?

85. Who was Mantronik's MC on the hits "Fresh Is the Word" and "Simple Simon"?

86. What group did DJ Muggs belong to before Cypress Hill?

87. Name the members of Stetsasonic, the "hip-hop band."

88. Who rhymes last on "Self Destruction"?

89. What former gang member was the key force behind "We're All in The Same Gang"?

90. Which member of the Ultramagnetic MC's got his start doing the "electric boogie"?

91. What NBA team jacket was Moe Love of Ultra wearing on the cover of *Critical Beatdown*?

92. How was EPMD's name spelled on their first 12-inch single?

93. To which Texas-based group did the D.O.C. belong before he hooked up with Dr. Dre?

94. For which group did Funkmaster Flex originally DJ?

95. What artist was Pete Rock's first production on wax?

96. What talented producer/rapper first appeared on a cut called "Breaking Atoms"?

97. What was Brand Nubian's first video?

98. Who play the reporters in the classic PE video "Night of the Living Bassheads"?

99. Identify the main dancer in the EPMD "You Gots to Chill" video, and name his first single.

100. Who was the first rapper pictured on the cover of *The Source*?

ANSWERS

If you got more than 80 correct, you're a true hip-hop historian. More than 60, you're on point. Between 40 and 60, pretty cool. Between 20 and 40, just decent. Under 20, you need to brush up, kid.

1. DJing, MCing, graffiti writing, and B-boying (break-dancing). 2. The Herculoids. 3. Old School legend Busy Bee. 4. "Christmas Rappin'." 5. Scorpio, Cowboy, Melle Mel, Kid Creole, and Raheem. 6. Rock Steady v. Dynamic Rockers at Lincoln Center in August 1981. 7. DJ Jazzy Jeff. 8. "Son of Kurtis Blow." 9. Kurtis Blow on Mercury Records. 10. "It's Yours" by T La Rock and Jazzy Jay (produced by Rick Rubin). 11. "Give It Up or Turn It Loose." 12. Afrika Bambaataa collaborated with James on "Unity." 13. *Flashdance,* **featuring the Rock Steady Crew. 14. Charlie Ahearn. 15. Busy Bee. 16. Martha Cooper and Henry Chalfant. 17. Skeme-TNT. 18. Shabba Doo (Ozone) and Bugaloo Shrimp (Turbo). 19. "Reckless" with Chris "The Glove" Taylor. 20. Produced by Harry Belafonte and David V. Picker; directed by Stan Lathan, now an executive at** *Def Comedy Jam.* **21. The Treacherous Three and Doug E. Fresh. 22. Blair Underwood. 23. Shelia E. 24. Run-DMC v. Kool Moe Dee and Special K of the Treacherous Three. 25. The Funky 4 + 1 on** *Saturday Night Live* **in February, 1981. 26.** *20-20.* **27. Harlem-based Enjoy Records. 28. Grandmaster Caz of the Cold Crush Brothers. 29. 149th and Grand Concourse in the Bronx, where the 2's and 5's ran. 30. The Disco 3, later known as the Fat Boys. 31. Harlem World on 116th and Lenox. 32. The Force MCs; before that: the LDs. 33. D.ST., who got down with Herbie Hancock on "Rockit." 34. Melle Mel, on Chaka Kahn's "I Feel for You." 35. Kurtis Blow. 36. Mr. Magic on WHBI in 1980. 37. World Famous Supreme Team, Sweet G, the Awesome Two and Afrika Islam's "Zulu Beats" were all broadcast on WHBI, which later changed its call letters to WNWK. 38. KGFJ. 39. CIA; Sir Jinx. 40. "The Terminator" on Electro Beat Records. 41. Bobcat, Mr. Prince, Egyptian Lover, Dj Pooh. 42. Andre "Dr. Jeckyl" Harrell is CEO of Uptown Entertainment;**

Alonzo "Mr. Hyde" Brown is VP of Film and Television at Uptown Entertainment. 43. "Roxanne, Roxanne" by UTFO. 44. "Ego Trippin' " by the Ultramagnetic MC's. 45. 75 Girls Records. 46. Double Dee & Steinski. 47. Rick "DJ Double R" Rubin; then Dr. Dre of Original Concept/*Yo! MTV Raps* fame. 48. "Body Rock" by the Treacherous Three, 1981. 49. The Ku Klux Klan; Total Rule (or Reign) Over Oppressed People. 50. L.L. Cool J. 51. Tony-Tone, Easy A.D., Charlie Chase, Whipper-Whip, Mr. T, Dotarock. 52. "The Weekend," "Punk Rock Rap," "Fresh, Wild, Fly and Bold," "Heartbreakers." 53. Tuff City, 1983, EPA (Epic Portrait Associated). 54. "Here Comes That Sound" by Sun. 55. Eddie Cheba. 56. Bassist Doug Wimbush—he played for the Sugar Hill Records house band that made tracks for many of the label's early recordings. He was also involved in the recording of the "No Sell Out" Malcolm X single released by Tommy Boy in 1982. 57. Mean Gene and Grand Wizard Theodore; the *L* stood for Livingston, the brothers' last name. 58. The Nigger Twins—they were B-boys who made their reputations dancing at Kool Herc's parties. 59. "La-Di-Da-Di" by Doug E. Fresh and Slick Rick. 60. "Rapper's Delight"; Big Bank Hank/Grandmaster Caz's line: "He can't satisfy you with his little worm/ But I can bust you out with my super sperm." 61. "King Holiday" by the King Dream Chorus and Holiday Crew. 62. William "Refrigerator" Perry of the Chicago Bears. 63. Ecstasy has a brother named Dynasty. 64. Radio DJ Mr. Magic. 65. "Punk Rock Rap" by the Cold Crush Brothers. 66. "Chillin' at the Spot" by Jazzy Jay. 67. "That's a Lie," with L.L. Cool J on the *Radio* album. 68. "She's Wild" by Hiko and Peso. It was the first hip-hop recording collaboration of an African-American and a Japanese artist. 69. "Request Line" by Rockmaster Scott and the Dynamic Three. 70. L.L. Cool J. 71. Paula "Sweet Tee" Winley; "Vicious Rap." 72. Diamond D on "Best Kept Secret." 73. 1983; "Bad Times (I Can't Stand It)"; Captain Rapp. 74. He was called "Little Billy," and he was a dancer. 75. Antionette. 76. Masta Ace, Craig G, Big Daddy Kane, Kool G Rap. 77. "Get Retarded" by Roxanne Shante. 78. The New Style on Bon Ami/MCA Records. 79. The slamming "Turn Out the Lights." 80. Masters of Ceremony. 81. DJ Cash Money. 82. The Singing MC Breeze. 83. Schoolly D Records. 84. "This Cut's Got Flavor" by Latee. 85. MC Tee. 86. 7A3. 87. Daddy-O, Delite, Fruitkwon, Prince Paul, the DBC, Wise, and drummer Bobby Simmons. 88. Chuck D. 89. Michael Conception. 90. Kool Keith. 91. Boston Celtics. 92. EPee MD. 93. Fila Fresh Crew. 94. Deuces Wild. 95. Groove B Chill. 96. Large Professor. 97. "Feels So Good." 98. Chris Thomas and MC Lyte. 99. Stezo, who dropped the phat "It's My Turn" b/w "To the Max." 100. KRS-One.

TRIVIA EDITOR: Jon Schecter CONTRIBUTORS: Harry Allen (numbers 47–49, 51–61, 65–68, 71–73), Crazy Legs, Reginald C. Dennis, Jon Schecter, Pee Wee Dance, DJ Mighty M., Burn 1 and Mike Nardone (38–41).

The Source is the magazine of hip-hop music, culture and politics. Subscription rate: 1 year (12 issues), $19.95. Send orders to P.O. Box 586, Mt. Morris, IL 61054, (800) 827-0172.

(November 1993)

Word from the Motherland: Rap, the Dozens, and African Griots

by Khephra Burns

"Brothers!" my wife hollered. Neither of us could believe what we were seeing—Arsenio Hall and rapper Will Smith, the Fresh Prince, playing the "dozens," dissing each other's mama on late night television. It was a first. It was funny. And, thankfully, as the dozens go, it was G rated.

Playing the dozens is part of a long tradition of verbal shootouts, rap acrobatics, loud lying, and a lot of poetic license word-slinging brothers and sharp-tongued sisters have taken with the language. Be we preachers, players, or just plain folks, our ability to wield words with wit and rhythm has given us power when there was little within our grasp. We are a race of rappers from way back.

In the 1950s, when the brothers on my block were rhythmically slapping their chests and thighs, "doin' that crazy hand jive," it seemed as novel to us then as rap must have seemed to kids in the South Bronx a generation later. Come to find out, we were "rapping" in the 1850s— trading tall tales, handing out verbal abuse in rhymes, and providing our own rhythmic, chest-whacking, thigh-slapping accompaniment. Back then it was called "pattin' juba." Juba faded, only to resurface like a race memory a hundred years later. In the meantime the tradition of rhyming and trading insults evolved into "signifying," the "dozens," and epic tales called "toasts." At least one well-known rhyme from the folklore, the Signifying Monkey, has its roots in West African animal tales.

> **Signifyin' monkey told the lion one day,**
> **"There's a bad motherfucker comin' down your way.**
> **He talked about your family and I'm sorry to say,**
> **But he talked about your mama in a hell of a way.**
> **Talked about your sister and your grandma, too,**
> **And he didn't show too much respect for you. . . ."**

The lion goes off in search of the elephant whom the monkey says has been doing all this bad talking, and the elephant hands the lion a royal ass whipping. To make matters worse, it turns out the elephant wasn't even studyin' the lion.

Signifying is not widely condoned among right-thinking folks. In order to avoid charges of signifying and stirring up shit, folks carrying tales (gossiping, that is) will often swear, "If I'm lyin', I'm flyin'." Still, the tale of the signifying monkey acknowledges that the word is mightier than tooth and claw, and that those with little power can use language to manipulate and overcome the powerful.

Most toasts celebrated mythical badmen like Stagolee and tricksters like Shine. Stagolee (aka Stackalee, Stacker Lee, etc.) was the baddest

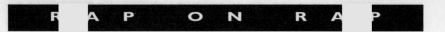

of the badmen—badder than Shaft, badder than Trouble Man, badder than anything L.L. Cool J could imagine. In some toasts he shoots Billy Lions, another badman, for cheating him at cards or dice. In others he shoots Billy just to prove which of them is the baddest. And in others still, he "perforates" the bartender and assorted others with "six .44 rockets" (bullets in typically phallic toast hyperbole) for daring to challenge him, verbally or otherwise. He breaks the white man's rules in grand style and flaunts power at the point of a gun for real-life black men who have no power. Stack's don't-give-a-damn attitude is summed up in the lines

> **I'm Stackalee**
> **Mean as can be.**
> **Trouble I crave.**
> **Born in a open grave**
> **When the earth quaked.**
> **Suckled by a black snake**
> **On poison and hoecake.**
> **Got no compassion,**
> **Ain't got no fears.**
> **The moans of widows and orphans**
> **Is music to my ears.**
> **I got a tombstone disposition**
> **And a graveyard mind.**
> **I'm a bad muthafucka**
> **'Cause I don't mind dyin'.***

Some of the impact of such toasts may be lost today when life too often and too tragically imitates art in our communities. Today, L.L. Cool J raps, "I explode / And my nine [millimeter handgun] is easy to load. . . ." (from "Mama Said Knock You Out"), but the vicarious experience of power through the toast or boast seems increasingly to be an insufficient fix for the pain of powerlessness. Especially when nine-year-olds can put their hands on a real nine-millimeter. In an article from the *Journal of American Folklore*, "Circus and Street: Psychological Aspects of the Black Toast," Bruce Jackson makes the case simply and succinctly that Stagolee's "style is not viable, for the population in the land of irrational badmen is constantly decreasing, and that is, in any society, intolerable."

From the author's play, *Stackalee

Unlike the badman, who cannot use words to cope with conflict—for whom, in fact, the words are typically unavailable—those who toasted them, and the rappers like L.L. Cool J who assume the badman persona, employ words as the weapon of choice. Likewise, tricksters, like Shine, use wit and cunning, guile and banter, to attain their goals, which are generally to get sex and to outsmart the white man. In the toast *"Titanic"* Shine outthinks the white folks, swims the ocean, outswims sharks, and (untypically) even resists the temptations of the flesh in order to save his ass when the great *Titanic* hits an iceberg and sinks.

All the old folks say
The fourth of May was a hell of a day.
I was in a little seaport town
And the great *Titanic* was goin' down.
Now the sergeant and the captain was havin' some
**   words**
When all of sudden they hit that iceberg.
Up come Shine from down below,
Sayin' "Captain, Captain, you don't know,
We got nine feet of water over the boiler room floor."
The captain said, "Go on back and start stackin'
**   stacks,**
We got nine pumps to keep that water back...."

Shine tells him:

"This ship may be big and this ship may be fine,
But where this ship is takin' you,
It ain't gonna take Shine."
Now a thousand millionaires was lookin' at him
When he jumped in the ocean and started to swim.
A rich man's daughter came up on deck
With her drawers around her knees and her skirt around
**   her neck.**
Shine shook as he stopped to look....
She said, "Shine, oh, Shine, save me, please,
And I'll give you everything your eyes may see."
He said, "Lady, your pussy looks good, it's true,
But there's some girls on land got pussy too."

> Up come a shark from the bottom of the sea,
> Said, "Look what the Lord done sent to me."
> But Shine wasn't jokin', he was double strokin',
> And after ol' shark seen that Shine had him beat,
> He said, "Swim on, motherfucker, 'cause I don't like black
>   meat."
> About four-thirty when the *Titanic* was sinkin',
> Shine had swimmed clear to Los Angeles and was in a bar
>   drinkin'.

Toasting Shine and Stagolee was one means by which black men identified with power. And toasting with style and clever rhymes gave one status and power among one's peers.

Like much of today's rap many of these toasts were shamefully misogynistic. Some even celebrated pimps, though not so much for their alleged sexual superiority as for their verbal prowess. On some level those who toasted knew—as do the pimps, politicians, and Madison Avenue advertising firms—that with the right words you can control the minds of others. *The Mack*, the title of the 1970s blaxploitation flick, was a synonym for *pimp*. "To mack" meant to seduce a woman with talk, as did *rap* before it finally came to signify rhyming in rhythm. (An interesting aside: The links between the sexual urge, the art of seduction, and the development of language go way back. It's no accident that the words *language*, *lingual* [tongue], and *lingam* [phallus] all have the same root. The word *language* can thus be read as a one-word poem; buried deep beneath its layers of centuries of civilizing usage is the powerful image of the tongue in the ear when *tongue* equals penis, *ear* connotes vagina, and words are the seeds that inseminate the mind.)

Quiet as it's kept, sisters have played the game too. And no amount of male muscle can ever hope to match the power that resides in a woman's mouth. Case in point: A brother stopped dead in his tracks. He'd been spotted by a group of women coming out of the men's room with his fly open. After zipping up he made the mistake of approaching one of them and asking, "Hey, baby, did you see my big brown Cadillac ready to roll into action just for you?" "No," she said, "but I saw a little gray Volkswagen with two flat tires."

Linguists say black folks place much more emphasis on effective talking than whites do. With us it's always been "not what you say, but how you say it" that has made the difference between seriously rapping and

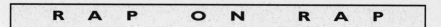

just flapping your gums. In the 1930s and '40s, before it came to signify someone who is trifling, "jive" was the black progenitor of American slang. And it was often rhymed. A "zoot suit with a reet pleat and a drape shape with a stuffed cuff" was a seriously hip fashion statement. While the vocabulary of the hip is constantly changing, and rap is the primary conduit of new slang today, the impetus for improvising with words originated with jazz improvisers in the thirties and forties. Over time many black slang terms have seeped into the mainstream culture and have helped to keep American English interesting and fresh. And some form of rapping, toasting, and verbal dueling can be found wherever we are.

Among the Rundi of Burundi in east central Africa, everyone plays the game of matching wits through verbal thrusts and parrying. Eloquence is highly prized, and the Rundi place a great emphasis on the ability to use *ubgenge*, which means something like "successful cleverness" in language, and *imfura* or "speaking well." News, gossip, social satire, and whole histories of the Mandinka and Ibo peoples were wrapped up in the epic narratives of savannah griots. Among the Yoruba, the trickster god, Eshu, is also the master of the principles of speech and language. And quarreling Yoruba women sing the dozens at each other in the laundry place, publicly airing each other's "dirty laundry." In the Caribbean, Trinidadians put music to the dozens and invented Calypso. Among the Efik of Nigeria, typical slams include *engwi imiäng urua* ("you fart in the market") and *eyen ntime nsene* ("child of mixed sperm"—in other words, you were conceived by more than one father). The person thus dissed might reply with a snappy comeback that translates as "Your mama."

According to brother Morgan Dalphinis, author of *Caribbean and African Languages*, this is the ultimate pan-African insult. The Hausa say *uwarka* ("your mother"), which is really short for *ka ci uwarka* (unprintable). In the Creole-speaking Caribbean, *manman ou* and *koukoun manman ou* mean roughly the same thing.

"Shameful," some folks say, and shake their heads. "Ign'ant." "And disrespectful." "A confused reaction to matriarchy on the part of adolescent boys searching for masculinity," say the sociologists. But the dozens is a high-stakes game where Mama's honor is worth more than anything, including your own physical safety. Fact is, insulting someone's mother, even in defense of your own, is ordinarily enough to provoke an immediate, highly emotional, and decidedly physical response. In other words, a fight. But resorting to violence is ultimately an admis-

sion that you aren't hard enough to hang. Not ready for the real world. More often than not, tensions are dissipated through words that fly fast and sting but also provoke laughter and inspire admiration for our cleverness and skill in using language creatively. It tests our ability to remain cool under pressure. And verbal dueling provides young brothers and sisters with a training ground for adulthood in a society where firepower and sheer numbers dictate that we do battle with whites verbally rather than physically. These are war games, with the only weapons we will be permitted in mainstream society.

The dozens is a kids' contest, in the main. Some of the same language strategy used in the dozens can be heard earlier on in the taunts and tricks of small children.

Red, red, peed in bed,
Wiped it up with jelly-bread.

Brown, brown, go to town,
With your britches hanging down.

African-American adults generally don't play the dozens. When adults "sound" on one another the proverbial response is "I laugh, joke, and smoke, but I don't play." Yet the game is never really forgotten. Clearly, it has served as schooling not only for rappers and others who see themselves as machine-gun poets and wordslingers for hire, but for all who, on whatever level in their daily lives, choose the mode of the trickster over that of the badman.

Ultimately, to update the old aphorism about pens and swords, the book is badder than the bullet. Traditionally, colonialists have relied for the long term not on the bullet but the Bible to control the colonized. Nations insist that their populations speak a single approved language as an expression of loyalty and are suspicious of foreign tongues and even dialects of the official language. The state can neither prohibit nor encourage behavior it cannot name. And there is a deep-seated, perhaps primordial, awe and fear of strange words and words used in strange ways. It is built right into the language, hidden in words like *curse* and *profane*. The word *grammar* itself derives from a very old term for occult learning and the casting of spells. Before inflationary use devalued it, the word *motherfucker* could be wielded with a force and rhythm by black men to put whites at unease. The same word has been used by black women as a term of endearment to their men. *Motherfucker* embodied the universal masculine and feminine principles, the yin/yang mother/father with a twist that turned the latter into a verb for the eternal whirlwind of creation. Words have power. The Bible says that "In the beginning was the Word," and that God created everything from the word. In fact, the word *god* has its origin in the Indo-European root *gheue,* meaning "to call." A word is nothing more than a sound which is nothing more than a vibration which is nothing more than a rhythm of waves. The rhythm on rhythm, the sound, the magic, and what we do with words—the way we turn "bad" into good— make African-American speech a wild card in the English language. It keeps American English alive and vital, though perhaps at the expense of white culture, by contributing culturally and linguistically to the blackening of the mainstream mode, and ultimately to what Public Enemy termed "Fear of a Black Planet." With that blackening, the language we have adopted and adapted will in the long run become for whites less the instrument of control and, to some, more a curse and instrument of retribution. (*Karma* was a word they should have got hip to in India, but were too busy oppressing the people of color there.) Even when we don't articulate it according to the standard grammar, we can still improvise some potent magic in this language. When Nina Simone shouts, "I put a spell on you," it's already on you.

In *The Healing Drum,* Yaya Diallo, a member of the Bamana tribe in Mali, West Africa, describes a scenario in which two children start to fight. When an elder breaks them up and asks why they are fighting, the first child says, "He insulted me." The elder asks, "Was it a new insult he invented?" "He insulted my mother," the offended boy says. "Oh, that is an old insult," laughs the elder. "It has never killed anyone here. I would have worried if it were a new insult. That one is nothing to worry about. We have tested all the old insults, and they are harmless. Look around you. All of these people you see have been insulted, but they are fine."

When I had similar complaints as a child, my mother used to recite, "Sticks and stones may break my bones, but words will never hurt me." With all due respect to Mama, the wisdom of this proverb seemed dubious to me. But, as words were the only socially acceptable weapons of war, the only thing left to do was build up my own arsenal.

Language is competitive. Even grown-up, everyday language is a game, a contest between speakers. And the limits of our language define the limits of our world. There is no thought that can be thought without it, no concept that can be grasped without the handle that words provide us. There are certainly things we feel profoundly that cannot be put into words, but there is no other way than with words to construct a thought. Thought is language spoken to oneself.

Beyond racism, Spike Lee's *Do the Right Thing* illustrates how the inability to communicate verbally leads to frustration, verbal violence, and, ultimately, physical violence. The stuttering Smiley symbolizes this frustration, and it is further illustrated in Radio Raheem's demands that the Korean grocers he patronizes speak English. Ironic, since he doesn't speak English much better than they. When the grocer calls him a motherfucker, Radio Raheem smiles. Now they are beginning to communicate. In the film Radio Raheem dies in a policeman's choke hold, but his fate is sealed earlier when the pizza shop owner smashes his radio/cassette player with a baseball bat. "You killed my radio!" he says, stunned. And with that the shop owner has effectively destroyed Raheem's identity. He is no longer Radio Raheem. Never again will the sounds of Public Enemy's rap "Fight the Power" give voice to his frustration. He is silenced. That frustration, which is to some degree the frustration of all African Americans, can be heard as well in the stylized emphasis that rappers and our young folks in the hip-hop culture place on what linguists call "plosives," consonants that appear to explode upon the eardrums.

Rap, the dozens, signifying, jive talking, and the other uniquely black modes of communication are just that, modes, best employed strategically and not exclusively or in every context we find ourselves in in America. Some of the more conscious rappers have begun to recognize that black people are (at least metaphorically) at war with the dominant culture in America. But it's a guerrilla war in which we all might serve as more effective agents and spies if we were only more fluent in the mainstream language mode. Ignorance of the rules of white folks' language games would mean I wouldn't know when sarcasm is intended or when I've been insulted. But that works both ways. To William F. Buckley, with all his verbose rodomontades and etiolated dialectics, a simple response like "Your mama" would seem to be an incomprehensible non sequitur. Slang, the invention of black jazz musicians in the thirties and forties, was, in fact, consciously employed to separate the hip folk from the squares and even up the score a bit. In Egypt, four hundred prophets are said to have spoken incoherently before the gates of Samaria in 853 B.C. Incoherent to whom? All depends on who's listening. Noamsain?

(August 1991/1995)

The Rap on Hip-hop

by William Safire

"But the Czar Never Knew About Hip-hop" was the headline in a recent *U.S. News & World Report.* The article was about the Siberian Cadets Corps in Novosibirsk, Russia, where students are learning the real history of Russia along with the cultural activities

associated with that country before the rise of Communism.

"We are learning the mazurka, polonaise, waltz," says fifteen-year-old Yevgeny Kondratiev, undoubtedly a good dancer, possibly an avid cyclist. "Later, they promise to teach us the hip-hop."

That opens some linguistic doors. First, to get hip on hip-hop: in the mid-seventies, Love Bug Starsky and DJ Hollywood and other pioneering rappers were developing a syncopation suited for improvisation. "[Hollywood] paced himself with a repeating refrain," wrote Robert Palmer in *The New York Times*, often "a variation on the nonsense formula 'hip, hop, hip-hip-de-hop.' " Rapping disc jockeys "created what were basically new musical accompaniments out of bits and pieces of funk hits."

Funk? I vaguely recall Louis Armstrong's singing "The Funkie Butt Boogie." Weren't smelly cigars called "funky butts"? "There was funk before there was hip-hop," explains Jim Steinblatt of ASCAP. "Funk is a variety of soul, from the James Brown school of soul. Hip-hop is an outgrowth of soul, yet it's very much related to rap. It's all connected, part of the R&B [rhythm and blues] tradition, which is related to gospel, country blues, and jazz."

Hippity-hop has for centuries been a reduplication describing the motion of a rabbit. In its shortened form *hip hop* (without a hyphen) first appeared in *The Rehearsal*, a 1671 play by George Villiers: "To go off hip hop, hip hop, upon this occasion."

Hip-hop is itself a prime example of a third-order reduplication. (First-order simply doubles a syllable, as in *boo-boo* and *bye-bye*, and second-order changes the opening consonant sound, as in *bow-wow* and *mumbo jumbo*; third-order changes the vowel sounds, as in *flip-flop, tip-top*, and our subject today, *hip-hop*.)

A rabbit hops along, or bops along, sometimes rhythmically, often jerkily; the reduplication describing it has been given a new twist, or metaphoric extension, by musicians. They have taken over the word *rap* the same way.

Rap began in the fourteenth century as an echoic noun, imitating the sound of a sharp blow. Early American English applied *rap* to a sharp rebuke, perhaps also the source of the 1903 sense of a criminal charge, along with the hope of "beating the rap."

As a verb *rap* has long meant "to express orally." The poet Sir Thomas Wyatt wrote in 1541, "I am wont sometime to rap out on oath in an earnest talk." British prison slang used *rap* for "to say" as early as

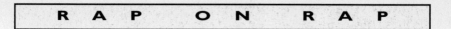

1879, and Damon Runyon may have picked up that *rap* to use in a 1929 story: "I wish Moosh a hello, and he never raps to me but only bows, and takes my hat."

According to one theory this talking *rap* came from British English into the American language, perhaps transferred through Caribbean English; another theory suggests that *rap* is a clipped alteration of *repartee*, a 1645 noun from French for "retort."

However *rap* entered American usage, it was widely adopted in black English by the 1960s. Eldridge Cleaver wrote in a 1965 letter, "In point of fact he is funny and very glib, and I dig rapping with him." Clarence Major, in his 1970 *Dictionary of Afro-American Slang*, defined *rap* as both verb and noun: "to hold conversation; a long, impressive monologue." Within a decade the noun was used attributively in rap music, labeling the rhythmic rhyming lines set to an insistent beat.

Covering this beat is Fred Brathwaite, known as Fab 5 Freddy, who hosts the weekly television show *Yo! MTV Raps*. This rapper-turned-lexicographer has collected hip-hop slang in *Fresh Fly Flavor* (Longmeadow Press), an alliterative title that joins three favorable terms.

Fresh, a shortened form of *fresh out of the pack*, is a compliment that's taken even higher by *fly*, a clipping of the 1960s slang *superfly* for "the brightest or flashiest." The noun *flavor* has a positive sense of "something good," but it also takes a neutral meaning of "the tone or vibe of a person, place, or situation."

As the best baddies know, *bad* and *dope* have turned around into expressions of praise. Mr. Brathwaite explains the positive sense for a drug term like *dope*: "A key ingredient in ultraurban, contemporary counter–youth-culture is to flirt with what's wrong, take the negative vibe and power, and turn it all the way around to make it serve a new purpose, yet with the shock value still intact."

Like the hare's bounce in *hip-hop*, rap terms stress action or excitement. To start doing or performing something is to *kick it*; if it's done well, it's *slammin'* (a forties bass player was Slam Stewart), which is also the term for playing loudly (the rhyming jammin', also eliding its *g* ending, means "partying" or "making good music"). *Pump it up* turns up that volume even higher.

The rap artist likes to clip words. *Dis* uses the first part of *disrespect* and means "to put down or show disrespect." Other terms, though, are clipped to their final syllable: *hood* for "neighborhood" and *tude* for "attitude," particularly a bad or negative disposition.

Rhyme and redundancy also have their place in hip-hop slang. In Tuesday's election, every candidate should have been *in it to win it,* a phrase using internal rhyme to express "trying your best." Deliberate redundancy rears its head in *quick, fast, and in a hurry,* infuriating the Squad Squad.

Boxers on the losing end of a bout may be down and out, but those terms take other senses in this lexicon. *I'm down* means "I'm ready" (get down is "to become culturally adjusted"), and *I'm out* means "I'm leaving," probably a shortening of "I'm outta here." (*I'm Outtie 5000* is a more insistent term for departure, playing on the name of the Audi 5000 automobile.) Leaving quick, fast, and in a hurry is a *breakout,* which has a curious parallel to the term used by arms-control negotiators for the sudden upsetting of a strategic balance.

Before I'm Outtie 5000, let me return to that *U.S. News* headline: "But the Czar Never Knew About Hip-hop." That's bottomed on a phrase that reverberates through political history: *If the czar only knew.*

"One of the oldest traditions in this nation's history," Murray Kempton wrote in a column from Russia in 1988, "is the voice of some victim of an administrative injustice, vast or little, saying that such things could not be 'if the czar only knew.' "

This aposiopesis—leaving the remainder of the thought understood after "If the czar only knew . . ."—is the classic way for a subject to excuse the inefficiency or barbarism of the highest authority. Many people prefer not to assign blame to the person at the top; thus the czar, or president, or ruler, can hip-hop away from responsibility.

(November 8, 1993)

Those T.I.R.E.D. Acronyms

by Mimi Valdés

BDP (Boogie Down Productions) was cool, and KRS-One (Knowledge Reigns Supreme Over Nearly Everyone) was even cooler. N.W.A (Niggaz With Attitude) was dope too. We could even get with EPMD (Erick and Parrish Making Dollars), and De La's D.A.I.S.Y. Age (Da Inner

Sound Y'all). Once initials were part of the fame-through-anonymity of brothas livin' underground. Now initials are becoming a bit T.I.R.E.D.—a lazy way to say too much and too little. The worst are the ones with "profound" hidden meanings, to say nothing of the N2DEEP's, and II D Extreme's. A trip to the record store is looking more and more like a game of Scrabble. You be the judge:

E.U.	(Experience Unlimited)
SWV	(Sisters With Voices)
TLC	(T-Boz, Left Eye, & Chilli)
INTRO	(Innovative New Talent Reaching Out)
TBTBT	(Too Bad To Be True)
B.B.O.T.I.	(Badd Boyz of the Industry)
UNV	(Universal Nubian Voices)
T.C.F. Crew	(The Chosen Few)
NKRU	(Naughty Kreations R Unified)
SSL	(Smokin' Suckaz Wit' Logic)
P.O.V.	(Point of View)
Get Set V.O.P.	(Voice of the Projects)
E.Y.C.	(Express Yourself Clearly)
RBX	(Reality Born Unknown)
DBG'Z	(Dank, Brew, and Guns)
UGK'S	(Underground Kings)
A.N.G.	(Ain't No Gains)
O.F.T.B.	(Operation From the Bottom)
SFD	(Six Feet Deep)
Boo-Yaa	
T.R.I.B.E.	(Too Rough International Boo-Yaa Empire)
Yaggfu Front	(You Are Gonna Get Fucked Up [If You] Front)
A.L.T.	(Another Latin Timebomb)
The B.R.O.T.H.A.	
Chilly-T	(Black Realist Out to Have Assets)

(December 1993)

Rhythmic Repetition, Industrial Forces, and Black Practice

by Tricia Rose

Unlike the complexity of Western classical music, which is primarily represented in its melodic and harmonic structures, the complexity of rap music, like many Afrodiasporic musics, is in the rhythmic and percussive density and organization.[1] "Harmony" versus "rhythm" is an oft-cited reduction of the primary distinctions between Western classical and African and African-derived musics. Still, these terms represent significant differences in sound organization and perhaps even disparate approaches to ways of perception, as it were. The outstanding technical feature of the Western classical music tradition is tonal functional harmony. Tonal functional harmony is based on clear, definite pitches and logical relations between them; on the forward drive toward resolution of a musical sequence that leads to a final resolution: the final perfect cadence. The development of tonal harmony critically confined the range of possible tones to twelve tones within each octave arranged in only one of two possible ways, major or minor. It also restricted the rhythmic complexity of European music. In place of freedom with respect to accent and measure, European music focused rhythmic activity onto strong and weak beats in order to prepare and resolve harmonic dissonance. Furthermore, as Christopher Small has argued, Western classical tonal harmony is structurally less tolerant of "acoustically illogical and unclear sounds, sound not susceptible to total control." Other critical features of classical music, such as the notation system and the written score—the medium through which the act of composition takes place—separate the composer from both the audience and the performer and set limits on composition and performance.[2] This classical music tradition, like all major musical and cultural developments, emerged as part of a larger historical shift in European consciousness:

[We see] changes in European consciousness that we call the Renaissance having its effect in music, with the per-

[1] John Miller Chernoff, *African Rhythm and African Sensibility* (Chicago: University of Chicago Press, 1979); Dick Hebdige, *Cut n Mix: Culture, Identity and Caribbean Music* (London: Methuen, 1987); Lawrence Levine, *Black Culture, Black Consciousness* (New York: Oxford University Press, 1977); Portia K. Maultsby, "Africanisms in African-American Music," *Africanisms in American Culture*, ed. Joseph E. Holloway, pp. 185–210 (Bloomington: Indiana University Press, 1990); Eileen Southern, *The Music of Black Americans* (New York: Norton, 1971).
[2] Christopher Small, *Music, Society, Education: An Examination of the Function of Music in Western, Eastern and African Cultures with its Impact on Society and Its Use in Education* (New York: Schirmer, 1977), pp. 20–21. See also Christopher Small, *Music of the Common Tongue* (New York: Riverrun Press, 1987).

sonal, humanistic viewpoint substituted for the theo-
cratic, universalistic viewpoint of the Middle Ages, expressed in technical terms by a great interest in chords
and their effects in juxtaposition, and specifically in the
perfect cadence and the suspended dissonance, rather
than in polyphony and the independent life of the individual voice.[3]

Rhythm and polyrhythmic layering is to African and African-derived
musics what harmony and the harmonic triad is to Western classical music. Dense configurations of independent, but closely related, rhythms
and nonharmonic percussive sounds, especially drum sounds, are critical
priorities in many African and Afrodiasporic musical practices. The voice
is also an important expressive instrument. A wide range of vocal sounds
intimately connected to tonal speech patterns, "strong differences between the various registers of the voice, even emphasizing the *breaks*
between them," are deliberately cultivated in African and African-influ-
enced musics.[4] Treatment, or "versioning," is highly valued.
Consequently, the instrument is not simply an object or vehicle for dis-
playing one's talents, it is a "colleague in the creation." And, most important for this discussion, African melodic phrases "tend to be short
and repetition is common; in fact, repetition is one of the characteristics
of African music." Christopher Small elaborates:

A call-and-response sequence may go on for several
hours, with apparently monotonous repetition of the
same short phrase sung by a leader and answered by the
chorus, but in fact subtle variations are going on all the
time, not only in the melodic lines themselves but also in
their relation to the complex cross-rhythms in the accom-

[3] Small, *Music, Society, Education*, pp. 9–10. See also John Storm Roberts,
Black Music of Two Worlds (New York: William Morrow, 1974).
[4] Rap's "human beat box" shares many vocal sounds found in African vocal
traditions. Marc Dery describes this link: "The hums, grunts, and glottal
attacks of Central Africa's pygmies, the tongue clicks, throat gurgles, and
suction stops of the Bushmen of the Kalahari Desert, and the yodeling,
whistling vocal effects of Zimbabwe's *m'bira* players all survive in the
mouth percussion of such 'human beat box' rappers as Doug E. Fresh and
Darren Robinson of the Fat Boys." Marc Dery, "Rap!," *Keyboard*,
November 1988, p. 34.

panying drumming or hand clapping. . . . The repetitions of African music have a function in time which is the reverse of (Western classical) music—to dissolve the past and the future into one eternal present, in which the passing of time is no longer noticed.[5]

Rhythmic complexity, repetition with subtle variations, the significance of the drum, melodic interest in the bass frequencies, and breaks in pitch and time (e.g., suspensions of the beat for a bar or two) are also consistently recognized features of African-American musical practices. In describing black New World approaches to rhythm, Ben Sidran refers to Rudi Blesh's notion of "suspended rhythm" and Andre Hodier's description of "swing" as rhythmic tension over stated or implied meter.[6] Time suspension via rhythmic breaks—points at which the bass lines are isolated and suspended—are important clues in explaining sources of pleasure in black musics.

Approaches to sound, rhythm, and repetition in rap music exhibit virtually all of these traits. Rap music techniques, particularly the use of sampling technology, involve the repetition and reconfiguration of rhythmic elements in ways that illustrate a heightened attention to rhythmic patterns and movement between such patterns via breaks and points of musical rupture. Multiple rhythmic forces are set in motion and then suspended, selectively. Rap producers construct loops of sounds and then build in critical moments, where the established rhythm is manipulated and suspended. Then, rhythmic lines reemerge at key relief points. One of the clearest examples of this practice is demonstrated in "Rock Dis Funky Joint" by the Poor Righteous Teachers. The music and the vocal rapping style of Culture Freedom has multiple and complicated time suspensions and rhythmic ruptures of the musical and lyrical passages.[7] Busta Rhymes from Leaders of the New School, reggae rapper Shabba

---

[5] Small, *Music, Society, Education,* pp. 54–55.
[6] See also Ben Sidran, *Black Talk* (New York: Holt, Rinehart & Winston, 1971), and Olly Wilson, "Black Music as Art," *Black Music Research Journal,* no. 3, 1–22, 1983.
[7] Poor Righteous Teachers, "Rock Dis Funky Joint," *Holy Intellect* (Profile, 1990). See also Ice Cube, "The Bomb," *Amerikka's Most Wanted* (Profile, 1990), and the Fu-schnickens, *Take It Personal* (Jive, 1992). Bear in mind that not all rap music deploys these characteristics equally. In particular, some of the earliest rap recordings used the instrumental side of a disco single verbatim as the sole musical accompaniment. This may, in part, be

Ranks, British rapper Monie Love, Treach from Naughty by Nature, B-Real from Cypress Hill, and Das EFX are known especially for using their voices as percussive instruments, bending words, racing through phrases, pausing and stuttering through complicated verbal rhythms.

These features are not merely stylistic effects, they are aural manifestations of philosophical approaches to social environments. James A. Snead, working along the same lines as Small, offers a philosophical explanation for the meaning and significance of repetition and rupture in black culture. As we shall see, musical elements that reflect worldviews, these "rhythmic instinctions," are critical in understanding the meaning of time, motion, and repetition in black culture and are of critical importance to understanding the manipulation of technology in rap.

> **The rhythmic instinction to yield to travel beyond existing forces of life. Basically, that's tribal and if you wanna get the rhythm, then you have to join a tribe.**
> **—A Tribe Called Quest**[8]

> **The outstanding fact of late-twentieth-century European culture is its ongoing reconciliation with black culture. The mystery may be that it took so long to discern the elements of black culture already there in latent form, and to realize that the separation between the cultures was perhaps all along not one of nature, but of force.**
> **—James A. Snead**[9]

Snead suggests that the vast body of literature devoted to mapping the cultural differences between European- and African-derived cultures, which has characterized differences between European and black cultures as a part of "nature," are in fact differences in force; differences in cultural responses to the inevitability of repetition. Snead argues that repetition is an important and telling element in culture, a means by which a sense of continuity, security, and identification are maintained.

due to limited musical resources, as disc jockey performances that predate these recordings demonstrate substantial skill and complexity in rhythmic manipulation.

[8] A Tribe Called Quest, "Youthful Expression," *People's Instinctive Travels and the Paths of Rhythm* (Jive Records, 1989/1990).

[9] James A. Snead, "On Repetition in Black Culture," *Black American Literature Forum*, vol. 15, no. 4, 153, 1981.

This sense of security can be understood as, in fact, a kind of "coverage," both as insurance against sudden ruptures and as a way of hiding and masking undesired or unpleasant facts or conditions. Snead argues quite convincingly that all cultures provide coverage against loss of identity, repression, assimilation, or attack. Where they "differ among one another primarily [is] in the tenacity with which the 'cover-up' is maintained . . . grafting leeway to those ruptures in the illusion of growth which most often occur in the déjà vus of exact repetition." He suggests that when we view repetition in cultural forms we are not viewing the same thing repeated, but its transformation: "Repetition is not just a formal ploy, but often the willed grafting onto culture of an essentially philosophical insight about the shape of time and history. . . . One may readily classify cultural forms based on whether they tend to admit or cover up these repeating constituencies within them."[10]

Snead claims that European culture "secrets" repetition, categorizing it as progression or regression, assigning accumulation and growth or stagnation to motion, whereas black cultures highlight the observance of repetition, perceiving it as circulation, equilibrium. In a fashion resembling Small, Snead argues that Western classical music uses rhythm mainly as "an aid in the construction of a sense of progression to a harmonic cadence (and) *repetition has been suppressed* in favor of the fulfillment of the goal of harmonic resolution." Similarly, musicologist Susan McClary points out that "tonal music" (referring to the Western classical tradition) is "narratively conceived at least to the extent that the original key area—the tonic—also serves as the final goal. Tonal structures are organized teleologically, with the illusion of unitary identity promised at the end of each piece."[11]

[10] Snead, "Repetition," 146–47. *Culture* is one of the most complex words in the English language. Culture, as I use it and as Snead uses it, is both a "whole way of life, which is manifest over the whole range of social activities but is most evident in 'specifically cultural' activities—a language, styles of art, kinds of intellectual work; and an emphasis on a 'whole social order' within which a specifiable culture, in styles of art and kinds of intellectual work, is seen as the direct or indirect product of an order primarily constituted by other social activities." From Raymond Williams, *The Sociology of Culture* (New York: Schocken, 1981), pp. 11–12. See also Raymond Williams, *Keywords* (Glasgow: Fontana, 1976).
[11] Snead, "Repetition," p. 152, my italics; Susan McClary, *Feminine Endings* (Minneapolis: University of Minnesota Press, 1991), p. 155.

To the contrary, Snead claims that black cultures highlight the observance of repetition, perceiving it as circulation and equilibrium, rather than as a regulated force that facilitates the achievement of a final harmonic goal. Drawing on examples in literature, religion, philosophy, and music, Snead elaborates on the uses and manifestations of repetition in black culture.[12] For our purposes his analysis of the meaning of repetition in black music is most relevant, specifically his description of rhythmic repetition and its relationship to the "cut":

In black culture, repetition means that the thing circulates, there in an equilibrium.... In European culture, repetition must be seen to be not just circulation and flow, but accumulation and growth. In black culture, the thing (the ritual, the dance, the beat) is there for you to pick up when you come back to get it. If there is a goal ... it is always deferred; it continually "cuts" back to the start, in the musical meaning of a "cut" as an abrupt, seemingly unmotivated break (an accidental da capo) with a series already in progress and a willed return to a prior series.... Black culture, in the "cut," "builds" accidents into its coverage, almost as if to control their unpredictability.[13]

[12] Snead also demonstrates that the recovery of repetition in twentieth-century European literature (e.g., Joyce, Faulkner, Woolf, Yeats, and Eliot) suggests that the dominance of nineteenth-century repression of European traditions that favored privileged uses of repetition and verbal rhythm in the telling "in favor of the illusion of narrative verisimilitude" may have "begun to ebb somewhat." Ibid., p. 152. For a range of discussions on form and meaning in black music and culture, see Graham Lock, *Forces in Nature: The Music and Thoughts of Anthony Braxton* (New York: Da Capo Press, 1988); Wole Soyinka, *Myth, Literature, and the African World* (New York: Cambridge University Press, 1990); and Henry L. Gates, Jr., *The Signifying Monkey* (New York: Oxford University Press, 1988). Gates affirms Snead's argument regarding the centrality of repetition in black culture: "Repetition and revision are fundamental to black artistic forms from painting and sculpture to music to language use," p. xxiv.

[13] Snead, "Repetition," p. 150.

Deliberately "repetitive" in force, black musics (especially those genres associated with dance) use the "cut" to emphasize the repetitive nature of the music by "skipping back to another beginning which we have already heard," making room for accidents and ruptures inside the music itself. In this formulation, repetition and rupture work within and against each other, building multiple circular musical lines that are broken and then absorbed or managed in the reestablishment of rhythmic lines.

Rap music uses repetition and rupture in new and complex ways, building on long-standing black cultural forces. Advances in technology have facilitated an increase in the scope of break beat deconstruction and reconstruction and have made complex uses of repetition more accessible. Now, the desired bass line or drum kick can be copied into a sampler, along with other desired sounds, and programmed to loop in any desired tempo or order. Rap music relies on the loop, on the circularity of rhythm, and on the "cut" or the "break beat" that systematically ruptures equilibrium. Yet, in rap, the "break beat" itself is looped—repositioned as repetition, as equilibrium inside the rupture. Rap music highlights points of rupture as it equalizesthem.

Snead calls James Brown "an example of a brilliant American practitioner of the 'cut' " and describes the relationship between established rhythmic patterns and the hiatus of the cut in Brown's work as a rupture that affirms the rhythmic pattern while it interrupts it. "The ensuing rupture," Snead claims, "does not cause dissolution of the rhythm; quite to the contrary, it strengthens it." Snead's reading of James Brown as a brilliant practitioner of the "cut" is a prophetic one. Published in 1981, a number of years before hip-hop producers had communally declared James Brown's discography the foundation of the break beat, Snead could not have known that Brown's exclamations, "Hit me!" "Take it to the bridge!" rapid horn and drum accents, and bass lines would soon become the most widely used breaks in rap music.

Snead's approach presumes that music is fundamentally related to the social world, that music, like other cultural creations, fulfills and denies social needs, that music *embodies assumptions* regarding social power, hierarchy, pleasure, and worldview. This link between music and larger social forces, although not widely held in the field of musicology, is also critical to the work of Susan McClary, Christopher Small, and French political economist Jacques Attali. McClary, Small, and Attali demystify the naturalized, normalized status of nineteenth-century classical musical structures and conventions, positing an understanding of music's role as a way of perceiving the world and suggesting that every musical code is rooted in the social formations and technologies of its age.[14] These historically and culturally grounded interpretations of technological "advances" shed light on naturalized aesthetic parameters as they are embodied in equipment, illustrating the significance of culture in the development of technology.

Grounding music as a cultural discourse dismantles the causal link between rap's sonic force and the technological means for its expression. Rap producers' strategic use of electronic reproduction technology, particularly sampling equipment, affirms stylistic priorities in the organization and selection of sounds found in many black diasporic musical expressions. Although rap music is shaped by and articulated through advanced reproduction equipment, its stylistic priorities are not merely by-products of such equipment.

On the question of repetition as a cultural force, Attali and Snead part company. For Attali and other cultural theorists, repetition is primarily considered a manifestation of mass culture, a characteristic of culture in the age of reproduction. The advent of recording technology signaled the emergence of a society of mass production and repetition. Repetition is, therefore, equated with industrial standardization and represents a move toward a single totalitarian code. At the point of mass production and industrial standardization, Attali claims, music becomes an industry and "its consumption ceases to be collective."[15] Similarly, Adorno describes the "break" in preswing jazz as "nothing other than a disguised cadence" and explains that "the cult of the machine which is represented by unabated jazz beats involves a self-renunciation that cannot but take root in the form of a fluctuating uneasiness somewhere in the personality of the obedient."[16] "In mass culture," Fredric Jameson claims, "repetition effec-

[14]Susan McClary and Richard Leppert, eds., *Music and Society: The Politics of Composition, Performance, and Reception* (New York: Cambridge University Press, 1989), and McClary, *Feminine Endings*; Small, *Common Tongue*, and *Music, Society, Education*; Jacques Attali, *Noise: The Political Economy of Music* (Minneapolis: University of Minnesota Press, 1985).
[15]Attali, *Noise*, p. 88.
[16]Theodore W. Adorno (with the assistance of George Simpson), "On Popular Music," in Simon Frith and Andrew Goodwin, eds., *On Record: Rock, Pop, and the Written Word* (New York: Pantheon, 1990), p. 313. Also see T.W. Adorno, "On the Fetish-Character in Music and the Regression of Listening," in Andrew Arato and Eike Gebhardt, eds., *The Essential Frankfurt School Reader* (New York: Continuum, 1982), pp. 288–89.

tively volatizes the original object—so that the student of mass culture has no primary object of study."[17]

Repetition does, in fact, function as part of a system of mass production that structures and confines creative articulation; along these lines Adorno, Jameson, and Attali offer vital criticisms of the logic of massified culture in late capitalist societies. Yet, repetition cannot be reduced to a repressive industrial force. Nor is it sufficient to understand repetition solely as a by-product of the needs of industrialization. I do not mean to suggest that any of the cultural theorists would claim that repetition was nonexistent in preindustrial society. However, their focus on repetition as an industrial condition encourages mischaracterizations of the black popular cultural phenomenon, particularly those forms that privilege repetition and are prominently positioned in the commodity system.

If we assume that industrial production sets the terms for repetition inside mass-produced music, then how can alternative uses and manifestations of repetition that are articulated *inside* the commodity market be rendered perceptible? Rap music's use of rhythmic lines constructed with sampled loops of sound are particularly vulnerable to misreadings or erasures along these lines. Working inside the commodity market and with industrial technology, rap music uses rhythmic forces that are informed by mass reproduction technology, but it uses them in ways that affirm black cultural priorities that sometimes work against market forces. Yet, none of this is visible if all mass-produced repetition is understood primarily as a manifestation of mass culture. If rap can be so overwhelmingly mischaracterized, then what other musical and cultural practices have been collapsed into the logic of industrial repetition, labeled examples of "cultlike" obedience? Adorno's massive misreading of the jazz break, beside betraying a severe case of black cultural illiteracy, is another obvious example of the pitfalls of reading musical structures in the popular realm as by-products of industrial forces.

Adorno, Jameson, and Attali, by constructing repetition as if it were a singular force, strongly suggest that mass production sets the terms for repetition and that any other cultural forms of repetition, once practiced inside systems of mass production, are subsumed by the larger logic of industrialization. Consequently, no other mass-produced or mass-consumed forms that privilege forms of repetition are accessible or relevant once inside this larger logic of industrial repetition.

[17] Frederic Jameson, "Reification and Utopia in Mass Culture," *Social Text*, Winter, 137, 1979.

Positioning repetition in late capitalist markets as a consequence of that market marginalizes or erases alternative uses of and relationships to repetition that might suggest collective resistance to that system. Repetition, then, is all too easily vilified, collapsed into the logic of the commodity system, and is employed as a means by which to effectively erase the multiplicity of cultures and traditions present in contemporary Western societies. I am not suggesting that black culture supersedes the effects of commodification. Nor is this meant to suggest that black cultural priorities lie outside of (or completely in opposition to) mass cultural industries. Quite to the contrary, this is a call for readings of commodification that can accommodate multiple histories and approaches to sound organization. I am mostly concerned, here, with facile and all-too-frequent readings of repetition that apply and naturalize dominant cultural principles and consequently colonize and silence black approaches, which, in the case of American popular music especially, have clear and significant problematic, dare I say racist, implications.[18]

(1994)

[18] Richard Middleton's *Studying Popular Music* (Philadelphia: Open University Press, 1990) attempts to grapple with the question of repetition in popular music in his chapter on pleasure, value, and ideology in popular music (see esp. pp. 267–93). He finds that "popular common sense tends to see repetition as an aspect of mass production and market exploitation but often also associates it with the phenomenon of being 'sent,' particularly in relation to 'hypnotic' rhythmic repetitions and 'primitive' audience trance. . . . How can we square a psychology of repetition and the historically specific Adornian notion of repetition as a function of social control?" (pp. 286–87). Middleton suggests that multiple determinations are operative at once. To illustrate his point, he compares Freud, Barthes, Deleuze, and Guattari, Jameson, Rosolato, and Lacan on the question of repetition. The multiple determinations he offers cannot accommodate the kind of black approach to repetition as articulated by Snead and Small. In fact, none of the approaches he offers grounds black practices in African traditions. Although he is quite aware of black cultural influences in popular music, in his mind these influences do not reflect an alternative approach to cultural production; they are discrete black practices that are not constructed as part of a larger approach. So, although he agrees that black music's privilege repetition (although not rhythmically complex uses of repetition, but "riffs, call-and-response, short unchanging rhythmic patterns"), it is a technique, not a manifestation of an alternative approach.

Stylus Counsel: The All-Time Record Player

by Gavin Edwards

When pioneering hip-hop DJ Grandmaster Flash recorded "The Adventures of Grandmaster Flash on the Wheels of Steel" in 1981, the "wheels" in question were turntables made by Technics. For club DJs twelve years later, a hit record still comes in one size only: twelve inches of vinyl. So a pair of turntables serves as the bedrock of any dance party, and DJs universally agree there are only Technics 1200s and imitations of the Technics 1200. This turntable is such a standard fixture among the hip-hop crowd that its outline served as the inspiration for Def Jam's stylized corporate logo. The Technics SL-1200MK2's most highly rated feature is the start/stop button, which has the instantaneous response needed to successfully cross-fade tracks. Because the direct-drive motor is more powerful than the average home turntable's, DJs can scratch, pinpoint a cue, or hold a record in place without skipping a beat. The 1200 is also known for being sturdy enough to lug from club to club without breaking down. Our only complaint? The night-light burns out too quickly.

(July 1993)

Larcenous Art?

by J. D. Considine

Despite what they say about imitation—is sampling really flattery? How ethical is it to swipe a piece of another artist's recording—slicing off a sliver of sound as if it were just so much sausage—and drop it into your own? Is sampling something inventively postmodern, an appropriate, artistic response to expanding technology and the quick-cut pace of modern culture? Or is it simple theft?

Such questions would be easier to answer if sampling were merely a matter of quotation. After all, there's a world of difference between echoing a famous phrase—say, Shakespeare's "Who steals my purse steals trash"—and claiming it as your own. But a sample doesn't simply reprise a melody the way a literary citation repeats someone else's words; it blurs the line between quotation and plagiarism by parroting bits of a recorded performance.

Imagine if John Lennon, instead of borrowing the lines "Here come ol' flattop/He comes groovin' up slowly" from Chuck Berry's "You Can't Catch Me" had actually dropped a chunk of the original Chess single—not only Berry's words but also his voice and guitar—into "Come Together." That's the difference between sampling and quotation.

So sampling is theft, right?

Well, not exactly. Easy as it is to read larcenous intent into this wholesale appropriation of other recordings, what makes sampling so attractive isn't that it's easier to pinch a James Brown scream than to learn how to make that sound yourself. Rather, it's the fact that there's something immediately recognizable about that scream, that it carries a specific association: Soul Brother No. 1. And hearing that scream outside the context of a James Brown record changes its meaning—reducing its emotional resonance to the level of mere recognition—just as surely as hearing Chuck Berry's voice in the middle of "Come Together" would change our understanding of the song.

"Recontextualization" is what the media critics call it, and though it used to be the domain of visual artists (think of Andy Warhol's soup-can paintings), it has started to put a new spin on a lot of old records. To a certain extent sampling has even managed to add a sense of history to the hit parade—as Stetsasonic argues in "Talkin' All That Jazz": "James Brown was old/Till Eric & Rak came out with 'I Got Soul'/Rap brings back old R&B."

It's not just rap that recontextualizes, either. House records routinely sample older dance hits; abrasive new beat acts like Ministry and My Life With the Thrill Kill Kult drop found sounds from radio broadcasts into their records; and ethnically minded rockers, from Jon Hassell to Peter Gabriel, use samples to add touches of traditional African or Asian music to their albums. Hell, Robert Plant even brought sampling into the guitar-crazed realm of heavy metal when he spat back traces of old Led Zep hits in "Tall Cool One."

Still, as our mothers used to point out, the fact that everyone else is doing something doesn't make it right for us to do it. Sampling can be exciting and evocative, but is it art?

Frankly, that depends on how it's used. Compare Janet Jackson's "Rhythm Nation," for instance, with De La Soul's "Buddy." The former owes much of its groove to a rhythm-guitar lick lifted from Sly and the Family Stone's "Thank You (Falettinme Be Mice Elf Again)"; the latter got its bottom by grabbing the bass line of Taana Gardner's "Heartbeat." But there's a difference in the way the two make use of what they borrow. Whereas "Rhythm Nation" creates a whole new groove out of a secondhand guitar hook, De La Soul simply spits back what it started with. It's not hard to figure out which is the more inventive approach.

Samplers, remember, aren't obliged to quote in context, the way reporters are. In fact, creative editing—manipulating a musical phrase so that it does what you want it to—is ultimately what turns the person behind the digital sampler from a technician into a musician. Saxophonist Branford Marsalis cites the work of Public Enemy as an example of how a sampler could be used as a musical instrument, calling PE "the only rap group that I know of that can take five or six snippets of a record, put it together, and make it sound like one band."

Nor is it hard to hear what he means. Public Enemy's "Fight the Power" builds its juggernaut groove out of the tiniest of scraps—for example the I from the chorus of Bob Marley's "I Shot the Sheriff." PE orchestrates each sample with the painstaking care of a symphonist, and the effect is devastating. Granted, there are no "instruments" being played (apart from Marsalis's saxophone solo), yet somehow the track seems infinitely more creative than a band-driven rap like Salt-N-Pepa's "Shake Your Thing."

Where sampling most obviously differs from other musical skills, though, is in performance. It may take longer to work out a guitar solo in the studio than it does to replay it onstage, but the physical effort involved is roughly the same. Playing back a sample, though, takes but a keystroke—not the most exciting thing to watch. Yet these days, bands from Milli Vanilli to the Rolling Stones are alleged to rely on samples for part of their onstage sound.

Granted, many of these acts are only trying to provide a reasonable reproduction of what the fans hear at home. As Geddy Lee of Rush explains, it's hard to replicate multitracked vocals onstage. "If you get an-

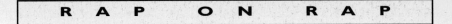

other singer," says Lee, "it's still not going to sound the same." But if you sample the studio vocals, it's better than Memorex.

Unfortunately, as an act's samples grow increasingly complex, music making ends up as something that takes place only in recording studios. And that may be the most insidious thing of all about sampling—that it takes the playing out of music, the life out of live performance. After all, if it's just like the record, why even bother going out?

(June 14, 1990)

How a Musicologist Views Digital Sampling Issues

by Judith Greenberg Finelli

The development of digital sampling technology[1] has resulted in new challenges for forensics—in detection, application of the law, and the definitions of origi-

[1] See Max V. Matthews, *The Technology of Computer Music II* (1969). Digital sampling is the conversion of analog sound waves into a digital code. The digital code that describes the sampled music or other sound can then be reused, manipulated, or combined with other digitized or recorded sounds using a machine with digital data processing capabilities, such as a computer or computerized synthesizer.

nality and infringement.[2] So far, most sampling claims seem to be initiated by recording companies, though music publishing companies should also want to protect their copyrights in the underlying music.

With sampling, many of the traditional standards for evaluating a copyright infringement claim do not apply. Access is obviously not an issue, since sampling establishes access to the sampled recording. Nor is copying an issue, since a sample is a copy, even if the original has been altered electronically.

Therefore, determining whether one recording has sampled another requires forensic methods different from those used in traditional copyright infringement. Many of the elements that are considered insignificant in conventional copyright-infringement cases take on greater importance in detection of sampling. In nonsampling cases one usually compares two songs' main melodies (pitches and rhythms) to determine similarity, then harmonies (chords), structure, and style. In a sampling case the identity of these key elements is a given.

On the other hand, tempo is rarely important in determining classic copyright infringement. Where sampling is in question, however, a good way to detect it is to clock precisely the speed of each song's related portion. If they are identical, and other factors sound identical, too, sampling is a strong possibility. If they are not the identical speed, and the second piece sounds distorted and in a slightly lower pitch, then sampling could still have occurred, but perhaps the sample was slowed down deliberately by the infringer.

Another change in the comparison process is in identifying the actual key of each piece. In classic copyright cases, whether two songs are in the same key is irrelevant to whether one is an infringement of the other. Where the issue is sampling, however, whether the related fragments of the two songs are in the same key bears directly on whether the second recording sampled the first.

A third factor in detecting sampling that does not exist in standard copyright cases is instrumentation. In a traditional copyright case, whether the allegedly infringing work uses the same instrumentation as the original is normally not relevant. In a sampling case, instrumenta-

[2] The first reported decision in a digital sampling case is Grand Upright Music, Ltd. v. Warner Brothers Records, Inc., 91 Civ. 7648 (KTD) (Dec. 16, 1991). See generally Robert G. Sugarman and Joseph P. Salvo, "Sampling Litigation in the Limelight," *New York Law Journal*, March 16, 1992, p. 1, col. 1.

tion takes on a new significance. One way to detect sampling is to determine if the supposed sampler has left a "footprint" that enables the second song to be traced to the first. These "footprints" include the underlying accompaniment parts. In one case a sampler had taken a fairly common piano passage from another recording. He might have escaped unnoticed had he not also included the first syllable of the singer-songwriter's next vocal passage from the original recording. This one syllable proved sampling.

Once sampling has been established, the main questions asked by attorneys for both plaintiffs and defendants are "How much was taken?" and "How important is the sampled fragment to the original and to the new piece?" At this point the attorneys are planning negotiation strategy and need to define the strength of their position.[3] Attorneys for defendants and plaintiffs ask for quantitative and qualitative evaluations in order to determine a reasonable fee to compensate the proprietor of the sampled recording. In making such evaluations the relevant questions include:

- What amount was taken from the original composition? Is it de minimis?

- What percentage of the original recording was sampled?

- What percentage of the infringing recording consists of the sampled material?

- How important is the sampled material both to the original recording and the infringement? For example, is it the "hook" (main signature melody) in either piece?

- Has the sampled material been changed or enhanced? If so, is it still recognizable as being derived from the earlier recording?

- Could the new recording maintain its identity without the sampled material?

- Has additional material in the new song evolved from the sampled material, thus enlarging the degree of copying?

Often, as is typical of rap music, a short musical fragment from the original song occupies a large portion of a new piece because it has

[3] "A New Spin on Music Sampling: A Case for Fair Pay," 105 *Harvard Law Review* 726, 1992.

been looped (repeated constantly). Because of its repeated use this fragment takes on greater significance in the infringing piece than it had in the original piece. Also, if the new piece is rap music, then it is mostly spoken rather than sung. Therefore, the sampled music fragment might be the only melodic material in the new song, and may be the musical glue that binds the piece.

(May 22, 1992)

Why Rap Doesn't Cut It Live

by Jonathan Gold

There may be nothing at this moment in pop music more exhilarating than a great new rap record—the street-smart immediacy, the juxtaposition of beat and funky-fresh politics. Even if you don't like the stuff, you can sense that it matters.

Nineteen-year-olds like De La Soul regularly come out of nowhere with mature, accessible, fully realized albums that radically shift the nature of the medium. Pundits and clergymen spend more time parsing the lyrics of certain rap songs than they do recent abortion decisions. Rap has been praised as a voice for the voiceless, an important mass medium for the underclass.

So why is rap so dull onstage?

When a new hard-rock band plays its very first support gig for, say, Whitesnake, it knows where to stand, what guitar licks work best, how the bass player should look when he bumps up against the guitarist.

Its album may be—probably will be—truly banal, indistinguishable right down to the cover from Skid Row's latest or a copy of Golden Earring's greatest hits; but onstage the group looks and sounds like what it is: a competent, professional arena band.

All the years of rehearsal and recording lead up to the moment when the singer can finally ask a Palace crowd, "Los Angeles, are you ready to rock?" And the crowd, insofar as it likes that stuff, is entertained.

But the simultaneous rise of record-company demand for new rappers and the national shortage of clubs willing to let new rappers play has all but ensured that rap remain almost exclusively a recorded medium.

Young bands, while baby geniuses in the studio, are often in the position of going out on the road with a gold album but almost no live experience. Hard-core rappers with gold albums and plenty of live experience are often wretched onstage. Certain splendid rap entertainers—Doug E. Fresh, for one—are fairly obscure. Where a rocker lives or dies by what he does onstage, a rapper rarely does.

Been to a rap show lately?

Here's what you might find: Two guys in sweats and Afrika medallions shamble onto the stage at the Palace, slump and mumble into their microphones over beats overamplified to the point of being indiscernible.

It takes nearly three full songs before you realize that this is the brilliant young act you came to see, not the no-name openers. The group's debut LP has been universally praised as subtle and complex, but you'd never know it from their concert.

On a different night perhaps a certain famous political rapper is on the bill, bellowing along with his hits like a pledge at a frat party.

Or:

- The multiplatinum hard-core rapper who's structured his show like a second-rate Las Vegas revue.

- The pioneer gangster rapper who attempts to enliven his audience by shouting, "All the people with AIDS keep quiiii-et."

- The rapper who brings dozens of his friends onstage, then can't seem to find his microphone.

- The many, many rappers who perform perfunctory medleys, as if one halfhearted chorus from each of their popular songs is all the audience wants to hear.

Out of the fifty or so major rap shows in the Los Angeles area over the last several years, perhaps half a dozen have been engaging on any level at all.

N.W.A. was dull. Eric B & Rakim were dull. Young M.C. was dull. M.C. Hammer was dull. Even Public Enemy has been dull.

Consider the basic nature of live rap: a guy onstage talking over recorded music, as exciting as *Sing Along with Mitch.* The format allows little room for spontaneity—the rappers considered "good live acts" are those who sound the most like their records.

Since almost all of the backing tracks you hear in concert are their records, the show adds little or nothing to the experience of the music. (Today's complicated hip-hop mixes, sometimes featuring samples from dozens of records per song, would be impossible for an octopus to replicate live.)

The craft of rap these days is the recording studio, and in the history of the genre, no one has defined the state of the art of rap performance the way Mick Jagger did for rock or James Brown did for R&B.

Rap was a strictly live medium when it began about fifteen years ago in Bronx discos, four years before the first rap record was released. The essence of "hip-hop" (an umbrella term that includes both rap and the culture associated with rap) was the larcenous borrowing of music from a number of different sources, to be recombined into something totally new.

The heroes of first-generation rap were the deejays who made the new sound—Grandmaster Flash, D.J. Kool Herc, Afrika ("Planet

Rock") Bambaataa—by playing turntables as if they were magnificent synthesizers of unlimited capacity. The spontaneity of a good deejay's invention was thrilling. The rappers, or MCs, who talked over the beats were considered subsidiary, there to pump up the party, while their deejays pumped ten seconds of an old Jimmy Castor record into art.

But the anticipated expense of purchasing rights to the records deejays borrowed from kept the number of samples to a minimum (or none: Sugarhill Records, the dominant label of the time, used a house band) and hip-hop records spotlighted rappers above all. (The first mix record, "Grandmaster Flash and the Wheels of Steel," wasn't released until 1981.) The producer supplanted the deejay as the dominant creative force. And along with the demise of the live deejay went any opportunity for spontaneity on the part of the rapper.

When you listen to early rap records, which were basically denatured re-creations of live performances, it becomes clear that the clichés of present-day rap performance were already well established in the seventies. At least half the songs praise the deejay; half invite the audience to party down.

By the beginning of the eighties hip-hop had degenerated into a dog-and-pony act, gimmicky disco for kids to spin on their heads to . . . Break Dance!

With the release of Run-DMC's first record in the middle of the decade, the cutting edge of recorded rap essentially became beat-box rock 'n' roll—rebellious attitude, dangerous edge, and all. Rap performance remained a dance-hall novelty, complete with the outdated call-and-response routines and unrestrained deejay worship. The sound changed, but the vision hardly at all.

(The aggressive nature of rap battles and unstructured deejay-centered hip-hop may have continued on a local level in the New York clubs but hardly made it onto the concert stage.)

Run-DMC's stage-stalking, crotch-grabbing, gangster-style yelling, which became the model for a generation of hard-core rappers, was entertaining at first—DMC is a powerful live rapper—but quickly grew clichéd. Such poppy rappers as M.C. Hammer and Jazzy Jeff & the Fresh Prince rely on energetic dancing rather than music to carry their shows, like old soul-revue bands. Guys like Tone Lōc—well, maybe just Tone Lōc—can carry a crowd with just the sheer weight of their personalities.

Deprived of the element of surprise that even the hoariest rock 'n' roll acts can count on to relieve the monotony of their sets, rappers—all of them—rely on the same old formulas. They exhort their audiences to scream, to stand, to yell louder than the kids on the other side of the auditorium, as if they were rocking a disco instead of the Sports Arena.

They have their deejays, who are at this point in rap history basically there to drop the needle on the backing tracks and perform interminable turntable scratch solos, like the drum solos in seventies stadium rock. And always, inevitably, sometimes several times an evening:

Throw your hands in the air
And wave them like you just don't care
And if you want to get rocked tonight
Everybody say, "Oh, yeah!"

Public Enemy makes its shows exciting with the unpredictability of its oratory, not of its music. You never know if Chuck D is going to go off on the Supreme Court, or if Professor Griff (when he was still a member) would suggest, as he did at USC two years ago, that black men who date white women be burned alive. Each show is a potential media event. If you follow the band, however, you do know exactly what Flavor Flav is going to say to Chuck when it's time to do "Cold Lampin' With Flavor," because the basic stage show is the same every night.

L.L. Cool J is among the most talented performers in rap, a man who recorded three million–selling albums before he was out of his teens, and whose polysyllabic hard-core rhymes have been matched neither in ferocity nor virtuosity.

But he scored a major crossover hit a few years ago with rapped love ballads and tailored his live act to his new audience of young girls . . . to the extent that it became a slick, bloodless revue, complete with mirrors, lasers, and an onstage Ferrari, though without passion.

This winter he showed up at the Palace to jam on an encore with Def Jam label-mates 3rd Bass. Over a funky beat, just him and a turntable, he spun a freestyle improvisation. "I juice the party like jumper cables," he rapped, and he did. Without the smoke machines or a prepared backing track, his clear tenor and astounding machine-gun articulation cut through the torpor of the room like an electric knife; it was a great rock 'n' roll moment. This was live rap as it should be but hardly ever is.

(June 3, 1990)

PART 2

The Message

I'M LOW IN THE WATER, BUT I AIN'T DUMB. YOU SEEN WHAT I DID WHEN THE TITANIC COME...
P. Steiner
ICE BERG

Rolling Out an Agenda for Rap

by Rev. Dr. Calvin O. Butts III

On Mother's Day I announced from the pulpit of the Abyssinian Baptist Church my plan to protest against particular rap lyrics, other music, and music videos that I and a broad cross-section of people consider vulgar, offensive to women, and contrary to the progress and goals of African Americans.

At that time I also pledged to take issue with the music industry for encouraging and promoting these lyrics and videos. My frustration about specific rap lyrics is what the media have given special attention. Indeed, there are many black rap artists whose words are positive, express the rich heritage of African Americans, provide valuable political and social commentary, and genuinely portray the importance and role of African-American women in our society.

But then there are other talented artists who are influenced by the power elite of the music industry and are lured with money to use their craft both to exploit the negative conditions that exist in some inner-city communities and to debase African-American women.

My objection to these lyrics and videos is spurred not only because I am a minister but because I am a black man, husband, and father. I want to supplant these negative music lyrics and videos with positive ones.

Let there be no mistake—this protest against offensive lyrics, videos, and companion products, such as T-shirts, is not an assault on our First Amendment right to free speech and expression. I cherish this very important privilege, but I also believe that African-American women such as Harriet Tubman, Rosa Parks, Ella Baker, Soujourner Truth, and Fannie Lou Hamer, among others, did not struggle and jeopardize their lives to give young black music artists the temerity to refer to black women as bitches and whores and, with abandon, characterize African-American people as niggers.

This was not the dream of Dr. Martin Luther King, not part of Marcus Garvey's plan for black improvement, nor Malcolm X's push for African-American self-determination and empowerment.

On a recent Saturday, as part of my campaign against explicit rap music, I held a rally in New York that attracted more than seven hundred supporters, and had planned to steamroll negative rap recordings that were turned in to the church. I got behind the wheels, but did not roll over the tapes and CDs that lay on the ground, because there were counterdemonstrators and police and I did not want to cause a confrontation. That was not my intention. I did, however, dump those tapes and CDs in front of Sony's midtown headquarters, because that recording company is a major contributor to the production of offensive music.

I am willing and hope to meet with all the rappers whose lyrics I consider repugnant in order to help make these artists understand the impact their negative words have on African-American young people, in particular, and black people in general.

This campaign has the support of major organizations, including the NAACP, Urban League, and 100 Black Men and Women, to name a few.

In the fall, outstanding leaders from various groups will be invited to a meeting I will convene of people representing academia, religion, politics, the African-American community, civil and human rights organizations, and the music industry, among others, to discuss ways to accelerate the improvement of conditions in inner-city neighborhoods and thus provide an impetus for the music industry and African-American rap artists to work in partnership to create music bare of negative attitudes and language.

(1993)

The Politics of Gangster Rap

by Brent Staples

The most dangerous myth facing African Americans today is that middle-class life is counterfeit and that only poverty and suffering, and the rage that attends them, are real.

Anyone who doubts the power of this myth need only think back to the Clarence

Thomas confirmation hearings, and how Judge Thomas's status as "a sharecropper's grandson" was put forth as a qualification for the Supreme Court. The poverty fetish is also dangerous; anyone who doubts this might recall Edmund Perry, the black Exeter graduate who was shot to death by an undercover cop in Morningside Heights. At Exeter, Edmund had played the swaggering tough without risk. At home, in the streets of New York, the role reared up and killed him.

Tom Wolfe's essay "Radical Chic," published in 1970, is still the best window into the notion that a magical nobility is somehow conferred on the dispossessed. The essay lampoons the party thrown by the conductor Leonard Bernstein for a group of Black Panthers at which the Panthers were fawned over by New York's elite.

It was there, Mr. Wolfe wrote, that "a Park Avenue matron first articulated the great recurrent emotion of Radical Chic: 'These are no civil rights *Negroes* wearing gray suits three sizes too big—these are *real men.*'" The central tenet of radical chic is that urban primitivism is romantic and that middle-classness is passé.

A generation has passed since Park Avenue swooned for the Panthers. The black middle class is larger than ever, but its influence is much diminished in the inner city. The ghetto, once a palatable mix of the middle class, the mildly poor, and the very poor, is now made up of the very poor alone. Adolescent murder and pregnancy are endemic; more black men go to jail than to college.

And then there's gangster rap.

For those who haven't caught up, gangster rap is that wildly successful music in which all women are "bitches" and "whores" and young men kill each other for sport. It's hard-core, and bristles with guns. Hear a band called Onyx, recently number one on the charts, urging its listeners to "Throw ya gunz in the air/ And pop-pop like ya just don't care." Hear the rapper called Dr. Dre: "Rat-a-tat and a tat like that/ Never hesitate to put a nigga on his back."

Hear the Beatnuts, in an ode to the machine pistol: "It ain't nothing you should laugh to/ I'll shoot your moms if I have to." These lyrics go out to an audience of young black men who are being murdered at five times the national average.

The rappers claim variously that they are "telling it like it is," or "reporting what we see in the streets," or "creating characters" that listeners misinterpret. The most effective rejoinder comes from Mike Davis's *City of Quartz*, a history of Los Angeles, where gangster rap was born. "In supposedly stripping bare the reality of the streets, 'telling it like it

is,' " Mr. Davis writes, "they also offer an uncritical mirror to fantasy power trips of violence, sexism, and greed."

Rappers, take note: The key phase is *uncritical mirror*. The music "plays" at rape and murder in a way that celebrates them.

The final irony is that some gangster rappers are middle-class guys posing as inner-city killers. A rapper from Onyx recently took offense when accused of middle-class origins: "That's bull, I'm a real [expletive deleted]," Onyx's Suave told Frank Owen of New York *Newsday*. "I've been seeing people get shot all of my life."

Here, by way of Suave, is the problem simply put: In the streets, middle-class normalcy for blacks is portrayed as an inferior state of being. The news and entertainment industries are often in complicity with this. That's bad news because cultural ideology is powerful, especially in the lives of the young. It determines how we see them, how they see themselves, and, to a large extent, what they aspire to become.

When middle-class blacks fabricate violent urban pasts, they pay homage to murder. When record company executives pose for pictures with gun-toting rappers, and when they push that murderous music, they trade in blood.

(August 27, 1993)

Both Sides with Jesse Jackson

JESSE JACKSON, Host: Welcome to *Both Sides.*

[Rap Video from EMI Records]

JACKSON: The rhythmic rhyme of rap. We know it when we hear it. It's a driving force. Music with a message. But sometimes that message calls for violence against police, against whites, against women. And increasingly, people are saying that's when the rap goes too far. The subject tonight is that type of rap. It's called gangster rap. Is it polluting the minds of our young people, or is it just another form of artistic expression? Before we meet our guests tonight, here is some background.

[voice-over] In Austin, Texas, nineteen-year-old Ronald Ray Howard was sentenced to death for killing a state trooper. Howard's defense: Rap music made him do it. The jury rejected an argument that Howard's inner-city life and lifelong exposure to so-called gangster rap were contributing factors. Immediately before the crime Howard was listening to rapper 2Pac.

ROBERT BELL, Jackson County, Texas, District Attorney: I can tell you that some of the first words out of this defendant's, Ronald Ray Howard's, mouth as to why he shot that trooper was "He stopped me for no reason," and that's exactly what 2Pac is conveying in the lyrics that he's got in that song.

JACKSON: [voice-over] Around the nation some police are calling rap the music of murder. Police went on the offensive when Ice-T came out with his violent rap, "Cop Killer." Not all rap is violent. Even critics say they can enjoy the music when it does not promote violence against police, women, or others. Critics say the music industry is part of the problem. Rap accounts for nearly ten percent of its $7.8-billion gross and that bottom line includes gangster rap, so the record companies have a major stake.

REV. CALVIN BUTTS, Abyssinian Baptist Church, New York: This trash that has been pumped into our living rooms and our communities belongs rightfully to the record industry.

JACKSON: [voice-over] It's part of a groundswell against violent rap even in the black community from which the music grew.

ANTIRAP ACTIVIST: To hear some of these rappers say it's all right to tear down your neighborhoods, to stick up people, to kill people, to disrespect each other—well, it's not all right!

JACKSON: [voice-over] But there are also defendants [sic] of violent rap. Both sides at odds. Both sides with powerful feelings.

[on camera] With us to talk about rap in all of its forms is rap artist Yo-Yo. She joins us from San Francisco. Also with us, Harry Allen, who's a writer and close associate of one of the most controversial rap groups, Public Enemy. Dr. Spencer Holland is with us. He's a psychologist at Morgan State University. Also with us, Officer Gary Hankins of the Washington, D.C., chapter of the Fraternal Order of Police. Dr. Holland, you are a psychologist. You've studied the impact of these sound waves upon people's minds. Has violent rap or gangster rap gone too far?

DR. SPENCER HOLLAND, Psychologist, Morgan State University: Well, I wouldn't go as far as saying that I've studied this. I'm the director of the Center for Educating African-American Males at Morgan, and one of the—and my area of specialty in psychology is social learning behavior, and one of the things we know about why we imitate and model and identify with certain kinds of people is their prevalence in our lives. I'm not going to say that rap is the cause of what we just saw, the guy killing, but what I'm seeing in terms of the way young boys and teenage boys are treating women, are treating their girlfriends, and the way these girls accept these definitions of themselves, or descriptions of themselves, in this rap is very, very dangerous. We have younger boys raping little girls. We have the incredible increase in date violence, physical abuse of girls by boys. Something is driving this, and I wouldn't suggest that it is all rap, but it's—there's a part of it there.

JACKSON: Harry, as a writer and a thinker, how does this play out in your own mind as you write?

HARRY ALLEN, Rap Activist: Well, what's notoriously absent from all of this discussion that I hear about hip-hop music and what it's doing to black and white people is a cogent and clear analysis of the problem of racism. I think even in this discussion here, it would do well and save your time and the viewers' if we would move immediately to that—because when we do, we will answer the questions of psychology, law enforcement, and these other issues.

JACKSON: But, Harry, is racism why a young black rap artist calls a black woman bitch or says, "I am a nigger with an attitude"?

MR. ALLEN: Absolutely.

JACKSON: And there is no burden on the part of that person to rise above that demeaning process?

MR. ALLEN: Well, his burden is to eliminate racism, to understand it and to attack it, but really—see, the problem with a lot of these attacks is that people are saying, "End this kind of gangster rap," and gangster rap is a term that I don't use. I don't find it accurate. I don't find it useful because, first of all, who came up with it? Second of all what does it mean? What is it?

JACKSON: It means people acting like gangsters, killing people, and blowing up cars, and demeaning—that's what—it means—it's the gangster psychology, and it seems that many young people are acting out that life-style.

MR. ALLEN: Black people are attempting to compensate for their lack of power under white supremacy, and it comes out in our art, it comes out in our music. They're trying to make up for what's missing. What's missing is order. What's missing is power.

JACKSON: Yo-Yo, from your point of view as a rapper, is the lack of power or lack of place of black people a justification for black male rappers calling black women bitches?

MR. ALLEN: The greatest white—

JACKSON: Yo-Yo.

YO-YO, Rap Artist: I feel as if rappers have—rappers have their own way of—rappers have their own way of putting out their music from the way they feel and from their perspective. I don't think that a lot of people understand where rap comes from. Rappers are not out killing people. Rappers are not raping young kids and—rappers make statements. These statements get turned around and—

JACKSON: But, Yo-Yo, the point is we've always been called niggers and our women have been called bitches, but we disagreed with it, we resented it, resisted it, and for—this seems to be a concession to such a demeaning process.

YO-YO: So are you saying that rap is the reason for all of this?

JACKSON: No, I'm really raising a question. I'm raising—Harry, since you're a writer, where is the redemptive dimension? Where is the resistance to the racism?

MR. ALLEN: Well, we haven't yet formed—black people have not yet formed an effective resistance.

DR. HOLLAND: We're talking about rappers.

JACKSON: No, no. Speak for yourself now.

MR. ALLEN: Rappers are black people.

DR. HOLLAND: Well, don't speak for us. Don't include me in that "We haven't formed an effective defense against . . ." Jesse and I have been out this—at this too long to sit up here and tell us we haven't formed something that isn't as negative as what is coming across, and what I'm seeing affecting my—

MR. ALLEN: If I could finish my statement, what I mean by that is an effective resistance against racism would be one which eliminates the problem. We've not yet produced an answer to this problem yet.

DR. HOLLAND: So negative rap is a way of attacking racism head-on?

MR. ALLEN: It is a reaction to white supremacy in the state of powerlessness.

DR. HOLLAND: I wouldn't doubt that, but is—it's a reaction that is coming—is it being expressed by those who are oppressed as negative to themselves? I asked my young—I asked a group of high school students, boys, all boys, "Do you guys have sisters and mothers?" and they looked at me, and they said, "Yeah." I said, "Would you approve of guys calling your sisters and mothers bitches and whores and having them—inviting them to do the degrading things that seem to come from some of these rap—" and they said, "Well, no," and they said, "Well, it's only music." Well, it's like Dr. Deborah Prothro-Stith, one of our sisters who was in the forefront of the violence movement—she said, "There's no consequence." When the kids memorize your raps, there is no consequence. There is no blood. There is no pain. There's—that's what the violent movies and television does.

JACKSON: Officer Hankins, as policemen on the street, how does this manifest itself in street life where you live and work?

GARY HANKINS, D.C. Fraternal Order of Police: We see young people today—we see them executing other young people in a black community. The majority of the victims—and I think it's very self-serving to try to deflect the discussion away from the rap music and what it's doing to its receivers to a discussion of racism. I think we ought to focus on what's happening.

MR. ALLEN: I absolutely agree.

MR. HANKINS: What's happening out here is that the black community are the people who are buying and listening to most of these records. Black children are being victimized.

MR. ALLEN: That's not correct.

MR. HANKINS: Black children are dying in numbers far out of proportion to the population at the hands of other black young men, and they look at it—

8 6

YO-YO: It goes far more—it goes past rap.

DR. HOLLAND: Let me—

JACKSON: Yo-Yo, I'll ask you a question. When I see four white police beat Rodney King, I call that racism.

YO-YO: That's right.

JACKSON: When I see young blacks drive by in an all-black neighborhood and shoot blacks without mercy on a corner and kill them, I can't call that racism also.

MR. HANKINS: In the District of Columbia—

JACKSON: How do you see that?

YO-YO: The problem is bigger than rap. I mean, hey, rap is—

JACKSON: No, the problem is bigger than rap, but how do you define that act?

MR. ALLEN: It's part of the confusion of white supremacy. That's what it is.

YO-YO: That's right.

MR. HANKINS: Well, let me—

DR. HOLLAND: That's far too general—

MR. HANKINS: If we—

DR. HOLLAND: —for the fact that a black boy, sixteen years old, stood up on a hill and shot a whole swimming pool full of children here in Washington, D.C., about three years ago—three weeks ago, and he was a black boy, and all the children in that pool were black.

MR. ALLEN: Because he knew if he did it to a pool of white children what would happen.

DR. HOLLAND: The same thing should have happened to him when he did it to the pool of black kids.

MR. ALLEN: But that's part of the confusion of racism.

MR. HANKINS: That's not true. Now we arrest these kids, and I deal with these kids. These kids don't give a whit about race or sex or power. They are going to do what they want to do, and they have—

MR. ALLEN: Which ones don't?

MR. HANKINS: The ones that we arrest.

MR. ALLEN: All of them?

MR. HANKINS: The ones who are shooting people—

MR. ALLEN: Sir—

MR. HANKINS: The ones who are shooting people don't care what color the targets are. They happen to live in neighborhoods full of black people who become their targets of opportunity.

MR. ALLEN: That's part of the confusion of racism.

MR. HANKINS: Let's look at the Nazis.

MR. ALLEN: That itself is part of the confusion of racism.

JACKSON: We're going to come right back and ask about the responsibility of the record company in all of this because there is a commercial dimension. We'll be right back.

ICE-T: I'm 'bout to bust some shots off / I'm 'bout to dust some cops off / Cop Killer / It's better you than me / Cop Killer / Fuck police brutality.

[Commercial break]

FIRST RAP ARTIST: I would love to talk about blue skies and apple pies, but that's not what I wrote. I live here in the projects.

SECOND RAP ARTIST: To get censored of anything I had to say, it would be, you know, kind of like putting me in the closet and locking me away.

THIRD RAP ARTIST: Ice-T may not be doing the same thing Kid 'n Play's doing, but I think one another—we support each other, and I think, ultimately, we just want rap to be regarded and respected as a music form with a lot of different criterias just like any other music form.

[Commercial break]

JACKSON: Yo-Yo, you're a young African-American woman, twenty years old. You're rapping against what some others advocate. What is your message?

YO-YO: Well, my message is for the strength of women. I rap about all sorts of things. There's no limit to what I would speak about in my music. I think that sometimes rap do go overboard, and I try to focus—

JACKSON: For example?

YO-YO: I try to focus my music—

JACKSON: For example? For example? Yo-Yo, when you say overboard, what's the limit?

YO-YO: What's the limit?

JACKSON: Yeah.

YO-YO: The limit to me is just what I call ridiculous rap where it—they're just—it's just—it's just nonstop—

JACKSON: Is that when they're saying violent things against women? Is that over the edge?

YO-YO: Well, see, I'm not the one—I am not the one to critique somebody else's—to critique someone else's rap. I—what I consider overboard is those out there who's just be, be, be, be, you know, constantly and just—I mean, no meaning to the rap, no emphasis on it. I mean, you know, those are who I consider to be real ridiculous, overboard, I mean, but it's a lot of rap that you consider to be gangster rap that I could understand and I can relate to and I don't consider to be ridiculous.

JACKSON: You know, Harry, not that it is not comprehensible. This black experience did not start last year, you know. It's a pretty old experience, you know. Is the record industry, now that it is profiting from this, responsible for pushing it to the outer limits?

MR. ALLEN: Again, what I'm talking about is racism, and you can find—

JACKSON: Please answer this question. Is the record industry, now that it is profiting from it—

MR. ALLEN: Who is the record industry?

JACKSON: It may be Time Warner. It may—those who make money from it. In other words, if you come in with, say, degrees of rap, are they more likely to sign up Artist A that's into a violent, gangster rap or Artist B who is into romance?

MR. ALLEN: I don't want to limit this discussion. I think it's a very expansive program you've got here.

JACKSON: But you are limiting it. If you'll just answer my question, we can kind of move it. I mean, is the record industry a factor in—

MR. ALLEN: The racists are responsible, whether that's in the police department, the record industry—

JACKSON: But you keep limiting the—

DR. HOLLAND: See, what has just happened to the television industry has to happen to the record industry. The television industry has been brought to bear in front of the Congress, in front of the country, "You're going to have to clean up your act. Your violence on television is affecting our children. Your teachers are telling you. Your psychologists are telling you." Rap—the record industry which is promoted by rap in this capitalist system—one of the things I want to say that's positive about these black kids I see doing these—doing this rap is that it's very, very American. Their First Amendment rights are protected. You can say anything you want, but what is the effect on the children that memorize—I have children that won't memorize a poem that know—that can—that memorize a fifteen-minute rap song.

YO-YO: And why is that? Why is that?

MR. ALLEN: Because it relates to them. It relates to them.

DR. HOLLAND: Why is that? Most of what they memorize is full of sex and violence and all of that, you know, and—

YO-YO: That's what society is made of. We have—

DR. HOLLAND: Not all society is—[cross talk] There is a redemptive part of society, Yo-Yo.

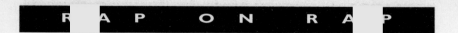

YO-YO: We have to overcome that. These kids will not memorize poems. These kids are not learning their spelling words; not—and memorizing rap not because of the fact that these rappers are out there or these rappers are being seen on TV. These kids go out and purchase these tapes. These kids go out and listen to these tapes. They rewind it. There is a demand for rap. You cannot blame that for everything, because after rap you're going to still have these same problems.

JACKSON: But, Yo-Yo, isn't there an attempt—

YO-YO: You will still have these same problems, and who would you blame? Who are you going to blame?

JACKSON: Yo-Yo, isn't that an attempt to make a distinction between the rap as an art form—perhaps the most phenomenal art form since jazz—this is a phenomenal rap form. We're talking about a content that lends itself to promoting self-destruction and violence. Is that overboard?

YO-YO: I'm not saying—I don't go on to say—I do—I do feel that rappers have a responsibility. I'm not saying that we don't have a responsibility, but I think that the responsibility on us should be the respons—like a drunk driver. A drunk driver—he might get in an accident. You have several cases every day. They don't ban liquor.

JACKSON: Officer Hankins, let me ask you a question.

YO-YO: You understand what I'm saying?

JACKSON: Now with all the talk about Ice-T, you know, and the "Cop Killer" rap, the—

YO-YO: I—it's not a rap—that's not rap.

JACKSON: Just one second.

YO-YO: That's not rap. That's—

JACKSON: But in—but the movie where you had all of these cops killed.

MR. HANKINS: *Terminator 2.*

JACKSON: *Terminator.* I mean, I didn't see the cops go berserk over *Terminator* but over Ice-T.

MR. HANKINS: Right, and we don't like either. Our—

YO-YO: That's right, and, also, we need to clean that up. You need to clean that up. That's a crash metal album.

JACKSON: Why didn't the cops react to *Terminator 2?*

YO-YO: It's not a rap album.

MR. HANKINS: If I can—we reacted to Ice-T's—he implored people to kill police. He went beyond showing it. He went out and implored people. We went—I went to the Time Warner stockholders meeting out there as part of the protest—

JACKSON: It's a heavy metal album, he's a rapper, but I'm asking the question why didn't the police go berserk over *Terminator?* They're just killing police. The whole thing was kill, kill, kill, kill.

MR. HANKINS: In *Terminator*—

MR. ALLEN: They shot them in the knees. They didn't kill them.

MR. HANKINS: In *Terminator* people—

YO-YO: They justified—

MR. HANKINS: If I can finish this, in *Terminator* the people who were shooting police were villains. In Ice-T's rap music the people who were shooting police are heroes, and therein lies the distinction.

MR. ALLEN: That's not a true statement.

MR. HANKINS: It is. I saw both, I listened to both, and I went—

MR. ALLEN: *Terminator 2*—

MR. HANKINS: —and I went to Time Warner—

MR. ALLEN: I want to get back to your—[cross talk]

MR. HANKINS: The Terminator is not a hero.

MR. ALLEN: Sure he is.

DR. HOLLAND: It's all violence. It's all violence, and the effect of that violence, whether it's video or music—

JACKSON: As this composed rapping conversation heats up, stay with us. We're going to come back and talk about rapping and free speech. We'll be right back.

[Commercial break]

JACKSON: Yo-Yo, let me ask you just a very basic question. Is this music hurting or helping our community?

YO-YO: I feel like this music is helping in a way, and in a way, I feel as if it might be dangerous be—only because a guy can say—only because the media is making it so rough on us, enabling people to blame their actions on us. That's the only part that I feel is really hurting us.

JACKSON: Gary, is this exercise in free speech—it is a free speech—helping or hurting?

MR. HANKINS: It's hurting. In Nazi Germany, in World War II—before World War II—

YO-YO: You—

MR. HANKINS:—the Nazis used the expression of free speech in order to poison the minds of a country to rise up and kill millions of people. The German people didn't open—wake up one morning and say, "Let's kill every Jew we can find." They were taught to do that. That was—and if you lis—if you study Goebbels, he said that they began a propaganda campaign to change people's minds ten years before the Nazis came to power. The power of the spoken word is as great today as it was then.

JACKSON: But, Harry, in this hurting process, do you make a distinction between a rap that describes the ugliness of police brutality on the one hand or a violent rap that in substance justifies drive-by shootings?

MR. ALLEN: I think—

YO-YO: What do you consider a violent rap? I don't understand.

MR. ALLEN: I'd like to make the—I'd like to clarify one thing first for the record, for your 164 countries watching, is that the comparison of hip-hop to the decimation of Semites by white Germans is ludicrous and obscene.

MR. HANKINS: It is illustrating—

MR. ALLEN: How you can even bring something like that into a discussion of—

MR. HANKINS: —and your self-serving denial in trying to deflect this discussion to racism when, in fact, you're making a fortune of inflicting pain on your own people inside ghettos where you're making heroes of killers—I—you know, that's inexcusable.

YO-YO: We're not making—

MR. ALLEN: Those black people watching this understand what I'm talking about.

DR. HOLLAND: Oh, I doubt that. I'm black, and I certainly do not understand what you're talking about, because I deal with children on a daily basis—

MR. ALLEN: Like me.

DR. HOLLAND: —little children, the older children, high school children, college children, you know, and their behaviors are reflecting their acceptance of what we call pass—this passive learning that comes through this incredible repetitiveness, and even though he—Officer Hankins was stretching and reaching, there's an analogy of what he says that—

JACKSON: Let me express—Harry, let me say—I want to thank my guests, Yo-Yo in San Francisco, rap activist and writer Harry Allen, Dr. Spencer Holland of Morgan State, and Officer Gary Hankins. This tremendous genius called rap at its best can revive and redeem, at its worst it really can hurt. Let's choose hope over hurt. Good night. We'll be back next week, and we'll see you then.

(July 24, 1993)

Gangsta Rap Loves You

from Rock & Rap Confidential

The lastest assault on gangsta rap began in November when a handful of self-appointed Los Angeles "community leaders" threatened KPWR-FM with an advertiser boycott if it didn't ban all songs using the words "nigga," "bitch," or "ho." On

December 7, KPWR gave in and began to mask or delete the three words.

During the same week, WBLS/New York announced it will no longer play songs it feels encourage violence, misogyny, or vulgarity; WPGC/Washington, D.C. reaffirmed a bleep-and-ban policy; BET unveiled a ban on "violent" rap videos; and WCKZ/Charlotte exiled gangsta rap to late night airplay. On December 11, President Clinton used his weekly nationwide radio address to congratulate radio for meeting "the obligations we all share to fight violence with values."

But this isn't about words in a song. WCKZ program director Tim Patterson admitted to *USA Today* that, although his station takes some of the words of most-requested artist Snoop Doggy Dogg and flips them backwards, "We know what he's saying."

KPWR program director Rick Cummings defended his station's cave-in by saying, "Even though it's [*nigga*] sort of a greeting, and I can't tell Snoop Doggy Dogg how to address his homeys, we may be doing more harm by legitimizing the word for other cultures that can't or don't understand the black culture."

But if gangsta rap is so hard to understand, why does KPWR's own research show that sixty-five percent of its listeners are Latino? Why is the music so popular that there are now upwards of fifty major market stations featuring it? "We can't ignore the songs," Tim Patterson explains. "They get such a huge response."

Millions are attracted to the brilliant production style of Dr. Dre, the vocal skills of Ice Cube, or the sheer beauty of a modern-day spiritual like D.R.S.'s "Gangsta Lean."

Part of gangsta rap's lyrical appeal stems from its uncritical embrace of the youth abandoned by society. When Ice Cube spoke at Locke High School in South Central Los Angeles on December 6, he took the mic right after the principal had explained that only students who had shown "academic improvement" had been allowed into the gym. "I'm here to talk to everybody outside," Cube said, "everybody who's ditching school today." On that firm foundation, gangsta rap is evolving into America's most important voice for unity.

It begins with the rappers themselves, as they move from boasting and putting each other down to giving each other respect (check 2Pac's "Representin' '93," in which he gives shout-outs to at least one hundred other artists). From there it expands to peace among the black gangs

(check Scarface's "Now I Feel Ya" or Snoop's liner notes), unity between the generations (check Ice Cube's "Lil Ass Gee"), and unity between those inside and outside of prison (check "Gangsta Lean"). Moving on, black rappers now extend a hand to Latinos (check anything recent by Ice-T). This call for unity is echoed by the Latinos of Cypress Hill, the Funky Aztecs in Oakland, Spanish People in Control in Miami, and LA's Brotherhood From Another Hood (produced by Japanese-American Kevin Nakao).

Whites, although often dissed in gangsta rap as cops and Klansmen, respond to the music both for its irresistible sounds and because they have problems with cops and making the rent too. "Gangsta rap is following the same course as the L.A. Rebellion," author Luis Rodriguez explains. "The blacks started it, then the Latinos jumped in, and before it was over the whites hit the streets."

Despite its overt sexism, gangsta rap promotes unity of the sexes by standing up for women. It begins with love for the same mothers that district attorneys often try to prosecute for their kids' run-ins with the law (check "Bang Bang Boogie" by DBG'z, as lovingly sentimental as "Mother and Child Reunion" or even "My Yiddisha Mama"). Gangsta rappers are the most visible and consistent defenders of the L.A. Rebellion and the women who took to the streets to steal food and diapers for their kids (twelve percent of those arrested were female). The Rebellion was caused in part by the unpunished murder of a young woman, Latasha Harlins, who's been forgotten by everyone except gangsta rappers (check 2Pac's "Something 2 Die 4").

2Pac also spits in the face of Bill Clinton's utterly misogynist welfare schemes when, on the prochoice "Keep Ya Head Up," he gives love and respect to all women on welfare. Surely gangsta rap will spread the word as such women find common cause with the kind of men who Coolio's "County Line" portrays being humiliated in a welfare office.

This isn't to say that anyone offended by gangsta lyrics shouldn't speak up, and there are productive ways to do it. On Queen Latifah's new *Black Reign* she is unrelenting in her demand that no one call her a "bitch" or a "ho." Yet Latifah appeared on KPWR to defend gangsta rap, explaining how much she'd learned about it simply by moving to L.A. Backstage at the recent *Billboard* awards, Latifah said: "A lot of that stuff has got to be heard. I wonder who's pulling those radio programmers' strings?"

(November 1993)

Number One, with a Bullet: Songs of Violence Are Part of America's Folk Tradition

by David Hershey-Webb

When rock and blues musician Eric Clapton was honored recently with six Grammys, there were no cries of outrage from the law-enforcement community. Wasn't this the same Eric Clapton whose big hit a number of years ago was a song about killing a cop?

While black rapper Ice-T's song "Cop Killer" has been relegated to the Orwellian dustheap after protests by police officers' organizations and former Vice President Dan Quayle, white pop star Clapton's "I Shot the Sheriff" (written by reggae legend Bob Marley) has escaped condemnation.

Perhaps Clapton's hit will be spared because the killer "didn't shoot the deputy"? Or because he swore "it was in self-defense"? (Don't they all?) Or was the pressure to pull "Cop Killer," while ignoring other songs (and countless movies) that contain similar messages, another reflection of the racial bias that Ice-T and other rappers denounce in the legal system? The National Black Police Officers Association thought so and opposed the threatened boycott that led to the song's demise.

While the censors have their fingers poised over the erase button, there are a number of other songs by white nonrap artists that might deserve deletion for either glamorizing crime or undermining people's faith in the criminal justice system. Following the logic of the opponents of "Cop Killer," removal of these songs from record catalogs and songbooks would be a significant contribution toward restoring respect for law enforcement in an increasingly violent society and may also bring down the crime rate. Similar treatment of white and black recording artists would also demonstrate society's commitment to equal justice before the law.

Woody Guthrie is probably the best-known American folksinger. He has had a deep influence on songwriters from Bob Dylan to Bruce Springsteen. His classic "This Land Is Your Land" has become something of an unofficial national anthem. Like Ice-T, however, Guthrie also wrote a song about killing a police officer, called "Pretty Boy Floyd." In the song Pretty Boy is riding into town when

A deputy sheriff approached him in a manner rather
   rude,
Using vulgar words of anger,
And his wife, she overheard.

Pretty Boy grabbed a log chain,
And the deputy grabbed a gun,
And in the fight that followed,
He laid the deputy down.

After the deputy has been killed—unlike Clapton's or Marley's protagonist, Pretty Boy did "kill the deputy"—Guthrie proceeds to turn Pretty Boy into a hero in a way that surpasses Ice-T's cop killer. Pretty Boy's life on the lam is filled with acts of generosity toward the poor. He pays a "starvin' farmer's mortgage," and leaves a "Christmas dinner for a family on relief." Guthrie's final two stanzas suggest that those with the law on their side cause more suffering than those who break the law:

> **Now as through this world I ramble,**
> **I see lots of funny men,**
> **Some will rob you with a six-gun,**
> **And some with a fountain pen.**
>
> **But as through this life you travel,**
> **And as through this life you roam,**
> **You won't never see an outlaw**
> **Drive a family from their home.**

"Pretty Boy Floyd" is available on any number of recordings, by various artists. Shouldn't law enforcement officials be concerned with a song in which a deputy sheriff is killed simply for using "vulgar words in anger" and which suggests that such outlaws are heroes?

Bob Dylan was Woody Guthrie's biggest fan, in his early days self-consciously patterning himself after the folksinger. Dylan has written a number of songs about crime that display a deep distrust of the fairness of the legal system. "The Death of Emmett Till" is about the acquittal of two brothers for the torture and killing of a black youth in Mississippi. Dylan writes that "On the jury there were men who helped the brothers commit this awful crime/And so this trial was a mockery, but nobody seemed to mind."

The alleged frame-up of former boxing champion Rubin "Hurricane" Carter on a murder charge is the subject of another Dylan song. "Hurricane" helped bring the case to the public eye. Dylan sings

> **. . . If you're black you might as well not show up on the street**
> **'Less you wanna draw the heat.**
>
> **. . . The trial was a pig-circus, he never had a chance.**

**. . . The DA said he was the one who did the deed,
And the all-white jury agreed.**

And, recalling Guthrie's "Pretty Boy Floyd":

**Now all the criminals in their coats and their ties
Are free to drink martinis and watch the sun rise
While Rubin sits like Buddha in a ten-foot cell,
An innocent man in living hell.**

Dylan's songs are not calls to lawless violence like "Cop Killer," or seeming justifications of lawlessness, like "Pretty Boy Floyd," but aren't they just as dangerous? Don't they evoke in the listener a contempt toward the legal system that could easily lead to lawbreaking? The implicit message is the same in all of these protest songs—if the system is not fair, why play by the rules? What this means in the case of "Cop Killer" is that if police brutality will not be punished under the law, its victims will seek retribution on their own.

Guthrie and Dylan are not the only folksingers who treat criminals in a sympathetic manner. Killers of one kind or another abound in traditional folk music, suggesting that folk music is one of the primary causes of the high murder rate in this country.

Traditional folk songs do not overtly criticize the injustice of the legal system. Instead, like the movies, they perpetuate a myth of the outlaw as an American hero. The well-known folk ballad "Jesse James" is about a "lad" who "killed many a man." Like Pretty Boy Floyd, he had a philanthropic streak. "He took from the rich and gave to the poor." The ballad portrays him as a popular figure, recognizing his bravery and denouncing the "dirty little coward" who killed him. How many schoolchildren have been exposed to this and other folk songs that make a killer appear heroic?

Unlike Pretty Boy and Jesse James, "Stagolee" was no friend of the poor. He was simply a "bad man" who shot Billy de Lyons because "he stole his Stetson hat." Still, there is something alluring about the killer who spent "one hundred dollars just to buy him a suit of clothes." Could this song, in some small way, be responsible for the numerous homicides that have been committed because someone desired expensive sneakers?

Some of the most violent folks songs involve "crimes of passion."

Given the widespread occurrence of domestic violence in society today, these songs are ripe for depublishing. Their particular insidiousness stems from the fact that they tend to be sung in a sweet, lilting manner that contrasts sharply with the macabre details of the story.

In "Bank of the Ohio," a folk song from the early 1900s, the jilted lover sings of his victim whom he took "by her lily-white hand":

> **I dragged her down to the riverbank,**
> **There I pushed her in to drown**
> **And I watched her as she floated down.**
>
> **. . . I murdered the only girl I love**
> **Because she would not marry me.**

"Knoxville Girl" is even more vivid:

> **She fell down on her bended knees,**
> **For mercy she did cry;**
> **Oh, Willy dear, don't kill me here,**
> **I'm unprepared to die;**
> **She never spoke one other word;**
> **I only beat her more,**
> **Until the ground around me**
> **With her blood did flow.**

The tension between the sweetness of the melody and the luridness of the crime is perhaps one of the reasons why Mike Seeger of the New Lost City Ramblers writes that when he sang the song to college students in the early 1960s "it always brought forth laughs."

While the victims in crimes-of-passion songs are usually women, one of the most famous ballads, "Frankie and Johnny," is about a woman who kills her man because "he is doing her wrong." Bob Dylan sings another version of this song, called "Frankie and Albert," on his latest recording.

Like folk music, modern country music (sung almost exclusively by white people, for white people) has also had its share of celebrated outlaws. In Johnny Cash's "Folsom Prison Blues" the singer says he "shot a man in Reno/Just to watch him die." How many senseless murders were inspired by that line? Cash not only made a hit out of this bouncy tune about a killer, he also cultivated the outlaw image, dressing in black and singing in prisons. How would the law-enforcement establishment greet the news of Ice-T performing "Cop Killer" at San Quentin?

Another country-music legend, Merle Haggard, whose "Okie From Muskogee" and "Fighting Side of Me" made him the darling of the love-it-or-leave-it crowd during the Vietnam War, launched his career with crimes songs. Haggard's hits "Lonesome Fugitive," "Branded Man," "Mama Tried," "Sing Me Back Home," and "The Ballad of Bonnie and Clyde" are all songs that evoke sympathy for the perpetrators of crime.

Cash and Haggard's success with crime songs set the stage for a group in the 1970s, made up of Willie Nelson, Waylon Jennings, and others, which called itself "The Outlaws." Their album *Wanted: The Outlaws* was the first country album to sell over a million copies. One of Jennings's big hits was "Ladies Love Outlaws." How many men have been drawn into a life of crime after listening to this song?

Is there something that distinguishes these songs from "Cop Killer," that argues for their being spared, apart from the fact that the singers (and usually the listeners) are white? Only two of them ("I Shot the Sheriff" and "Pretty Boy Floyd") deal explicitly with the killing of an officer of the law. So it might be argued that it is the heinousness of the crime that separates an acceptable song from an unacceptable song. But is killing a man just "to watch him die," or drowning a woman in a river, really that much more palatable than murdering a police officer?

Another significant difference is that in most folk and country songs the killer is either paying the price for his deed ("Folsom Prison Blues," "Mama Tried," "Stagolee," "Banks of the Ohio," and "Knoxville Girl") or has been killed himself ("Jesse James"). Haggard's "Lonesome Fugitive" and Clapton's sheriff killer are both on the run. It could be argued, therefore, that these songs act as a deterrent, rather than encouraging crime. "Cop Killer" is quite different in this respect. The killer hasn't been caught or convicted. But that's because he hasn't killed anybody, either, he's only threatening to. Is the listener to believe that if he carries out his threat he's going to get away?

Does it matter if the killer gets away or not? The romance of the outlaw and the gangster is so deeply embedded in American culture that the distinction between a criminal who pays the price for his deed and one who gets away may not be so important. Either way, immortality has been achieved, in a song.

Probably what sets "Cop Killer" apart from even the protest folk

songs is the intensity and directness of the anger expressed. There is no question that this is a profoundly disturbing song. "I'm out to dust some cops off" is a long way from "I shot the sheriff." There is also no pretense of self-defense; Ice-T's cop killer is looking for retaliation. It is hard to argue that the character in the song is not advocating the killing of police.

If the anger is more extreme than in other protest songs, it is because the wrongs that have provoked such anger are more extreme. Ice-T is not concerned, like Woody Guthrie, with people being driven from their homes, or even, like Bob Dylan, with the conviction of an innocent man or the acquittal of a racist murderer.

Ice-T's anger stems from the unpunished and unjustified beating and killing of numerous African Americans by the police. ("Fuck the police/For Rodney King/Fuck the police/For my dead homeys"). It's hard to imagine a more effective expression of such anger than this song.

In the interests of law and order, and equal justice, the most prudent course of action may be to purge from the past, as well as the present, all those songs (and movies) that might encourage lawless behavior. Self-censorship by Ice-T, in response to the threatened boycott, was a good first step, but only a first step. The only reasonable alternative to this approach would be to allow "Cop Killer" to take its place alongside the legion of crime songs in the American songbook. A couple of slight changes might help—sing it as a country song and have the killer end up "stuck in Folsom Prison."

(April 21, 1993)

From *Urban Romance*

by Nelson George

The smell of mildew, marijuana, and Harlem garbage steaming in the June heat filled Joint-ski's Apollo Theater dressing room. The aroma was rank enough to turn the stomach of even the most insensitive diner, so all Dwayne could down was some potato chips and ginger ale, avoiding the courtesy spread of cold cuts and mushy potato salad. Joint-ski, however, wasn't so wise and was now in the bathroom vomiting.

It had been a long day. Shooting a music video had been the idea of B.C.'s London office since "Break It Down" was a budding United Kingdom hit. B.C.'s U.S. staff couldn't care less. To B.C., rap was a novelty and nothing else, which is why no one at the label told the Brits that the Apollo had profoundly lost its glory since its historic days and that they'd spend much of the shoot dodging chunks of falling plaster. Adding to the day's difficulty was that the gap between Joint-ski's onstage charisma and offstage insecurity had grown dangerously with each twelve-inch sold—they were up to 300,000 nationally. Vomiting was, in Dwayne's eyes, just one more manifestation of the strain.

Reggie didn't care. Well, Reggie cared but he cared more about his own peace of mind. Of all the rappers on the Dance Inferno scene, Reggie had picked Joint-ski to invest his money in. Reggie had given the kid a career, treated him like a son, and now both were reaping the rewards.

Reggie was in love as deep as his naturally cynical soul allowed. Time once spent scolding and tutoring Joint-ski after sessions was now spent riding the Metroliner to D.C. Reggie even missed the video shoot's start because his train was delayed in Wilmington.

Joint-ski came onstage in a red leather outfit, looking a bit pale but basically cool, and began rapping. The director tried to get him to wait, but he was feeding his ego, building himself up, banishing his demons, and he didn't care what anybody said.

"Mr. Robinson, could you please help us?" a Brit producer asked. "Your Joint-ski doesn't seem to want to stop talking, mate. He bloody well won't let us set up our shots." Dwayne peered at the Apollo stage, where Joint-ski, the microphone pressed to his lips, mumbled rhythmically about how "The sins of the father are visited on the son/And my black Daddy was a son-of-a-gun."

In the wake of "Break It Down" and a Dwayne Robinson piece in *The Village Voice*, The Dance Inferno was no longer an obscure ghetto club, but an "underground" spot, a designation that meant trend-pimpers of every variety—journalists, record executives, filmmakers, photographers, models, agents, visual artists—made pilgrimages to Inferno in search of thrills, spills, and greenbacks. Much of the art crowd was

knee-deep into its flirtation with graffiti as art. Break dancing had already begun its long climb from urban battle style to music video irrele-
vancy. But rap was still too foreign, unproven, and unmusical for effective exploitation. In short, the Inferno still stank of angel dust and
herb, but now a hint of designer perfume also hung in the air.

All this bothered the Inferno's back-room crew. Being a star in the
ghetto, a house-rocking party starter, celebrated from the Bronx's
Grand Concourse to Brooklyn's Belmont Avenue, was cool back when
that was the best that rap could earn you. A rep for turning parties out
meant quick cash—on a good night you could rock two or three jams,
plenty of pliant dirty-sock girls, and earn respect usually granted
ballplayers, pimps, and the dope man. Just as the Sugar Hill Gang's
"Rapper's Delight" and Kurtis Blow's "The Breaks" had changed things
for those kids, "Break It Down" revolutionized Joint-ski's life. To non-
Bronxites, Joint-ski "was" hip-hop because he'd put out a record and
none of the old-school crew had.

Soon that would change—all the back-room boys would eventually
get their shot (and years later be nostalgic for life before records). But
at this moment in time luck had conspired against them. They'd never
respected him. Joint-ski. He was a joke the girlies liked. Now he was
their worst nightmare—a sucka getting paid at their expense.

So the events that would transpire that July evening weren't a spon-
taneous explosion. It had been building since the Inferno regulars heard
Joint-ski was doing a special appearance at the Inferno, along with two
break-dance crews and a showing of work by the graffiti artist Samo.
Television crews from Belgium, Germany, and the United Kingdom
were to be in the house and everyone was encouraged to dress in their
freshest sweatsuits, gold chains, and Kangols.

Joint-ski, while by no means mature as a man, had grown tremendously as a performer. Despite the television crews and the hipsters and
the old-school rappers in the house, he felt in control enough to sit in
The Dance Inferno's minuscule dressing room with Rahiem, in a cus-
tom-made Gucci warm-up suit.

"Did you get the ass?" he queried Rahiem.

"What do you think, motherfucker?" said the usually taciturn dee-
jay-valet-bodyguard.

"I didn't ask you to ask me a question. Either answer my question
straight or we'll just squash the whole conversation."

"Yo, I got that ass, that mouth, the mole on her thigh, and both her
big titties. Satisfied? I got it all."

"You ain't all that, nigger. Bring that girl back here after the gig and I'll get it from her direct."

"Why you gotta talk to her?"

"Yo, if your shit was correct no need to worry. Am I right? Nigger, you know I'm right."

"Maybe," Rahiem said reluctantly.

"Maybe what?" Joint-ski demanded.

"Maybe I'll bring her back."

"Maybe!" Joint-ski laughed. "Yo, man, I know you been taxing that booty in the back ride. I know it. Least you can let me do is check out that pussy's aroma."

The way Joint-ski stretched out the word *aroma* made Rahiem laugh, though he really didn't want to. Joint-ski playfully hugged Rahiem around his neck. "Yo, you my nigger man. We been through a lot. Now we taking shit to the next level. We gonna bust out all the nonbelievers in here tonight."

An anxious Reggie entered the room, and Joint-ski's mood changed. "They're ready," Reggie said.

"No. The question is, Are you ready? Is the sound right? Are the few shitty-ass lights here coordinated? Since you got them D.C. skins, Reggie, your game has just gone left."

Joint-ski and Reggie's relationship had seriously deteriorated since Reggie had missed the British video shoot. He resented how Reggie's romance with Kelly Love Chase had changed him. Every free weekend was spent either in D.C. or in his Queens bedroom with her. No more club cruising at Leviticus or Othellos; no more pickup lines on the F train. Joint-ski understood it was Reggie's choice to live this way. But Reggie's obsession was hurting Joint-ski's career. Reggie was slow to respond to record-company phone calls. He was distracted in the studio because he was always thinking about calling Kelly or waiting for her to ring him.

At this key time in Joint-ski's life, when all his childhood dreams and adolescent insecurities were bubbling up through the prism of fame, he craved the fatherly authority that Reggie had provided and now didn't. So when Reggie reached over and grabbed Joint-ski by the collar, pulling him close to him, Joint-ski wasn't inclined to back down.

"Listen, boy." Reggie spoke with real menace. "Don't ever talk to me like that!"

"Fuck that, you fat bitch!"

Reggie slammed Joint-ski against the wall. Immediately he wanted to apologize, but he never got the chance. Rahiem pumped a right into his kidney and Reggie crashed to the floor.

"I'm sorry, Mr. Olds." Rahiem was genuinely contrite. "Real sorry, but I couldn't let you do my man like that. Here—let me help you up."

Rahiem lifted Reggie up and sat him on a chair in front of the makeup table. Reggie, in considerable pain, moaned and squeezed his side. Joint-ski stood behind him, adjusting his gold chains, ignoring Reggie's groans. Randy, The Dance Inferno's owner, entered the room. "C'mon, guys, everybody's ready. What happened to Reggie?"

"Nerves," said Joint-ski. "Yo, we ready. Let's take it to the stage."

As they walked out, Rahiem told Randy, "You better get Mr. Olds a ginger ale."

Joint-ski followed Rahiem's back as he pushed toward the stage past Kurtis Blow and Afrika Bambaataa. Blue, the white woman promoter who wanted to bring hip-hop downtown, was with the graffiti kid, Fab 5 Freddie. Dwayne Robinson patted his back and Joint-ski smiled. Suddenly there was the stage. Time to blow up.

———

Dwayne wondered where Reggie was. He usually stood stage right, looking on like an anxious father-to-be. In his spot tonight were some crazy gangster homeboys with their arms folded and show-me looks on their faces. As usual the girls were screaming, but this time the Inferno's stage was bathed in bright TV lights. Dwayne looked around at this strange mix of black and white, downtown and the Bronx, B-boys, Brits, and bohemians. *This is the joint! Something's going on here. Will it last? Hopefully long enough to get another* Voice *piece out of it. After that* . . . Dwayne never finished that thought.

"Yo, pussy! You nonrhyming, punk-ass pussy!" Joint-ski was about to introduce "Break It Down" when the hard-rock kid known as Sugar Dice, garbed in a green velour jogging suit, unlaced green Adidas, and a green Kangol, appeared stage left.

"Yo, homey, chill!" Joint-ski shouted. "You got beef, wait till the gig's over."

"No, pussy!" Sugar Dice jumped onstage. "You ain't no real rapper. Just a punk white boys be gassin'."

Somewhere in the back of The Dance Inferno there was a commotion. Two black kids in green velour suits yoked an astonished and complaining German soundman. A chair flew by, launched by an unseen hand. A girl screamed, "Get the fuck off my man!" The crowd, as though impelled by an invisible hand, surged toward the stage. Sugar Dice leapt at Joint-ski and in a sign of total disrespect used his open hand to mush the rapper's face. Somebody shoved Dwayne from behind and he smashed face-first onto the floor of the stage. More screaming. A few feet from him, Joint-ski struggled to free himself as Sugar Dice held his thick gold chain with one hand and smacked him one-two-three times. Dwayne saw Rahiem knock over a turntable, grab Sugar Dice, and begin to pistol-whip him about the head and neck with a .45 automatic.

Bam-bam-bam.

Rahiem let go of Sugar Dice and squinted out into the dim, smoky room, trying to spot who had fired the three shots. A boy lay on the stage, on his back, twisting in pain, his face covered with blood. Rahiem dove to the floor, expecting more gunfire. He looked up cautiously, then crawled over to Dwayne to see if he was okay. Joint-ski and Sugar Dice continued to wrestle.

Rahiem rose to his knees and raised the automatic. His eyes darted through the yelling, panic-stricken crowd. He turned and looked at Sugar Dice. "I should put a cap in that nigger."

"No, Rahiem!" Dwayne shouted.

"Over and out."

"No!"

(1994)

Hip-hop Flop: The Failure of Liberal Rap

by Stephen Rodrick

It's an old story in popular music that every threatening new sound is soon followed by a more docile clone. Buddy Holly's edgy melodies were appropriated by cuddly Ricky Nelson. The Beatles spawned the Monkees. Michael Bolton has created a lucrative career out of recording sanitized versions of soul classics. "Alternative rap" is continuing the trend. However, this process of banalization has a twist to it. To begin with, a fair amount of rap marketed itself to a mass white audience by actually accentuating its "blackness," hyping its offensiveness, misogyny, and antiwhite racism. But with that market conquered and a critical backlash beginning, hip-hop embarked on a new direction: "alternative rap," rap so sanitized and filled with uplift, even a policeman would like it. While other forms of hip-hop have predated and coexisted with gangster rap—from the pop/albino rap of Hammer and Vanilla Ice to the music of the original rap social commentator, Grand Master Flash, with "The Message"—alternative rap is the first conscious move within male hip-hop that directly attacks the machismo ethos of the gangsters.

Gangster rappers fashion themselves as angry, gun-toting outlaws, appealing to both urban blacks and suburban whites seeking vicarious thrills. Like the gangsters, alternative groups such as Arrested Development, Disposable Heroes of Hiphoprisy, Basehead, and Me Phi Me address the issues of the inner city, but without the familiar venom. Preaching social responsibility and espousing can't-we-all-get-along? themes in songs with titles like "Give a Man a Fish" and "Black Sunshine," alternative rap lyrics are a blend of do-good ethics and self-esteem hype. "Stop, evaluate what you have made of your life," go the lyrics to Me Phi Me's "(Think . . .) Where Are You Going?":

> **You have to do it right**
> **For these are the times that try men's souls**
> **There is no time to worry about a negative mind**
> **Positivity that's what we got to see**
> **As you teach your neighbor as you learn yourself—**
> **To be a navigator, an operator,**
> **Never another perpetrator. . . .**

No wonder Kemp Mill, a Washington record chain, displays Arrested Development's and Me Phi Me's CDs as "rap albums appropriate for children."

To reach a mass white audience, alternative rap is promiscuous, if not daringly so, in its musical appropriations. The performer Me Phi Me uses a tuneful acoustic guitar that conjures up images of James Taylor. Disposable Heroes of Hiphoprisy assimilates industrial punk

noises, jazz, and traditional rap into its songs. The platinum-selling
Arrested Development, by far the most musically credible of the alternative rappers, mixes in soul and R&B overtones to soften its
Afrocentric rhymes; its debut album found a place on many critics' top-
ten lists for 1992.

Alternative rap has drawn little more than barely concealed yawns
from other rappers and urban audiences, but it's gone down rather well
with the usual suspects. *The Wall Street Journal*, a newspaper not
known for its praise of Afrocentrist philosophy, recently ran a glowing
front-page story on alternative groups: "Rap Music Is Taking a Positive
Turn and Winning Fans." The piece commends Arrested Development
for its humanity, compares the group's political lyrics to early Bob
Dylan, and includes interviews with consumers proudly purchasing a
rap album for the first time in their lives. Likewise, Me Phi Me was recently praised as a "beat poet" in a *People* magazine puffer. The
Chicago Tribune, in a story about the new rap genre, ran the headline:
RAP'S NEW MESSAGE, FAINT SOUNDS OF HOPE CAN NOW BE HEARD IN THE
GHETTO. Noted hip-hopper Bill Moyers invited Michael Franti, who
heads up Disposable Heroes of Hiphoprisy, to ponder voter apathy on
the PBS program *Listening to America*. The show's highlight came
when rap master Moyers rolled a video of the Disposable Heroes' hit,
"Television, Drug of a Nation":

> **There's a reason why less than ten percent of our nation**
> **reads books daily,**
> **Why most people think Central America means**
> **Kansas,**
> **Socialism means un-American, and apartheid is a new**
> **headache remedy.**
> **Absorbed in this world, it's so hard to find us.**
> **It shapes our mind the most.**
> **Maybe the mother of our nation is sitting too close**
> **To the television, the drug of a nation,**
> **Breeding ignorance and breathing radiation. . . .**

Conventional rappers spin tales of drug busts and shootouts with evil
white coppers; alternative rappers try another tack, rhyming about PC
characters in need of a helping hand. Take Disposable Heroes'
"Language of Violence," a sermon against gay bashing:

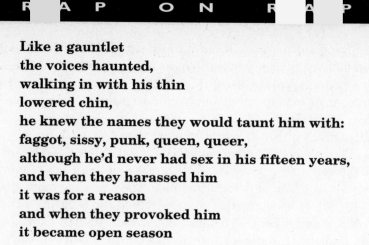

Like a gauntlet
the voices haunted,
walking in with his thin
lowered chin,
he knew the names they would taunt him with:
faggot, sissy, punk, queen, queer,
although he'd never had sex in his fifteen years,
and when they harassed him
it was for a reason
and when they provoked him
it became open season

"Sure the sentiments are good and I can appreciate that, but nobody wants to hear it," says one prominent New York rap promoter. "Everybody comes out to the clubs for a good time. They don't want to be preached to by some navel-gazing liberals. That song totally bombed."

Understandably, alternative rap's primary airplay has been college radio stations and crossover urban pop formats, which target middle-class whites and blacks in the sixteen- to twenty-five-year-old age group. A recent nationwide tour by Disposable Heroes, Me Phi Me, and Arrested Development played mostly white alternative rock venues like the Cabaret Metro in Chicago and the 9:30 Club in Washington, D.C. These critically acclaimed shows were largely ignored by rap's cultural elite, leaving bohemian college-age whites and Huxtable generation middle-class blacks gyrating approvingly to the reformist words.

These affluent would-be hipsters have adopted alternative rap as a reflexive reaction to the sudden liberal distaste for the message their street-wise counterparts promote—the racism, violence against women, and homophobia that are often inextricable from "authentic" hip-hop. At its core, alternative rap is a way to make rap safe for white liberals. *Vibe*, perhaps the rap bible for white people—edited by a white gay male—ran an essay in its premiere issue by Greg Tate, an African-American writer. Wedged in the latest Time Warner marketing venture, Tate's essay blamed the L.A. riots on rampant consumerism, bemoaned the "agendaless" nature of rap, and urged rappers to address the issues of misogyny and demagoguery in the hip-hop culture. In fact, in the song "Famous and Dandy (Like Amos 'N' Andy)," Disposable Heroes addresses many of the same issues in a stinging in-

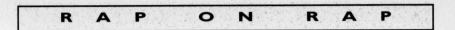

dictment of other rappers who have gained platinum record sales by fulfilling black stereotypes: a laudable message, but fairly useless when your target audience ignores it and white fans approve of it only for the sake of trendiness.

(February 8, 1993)

The Nigga Ya Hate to Love

by Joan Morgan

Snatch 1

Greg Tate calls and strongly suggests I do a piece on Ice Cube's new album, *AmeriKKKa's Most Wanted* (Priority) for *The Village Voice*. I refuse, which I suspect he expects. It's no secret that I found N.W.A.'s *Straight Outta Compton* nothing short of

demonic. "But someone needs to do this who grew up in the 'hood." I tell him for the umpteenth time that I'm not the one trying to reconcile my black middle-class intellectual complex with wanna-be down ghetto romanticization. What I don't tell him is I'm still weirded out from last summer when I found myself singing the chorus to "Gangsta Gangsta" in the kitchen long after I decided *Straight Outta Compton* was the most fucked-up, violent, sexist rap album I'd ever heard: "We wanna fuck you E-Z/I wanna fuck you too."

Snatch 2
The next night in Harlem, U.S.A., me and a posse of homeboys, ages ten to fourteen, check out a familiar scene. Two white Five-O's are busy looking terribly bored on the most well-lit block on Amsterdam Avenue, seemingly unaware that there's plenty to do a half a block away in either direction. Money Grip turns to his cadre and they break into a midsummer night's ghetto serenade: "911 is a joke/Ow-w-w/911 is a joke." The cop on the right fingers his holster absentmindedly while the one on the left reduces them to little black gnats and waves them away. The kids are not unaware of the gesture. Gnats turn into killer bees and chant "Fuck Tha Police" all the way home. Not thinking a damn about Philip C. Panell, Michael Stewart, or Edmund Perry.

Snatch 3
I'm doing the piece.

Snatch 4
I gotta hand it to Cube. Even if he weren't rap's most proficient raconteur since KRS-One, and even if *AMW* were straight-up wack, he'd still have to be congratulated on marketing strategy alone. Unmitigated black rage prepackaged for your cathartic or voyeuristic convenience. Hip-hop macabre. It's a brilliant concept. Peep this. . . .
    The first track. "Better Off Dead." The empty, echoing footsteps of a young black man's final walk down death row. He and a black (yes, black: turn to "Welcome to the Terrordome" if you need a refresher course, "Every brother ain't a brother 'cause a' color/Just as well could be undercover") corrections officer engage in the following discourse: "You got any last words?" "Yeah. I got some last words. Fuck all y'all." "Switch." Fry. Sizzle. Dead nigger. Then he evokes the specter of the

dehumanizing media by using the same emotionless newscaster's voice that matter-o-factly told us that black men in Harlem had a lower life expectancy than those in poorer than poor Bangladesh: "White America is willing to maintain order no matter what the cost." Execution, however, is not quite that easy. On "The Nigga Ya Love to Hate" Ice Cube reemerges as the quintessential Black Phoenix whom even the fires and electric chairs of white racist oppression could not destroy.

> **I heard payback you motherfuckin' nigger**
> **That's why**
> **Cause I'm tired of being treated like a goddamn stepchild**
> **Fuck a punk cause I ain't him?**
> **You gotta deal with the 9 double M**
> **The day has come that you all hate just think**
> **A nigger decided to retaliate. . . .**

He's back, he's black, and badder than ever. How's that for a Rude Boy/Revolutionary fantasy?

Snatch 5

I leave Yankee Stadium, full of good vibes and Mandela fever, and head for the Vineyard. Cape Cod is a sharp contrast to Africa Square but I'm willing to play cultural chameleon for a little sea air and solitude. *AMW* peeks out from my pile of dirty laundry and I shudder. Ice Cube and South Beach seem somewhat incongruous. Reluctantly, I put it next to my bag of black hair-care products so I don't "accidentally" forget it. We're in the car only twenty minutes before Kianga slips it in the Benzy. I don't riff too much, figuring that even that has got to be more bearable than this pseudoreggae UB-40 shit Leslie's making us listen to. It doesn't take long before Negra, Leslie's sweet, black, and respectably corporate car, is turned into a thumpin', bumpin', finger-poppin' Negro mobile. Yeah, boyee. This is work booty music in a big way. Great. Chuck D., Hank and Keith Shocklee, and Eric Sadler gave *AMW* all the kick that was sorely missed on *Fear of a Black Planet.* This is straight-up, hard-edged warrior music. Like the beats of African prebattle ceremonies, it either makes you want to dance into oblivion or go off and bumrush somebody. Kianga flips the tape to the B side. "Joan, you know this motherfucka must be bad if he can scream *bitch* at me ninety-nine times and make me want to sing it." Yep. This one's deffer than dope.

Snatch 6

> Some say the mob ain't positive
> Man fuck that shit cause I got to live how I live
> ...Some rappers are heaven sent but "Self Destruction"
>   don't pay the fuckin' rent
> So you can either sell dope or get your ass a job
> I'd rather roll wit the Lench Mob.
> —"Rollin' Wit the Lench Mob"

Things are not going as planned. How the fuck could I remember to bring Ice Cube and forget my bag of black hair-care products? There's not a bottle of T.C.B. anything anywhere to be found and the most tan we got today was in the parking lot, waiting three hours to get on the ferry. By the time we get to the beach I'm a walking time bomb. Leslie, Kianga, and I get into a thing because they think I overintellectualize everything. Maybe. But what's so cute about "A Gangsta's Fairytale"?

> Little boys and girls they all love me
> Come sit in the lap of M.C. I-C-E
> And let me tell you a story or two
> About a punk ass nigga I knew
> Named Jack
> He wasn't that nimble
> Wasn't that quick
> Jumped over the candle stick and burned his dick
> Went up the street cause he was piping hot
> Met a bitch named Jill on the bus stop
> Dropped a line or two and he had the ho
> At that type of shit he's a pro
> So Jack and Jill went up the hill to catch a little nap
> Dumb bitch gave him the clap.

Just what our community needs. Ghetto fairy tales. Andrew Dice Clay style. I ask Leslie if she would want her kids singing this? Exasperated, she asks if everything has to be political.

Snatch 6 ¹/₂

> **Not a baby by you**
> **The neighborhood hussy . . . all I saw was Ice Cube in**
> **court paying a gang of child support**
> **Then I thought deep about giving up the money**
> **What I need to do is kick the bitch in the tummy**
> **No cause then I'd really get faded**
> **That's murder 1 cause it was premeditated. . . .**

Leslie is appalled. "Do we have to listen to this shit?" I crank up the volume. The sense of pleasure I feel is almost perverse.

Snatch 7

The Vineyard is a romantic place. Leslie, Kianga, and I become products of the environment and spend three quarters of our "weekend away with the girls" talking about the men we left at home. We can't figure out whether it's the combination of the beach, the fog, the gazebo, and the lighthouse or the fact that the few brothers we did see on the island were all cut from the same soft, prep-school, young Black Republican cloth. Either is enough to make three street-wise, ex-prep-school sisters very homesick/horny for what they have at home.

"I need the element, my sister," says Leslie.

My mind races back to a scene that took place two weeks ago. I'm listening to AMW when my terribly significant other emerges from the shower, wet, glistening, and wrapped in a towel. My audio catches up with my visual and I hear him singing, albeit softly. "I'm thinking to myself, *Why did I bang her?*/Now I'm in the closet, looking for the hanger." That's great, Z. Just great. "Sorry, baby," he says, "it's crazy seductive." He reassumes gangster position and nods his head to the beat. I look up and see the beads of water dance around the slight snarl on his lip. Seductive? . . . Yes, Lord.

Snatch 8

We catch a four o'clock ferry. There's a carload of black folks behind us playing Ice Cube stupid loud. There are carloads of white folks looking over at the car, extremely uncomfortable.

"Damn, Kianga," Leslie says, "maybe that's what we should have done last night when that ignorant white waitress asked you if you didn't have an easier name to pronounce than 'Kianga'!"

"Word, that bitch didn't even want to take the order. What the fuck, is my name supposed to be Mary, or Sue?"

I suggest we run back up in there with a broom and cold-blast that shit. We all laugh. Bumrush fantasies. Kianga stops. She looks away and touches my arm. Homeboy is holding a baby girl in his arms. She's about a year old and nodding her head to the music. That's the problem with unmitigated black rage. It grabs white people by the jugular with one hand, and strangles black folks with the other.

Snatch 9

Yo, Ice Cube, man why you always kickin' the shit about the bitches and the niggers
Why don't you kick some shit about the kids man
The fuckin' kids.
—"A Gangsta's Fairytale"

I'm back on 125th Street. One week later folks are still buying Mandela T-shirts at almost the same rate they're buying the Black Bart T's. I stop in Sikulu, the record shop of the righteous, to find out how *AMW* is doing. Reluctantly, they tell me it's one of the top five sellers. I'm looking for a young urban male type to talk to about it. For some reason they're few and far between today. I move and stand in front of the children's clothing store that has those black mannequins. I realize that I've stood there umpteen times and never noticed how fucked up they are. I'm transfixed. They're all white models that were painted shit-brown. The boy mannequin has his head contorted to the side, like his neck is broken, and his hand is missing: it looks blown off. The bright red shoulder-length wig sadly parodies the weaves that keep the Korean hair store down the block in business. At least the "negative" images Cube feeds us are our own. A posse of youngbloods walks by. All of them have heard it but they're as reluctant to talk about it as the sister in Sikulu. Finally one asks me what it is I wanted to know.

"I want to know what you think about it?"

"What I think about it?" He looks at me like I'm from Mars or Martha's Vineyard.

"Yeah, do you like it?"

"Yeah, I like it. I like it a lot . . . Money can rap."

He reads in my silence that I'm waiting for him to say more.

"I like him."

"But why? . . . Why do you think he's good?"

It took me a while to realize that the look he was giving me was the same look Andy Kirk, the legendary swing bandleader, gave this young guy in my elevator when he asked him what made those old jazz greats so great. . . . Because they could play, son. They could play.

Homeboy mouths the words again for me, slowly.

"Because . . . he . . . can . . . rap."

(July 17, 1990)

Ain't a Damn Thing Changed: Why Women Rappers Don't Sell

by Danyel Smith

It's a fact. Women hip-hoppers can't sell as many records as their male counterparts. Salt-N-Pepa, MC Lyte, and one-hit wonders J.J. Fad are the only women who have ever had a single or album certified gold (sales of 500,000). No one else has reached that plateau—not Yo-Yo, not Boss, not even Queen Latifah. And as the hip-hop universe evolves and generates wave after wave of new male MCs, DJs, and producers, as far as women are concerned, the same names and sensibilities continue to pop up, with few exceptions, year after year.

Monica Lynch, president of Tommy Boy Records, attributes much of Salt-N-Pepa's and J.J. Fad's exceptional successes to the rare support of female buyers. "Their primary lyrical domain has sexual overtones," Lynch says. "They are pop-ish, not hardcore. Salt-N-Pepa, especially, have consistently made great music—music bought primarily by women." Jeff Sledge, manager of A&R at Jive Records, concurs. "Girls buy records, but not rap records. If there's a choice between the new Jodeci or the new Naughty by Nature, girls will buy Jodeci first." At the same time, says Jeff Fenster, Jive's VP of A&R, "males just don't want to hear hard things from women. They don't want to hear aggressive go-for-theirs sentiments from females."

Money and employee hours, of course, sell records as much as great songs and attitude do, so whether labels give female rappers equal financial support and company enthusiasm is also a pertinent issue. Fenster says, "In the past, female rappers have not been perceived as successful commercially, so they haven't gotten as much label support. As you get more breakthroughs with female rappers, the level of support will change." But Tommy Boy's Lynch disagrees. "It's not a lack of marketing dollars or promotional money that keeps women from selling hip-hop records," she says, "and I don't think that there's an inherent bias with label staff. Plus the media has been tremendously supportive. There are just a lot of biases to overcome in society, in rap as in rock. I don't know that this phenomenon is peculiar to any particular genre."

But in the almost exclusively male world of hip-hop, these biases seem especially close to the surface. Women's lyrics are often still viewed, by men and women themselves, as not valid—or simply "wack." Women's versions of reality are somehow suspect; men's interpretations of women and their motives and ideas are considered more "real" than women's own declarations.

In addition, the quality of women's hip-hop is often questioned. "There has been a perceived difference in the quality of female rappers' work," says Fenster. "Many female rappers have tried to be too hard—either trying to be just like men or trying to be raunchy beyond what

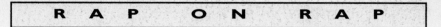

people would accept. We're just now beginning to see female rappers with skills who are not trying to be like men." He cites Boss as an example of this new style, and adds, "Mz. Kilo is a hard girl rapper who cannot in any way be accused of trying to be like a male. And there are interesting hybrids, like Smooth. She's assertive but still manages to be feminine."

Within Fenster's descriptions of "interesting hybrids" lie the contradictions inherent in the idea of being a female hip-hop artist: a girl rapper has to be soft but hard; sweet but serious; sexy but respectable; strong but kind of weak; smart but not too loud about it. The scale seldom balances and the line is always moving. A hip-hop girl, like a regular girl, has got to mix her own ingredients carefully.

Women writers and MCs are too often satisfied by simply responding to men's music—flipping over the proverbial coin ("They objectify me, so I'll objectify them") in a well-intentioned attempt to even the lopsided score. It's disheartening to think that women's love for and desire to be with men leads women to consistently offer their narratives conditionally—that is, self-censored and molded in the hope that they will still be desired. Like Salt-N-Pepa's intoxicating "Shoop": the sexual, assertive gender-flip is momentarily exhilarating, but ultimately leaves the listener feeling cheated and wondering why. It would be thrilling to hear girls go beyond trying to do to boys what boys do to them.

It's significant that the females who get the most respect in hip-hop's primarily male domain—Queen Latifah and MC Lyte—are relentlessly dogged by rumors that they are lesbians. Whether these rumors are true or not, the message is evident: a female can't be tough or strong or clear or exceptionally skillful at hip-hop unless she has sacrificed the thing that makes her a "real girl."

The words *double standard* are tired but still appropriate; the corner that girl rappers are painted into is a blatant manifestation of sexism. The music industry as a whole needs to look at the situation, call it what it is, and work to change it. Why are there still so few female DJs, producers, and label executives? Women label presidents like Monica Lynch, East West's Sylvia Rhone, and Perspective's Sharon Heyward are few and far between (though, to be fair, hip-hop is actually ahead of most of the pop industry on this count). We need to consider why women have to be touched with either dyke- or ho-ism in order to be marketable hip-hoppers.

Why do those who exist in between those labels languish saleswise? And finally, we need to ask why hip-hop, the new music that could have and should have been the music that challenged sexism, has punked out.

(February 1994)

Why Does Rap Dis Romance?

by Mark Naison

For better or worse, rap music is now the cutting edge of American popular culture. Created in the 1970s by deejays in Harlem and the South Bronx, it has become the dominant musical language of a generation of inner-city teenagers as well as captured the imagination of youngsters throughout the country who have never set foot in an urban ghetto. The syncopated rhyming of rap artists not only pervades MTV and pop radio, it sells everything from Pepsi to children's furniture and sets the tone at bar mitzvahs and sweet sixteens, house parties and school dances.

But amid rap's ferment and vitality one of the most precious themes in African-American popular music seems to have been lost—romance and tenderness. When black rhythm and blues took America by storm in the 1950s and 1960s under the name of rock and roll, it did so not only with the power of its beat, but with beautiful harmonies and lyrics propagating images of love and longing. Songs like the Five Satins' "In the Still of the Night," Jerry Butler's "For Your Precious Love," and Smokey Robinson's "The Love I Saw in You Was Just a Mirage" encouraged teenage boys and girls to regard their attraction to each other with reverence and caring. The music, or much of it, made people want to hug and caress each other, not force a partner into sexual submission.

For teenagers of the fifties and sixties, black or white, male-female relationships were often initiated or celebrated through slow dancing, usually to the backdrop of mellifluous music that affirmed the dignity and value of teenage love. Songs like Ben E. King's "Spanish Harlem" and the Shirelles' "Will You Love Me Tomorrow," despite their strains of sadness and anxiety, evoked a sweet innocence and hope of personal fulfillment, images that had as much meaning on the streets of the inner city as in suburbs or farm towns.

Like rock and roll in the 1960s, rap is a reminder of the prominent role African Americans have played in shaping the styles and images of American popular music. Blacks invented this music, and continue to be its major innovators. The rap format has become a battleground of conflicting personas, from artists promoting black unity and empowerment to those bragging of sexual exploits and acts of violence. So completely has this music captured the imagination of black teenagers that anyone seeking to communicate with them has to employ it. Rappers with fat gold chains are challenged by those with African medallions, "gangsta" rappers are denounced by those opposing drugs and gang violence, and rappers celebrating rape and sexual degradation are "dissed" by those with a feminist message.

Yet partisans of rap need to ponder why an earlier generation of black artists dealt with male-female relationships as the repository of hopes and dreams rather than an arena for violence, competition, and naked

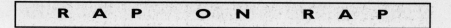

aggression. The journey from Otis Redding's "Try a Little Tenderness" to Slick Rick's "Treat Her Like a Prostitute" is not progress; it is a sad commentary on the decline of humanistic values in African-American communities and in American society as a whole.

Members of 2 Live Crew may have been acquitted of obscenity, but that doesn't mean their graphic lyrics about oral and anal sex aren't demeaning to women. Rappers like Ice Cube and the Geto Boys glorify rape and murder and even necrophilia.

The propensity of rap artists to employ clinical descriptions of sex, revel in violence, and refer to women as "bitches" suggests an extraordinary decline of community standards and a brutalized vision of life. Instead of defending such images for their poetic character or their roots in black culture, as the witnesses testifying on 2 Live Crew's behalf did, we need to view them as symptoms of a disease that is undermining communities, families, and the quality of personal relationships.

(October 29, 1990)

Hey! Valentine's Day? Walk This Way

by Run-DMC

Hey . . . won't you be mine today?
It's Valentine's Day and I wanna
say . . .
Understand me, I wanna hold
your hand, see, and give you
candy
Like Raggedy Ann and Andy, I
wanna be your man, G!

Cause Cupid must be stupid
For you I flipped and tripped, so I must troop it
Cause Darryl's arrow has been shot
It's not a messy dart shot through your heart
Cause if these words are a gift, then I'll be shootin'
Shootin' the gift because you are so cute and
If your name is in the game then I will be rootin' . . .
For you, and everything that you do
Cause Valentine's Day is the time to say
To the one that is true to you . . .
I love you!
Christmas Day is a holiday like New Year's Day and my birthday
And these Valentine rhymes should happen all the time
Twenty-four hours, seven days a week
These rhymes I speak
From me, DMC, cause you be so sweet
It's you with whom I want to play
And I'm praying for you when I do pray
I asked the good Lord, May I?
He said, Yes, you may
I said, I'd just like to say . . .
Happy Valentine's Day!
Me and you, we are in love
And you're the one I'm thinking of
I think of you all the time
Cause you are mine and, oh, so fine
We may get mad and argue, too,
But we're forever, me and you
That's the poem
Nothing else to say
From Run to the *Times* on Valentine's Day.

(February 14, 1989)

PART 3

Banned in the U.S.A.

DO THE RIGHT THING

SCENE 92 P. 78

CUT TO:

(COMING IN MID-SCENE)

CLOSE ON SAL'S HAND
GRABBING HIS BAT FROM
UNDER THE COUNTER.

AS HE PULLS IT OUT, CAMERA
PULLS BACK,...

TILT UP

92 A

SAME SHOT:

... SLANTS DIAGONALLY,...

TILT UP

92 A CTD.

SAME SHOT:

... AND TILTS UP WITH
HIM AS HE WINDS UP...

TILT UP

92 A CTD.

P. 1

SCENE 92 P. 78

SAME SHOT:

...AND SWINGS DOWN OUT
OF FRAME.

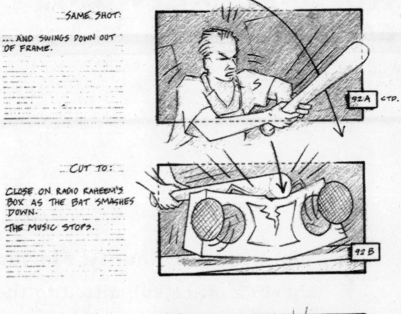

92 A CTD.

CUT TO:

CLOSE ON RADIO RAHEEM'S
BOX AS THE BAT SMASHES
DOWN.
THE MUSIC STOPS.

92 B

CUT TO:

RADIO RAHEEM - REACTION.

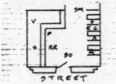

92 C

P. 2

Skyywalker Records Inc. v. Navarro, DC SFla, No. 90-6220-CIV-JAG, 6/6/90

The Broward County, Florida sheriff's office submitted to the circuit court a transcript of six of eighteen songs from the recording *As Nasty as They Wanna Be*, by 2 Live Crew. The court found probable cause to believe that the recording was obscene under Florida law.

Sheriff's deputies then warned Broward County merchants that they should refrain from selling the *Nasty* recording. Within days, all retail stores in Broward County ceased selling the record.

Members of the rap music group brought this action under 42 USC 1983, seeking an injunction and declaration of their rights. It must be emphasized that this decision does not criminalize the plaintiffs' conduct, nor does it charge anyone with a crime. Whether the album is criminally obscene is left for the determination of another court.

Obscene speech has no protection under the First Amendment. The message conveyed by obscene speech is of such slight social value that it is always outweighed by the compelling interest of society, as manifested in the laws enacted by its elected representatives.

Whether a specific work is obscene is governed by Miller v. California, 413 U.S. 15 (1973). To be obscene there must be proof of all three of the following factors: (1) the average person, applying contemporary community standards, would find that the work, taken as a whole, appeals to the prurient interest; (2) measured by contemporary community standards the work depicts or describes, in a patently offensively way, sexual conduct specifically defined by the applicable state law; and (3) the work, taken as a whole, lacks serious literary, artistic, political, or scientific value.

This court finds, as a matter of fact, that the *Nasty* recording appeals to the prurient interest. The U.S. Supreme Court has defined prurient as "material having a tendency to excite lustful thoughts" Roth v. U.S., 354 U.S. 476 (1957). *Nasty*'s lyrics and the titles of its songs are replete with references to female and male genitalia, human sexual excretion, oral-anal contact, fellatio, group sex, specific sexual positions, sado-masochism, the turgid state of the male sexual organ, masturbation, cunnilingus, sexual intercourse, and the sounds of moaning. Furthermore, the frequency and graphic description of the sexual lyrics evinces a clear intention to lure hearers into this activity. The depictions of ultimate sexual acts are so vivid that they are hard to distinguish from seeing the same conduct described in the words of a book, or in pictures in periodicals or films. It is an appeal directed to "dirty" thoughts and the loins, not to the intellect and the mind.

The *Nasty* recording is also patently offensive. It depicts sexual conduct in graphic detail. The specificity of descriptions makes the audio message analogous to a camera with a zoom lens, focusing on the sights and sounds of various ultimate sex acts. Furthermore, the frequency of the sexual lyrics must also be considered. With the exception of Part B of side one, the entire *Nasty* recording is replete with explicit sexual lyrics. This is not a case of subtle reference or innuendo, nor is it just "one particular scurrilous epithet" as in Cohen v. California, 403 U.S. 15 (1971).

Additionally, the *Nasty* lyrics contain what are commonly known as "dirty words" and depictions of female abuse and violence. It is likely that these offensive descriptions would not of themselves be sufficient to find the recording obscene. When these terms are used with explicit sexual descriptions, however, they may be considered on the issue of patent offensiveness. Also, the material here is music that can certainly be more intrusive to the unwilling listener than other forms of communication. Unlike a videotape, a book, or a periodical, music must be played to be experienced. A person can sit in public and look at an obscene magazine without unduly intruding upon another's privacy; but, even according to the plaintiffs' testimony, music is made to be played and listened to. A person lying on a public beach, sitting in a public park, walking down the street, or sitting in his automobile waiting for the light to change is, in a sense, a captive audience. While the law does require citizens to avert their ears when speech is merely offensive, they do not have an obligation to buy and use ear plugs in public if the state legislature has chosen to protect them from obscenity.

The final Miller factor—whether the recording, taken as a whole, lacks serious literary, artistic, political, or scientific value—is not measured by community standards. The proper inquiry is whether a reasonable person would find serious social value in the material at issue.

The plaintiffs' strongest argument is that the recording has serious artistic value as comedy and satire. It cannot be reasonably argued that the violence, perversion, abuse of women, graphic depictions of all forms of sexual conduct, and microscopic descriptions of human genitalia contained on this recording are comedic art.

The *Nasty* recording is not comedy but is, first and foremost, music. Music nevertheless is not exempt from a state's obscenity statutes. Musical works are obscene if they meet the Miller test. Certainly it would be possible to compose an obscene oratorio or opera, and it has probably been done.

The plaintiffs claim that this case is novel since it seeks to determine whether music can be obscene. The particular work here, although belonging to the general category of music, is to be distinguished from a purely instrumental work, or other more common recordings with a fairly equal emphasis on music and lyrics. The focus of the *Nasty*

recording is predominantly on the lyrics. Expert testimony indicates that a central characteristic of rap music is its emphasis on the verbal message. Rhythm is stressed over melody, not for its own sake, but to accentuate the words of the song. 2 Live Crew's music is explicitly clear as to its message. Although music and lyrics must be considered jointly, it does not significantly alter the message of the *Nasty* recording to reduce it to a written transcription. Kaplan v. California, 413 U.S. 115 (1973), is applicable here. It held that an expression by words alone, albeit in a written form, can be legally obscene even if there are no accompanying pictorial depictions. This case is an extension of the law to the extent that words, as lyrics in music, can be obscene. The *Nasty* recording, taken as a whole, is legally obscene.

(June 6, 1990)

Crossfire

moderated by Pat Buchanan and Michael Kinsley

ANNOUNCER: From Washington, *Crossfire*. On the left, Mike Kinsley. On the right, Pat Buchanan. Tonight, Bad Rap. In the crossfire, Jack Thompson, attorney and antiporn activist. In Miami, Bruce Rogow, attorney for 2 Live Crew. And in Chicago, rock musician Jello Biafra.

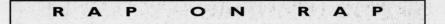

MIKE KINSLEY: Good evening. Welcome to *Crossfire*. Six sheriff's deputies burst into a record store in Fort Lauderdale, Florida, this afternoon, handcuffed and arrested the owner. His crime? Selling a record album to an undercover detective.

ARRESTED RECORD-STORE OWNER: Freedom of choice, freedom of speech. Remember that.

CORRESPONDENT: No regrets?

ARRESTED RECORD-STORE OWNER: No regrets.

KINSLEY: The album is Beethoven's Ninth Symphony. No. No, wait. The album is actually called *As Nasty as They Wanna Be* by the rap music group 2 Live Crew. It's a bestseller, over 1.7 million sold. But on Wednesday, a Florida federal judge ruled it obscene. Quote, "An appeal to the loins, not the intellect." And the local sheriff declared, "If you sell it, you're going to jail." Here's a little taste of the album video.

[clip of 2 Live Crew "Me So Horny" video]

KINSLEY: Gosh, Pat. That reminds me a bit of Julie Andrews in *The Sound of Music*. What's your problem?

PAT BUCHANAN: Well, let me talk to Jello Biafra out there in Chicago. Jello, I think the—there's a loose count of mine is there's some six hundred words in the album which are either—most people would consider dirty, obscene, filthy. Let me ask you something. The judge ruled that thing was obscene. The guy knew the judge had ruled that. He defied the law. I mean, if you do the crime, why not do the time? Why shouldn't he pay the price of having broken the law?

JELLO BIAFRA, Rock Musician: Well, because not everybody has the same definition of what is obscene and what is not obscene. And I'm getting an echo.

BUCHANAN: Well, I mean, the judge ruled it was a—all right. Look, Jello, the judge ruled it was obscene. He made that determination. This individual says, I don't care, I'm going to sell it anyhow. Why shouldn't he pay the price of breaking the law?

MR. BIAFRA: Well, I think it would be one way of seeing if the law itself is what is obscene. And it should be thrown out. The Beethoven analogy is not that farfetched when you realize how he was treated in his heyday by the same kind of right-wing fundamentalists who want to force their mind-set on us—

BUCHANAN: All right.

MR. BIAFRA:—by censorship of music as well as school textbooks, films, journalism, *The Simpsons*, what have you.

BUCHANAN: Right. Well, Jello, let me ask you this. I think there's going to be general consensus even on Michael's part that it is obscene or dirty or filthy, the record. Can you tell me—the judge couldn't find any artistic or social merit in it. Tell me the merit in an album which managed to use the *F* word 226 times.

MR. BIAFRA: Well, I'm not familiar enough with it to know how the word was used every time. Sometimes it's an expression of emotion, outrage, what have you. You know, some people drop something on their foot and guess what they're going to say. There's nothing on a 2 Live Crew album that hasn't been heard in a gym locker room in a Catholic school a thousands times already.

BUCHANAN: Well, if it's—it's been written on bathroom walls and all the rest of it. Let me ask you. Is your basic point, Jello Biafra, that there is no such thing as obscenity that should be outlawed even after it's been published, printed, or put on the air?

MR. BIAFRA: I agree because—I agree with what you're saying there. But I don't think it should be outlawed. No, if somebody doesn't want to hear what's on a 2 Live Crew record, don't buy the record. And if you don't want your kid to buy the record, ask the kid about it. Ask the kid what the lyrics are. If the kid can't remember the words, he's probably not listening to them. But to legislate the taste for everyone else through the law, I think that's what's obscene. I mean, it amazes me how as free—as more and more restrictions on artistic freedom and freedom of speech are lifted in the Eastern bloc, more and more of those same restrictions are being imposed—

KINSLEY: Okay.

MR. BIAFRA:—over here.

KINSLEY: Jello, let's let Jack Thompson in here. Jack, Pat is right. I—I heard 2 Live Crew for the first time this afternoon. I think it's pretty revolting. But, you know, if it weren't for you I would never have had to listen to it. And in fact, nobody has to listen to 2 Live Crew who doesn't want to. So, why do you want to prevent people who for whatever reason do want to be able to listen to it from doing that?

JACK THOMPSON, Attorney/Antiporn Activist: Well, let me—let me point out that the judge who found this album obscene after a full-blown trial with Skyywalker Records putting on their experts was appointed by Jimmy Carter, confirmed by a Democratic Senate, and this judge is in the mainstream. The reason that this album has been found obscene in large part is because it's been marketed to children. And in fact, six months ago, I found that throughout the country, after the Focus on the Family transcribed the lyrics of this album, this album was being sold to children as young seven years of age throughout Florida.

KINSLEY: Okay. But the guy was—the record-shop owner today was arrested for selling it not to a child but to a grown-up, to an adult.

MR. THOMPSON: Right.

KINSLEY: Now, what is wrong with selling a record album, a dirty record album, to an adult who wants to listen to himself, not—not play it for children, whatever? Do an—does an adult have the right to buy a dirty record album if he wants, in your opinion?

MR. THOMPSON: It's not my opinion that matters—

KINSLEY: Should he—should he have the right?

MR. THOMPSON: Of course. Dirty? Yes. Obscene? No.

KINSLEY: Why not? Why not?

MR. THOMPSON: Because the line on that—

BUCHANAN: Let me get to that point.

KINSLEY: I know—

MR. BIAFRA: I mean, here you are saying your opinion doesn't matter but you're trying to legislate for the rest of the country.

MR. THOMPSON: Let me—he got a certain amount of time, I have a First Amendment right to respond to your question.

KINSLEY: Not really. But go ahead.

MR. THOMPSON: The point is that the judge ruled that this album is obscene and the law is very clear in this country. I don't know what planet Mr. Jello is from, where he thinks obscenity is legal. But the court ruled, in fact, he sealed the courtroom, the judge did, and he said to the media, "You have so misinterpreted what the law is and the facts here, you're going to read the opinion and you're going to learn that obscenity is illegal."

KINSLEY: Well, what social purpose is served by denying adults, not children—let's just talk about adults—the right to listen to an album that you don't like?

MR. THOMPSON: Because the evidence is overwhelming which Mr. Jello and Mr. Rogow, whom you'll hear from later, who's from the ACLU, that this material, which combines sex, not just dirty words but sexual acts graphically described with violent acts, and encourages violent acts against women, actually causes some people to act out those violent sexual acts.

BUCHANAN: All right. Jello, I want to ask you this question. And it's—you have said that you don't think there should be laws against obscenity. But you like the idea of democracy, Eastern Europe is head-

ing our way. However, these laws were all passed against obscenity democratically. They were upheld by the Supreme Court of the United
States which says obscenity is not protected speech. The judge pur-
suant to that law being upheld is enforcing it. Now, what you seem
to be asking for is really suspension of those laws with which Jello
Biafra disagrees and dislikes even though they were passed democratically by a majority of American people.

MR. BIAFRA: Well, I would argue who actually got the laws passed and
why. I mean, some of the antiobscenity laws were courtesy of Jesse
Helms tacking them on to an antidrug bill that congressmen were
afraid to vote against—

BUCHANAN: But, you know, Jello—

MR. BIAFRA:—before the election.

BUCHANAN: Jello, there's a lot of folks that passed civil rights bills that
some of Jesse Helms's supporters might not have liked, either, and they
are required to obey the law. I want to know why this character running
this music store down there is somehow above the laws that apply to
everybody else.

MR. BIAFRA: I think maybe he's trying to call attention to a bad law in order to organize and galvanize some kind of feelings and forces
against it, perhaps even with an election coming up throwing out the
legislators who keep trying to take away our freedom of speech—

BUCHANAN: All right.

MR. THOMPSON: Let me—

MR. BIAFRA:—and instead impose an agenda from the religious right as
Governor Martinez has tried to do in Florida.

MR. THOMPSON: Let me point out that *The Miami Herald* today in the
wake of this decision which they cannot countenance came out, Pat
and Mike and your viewers, out on the proposition that the obscenity

should be legalized in the state of Florida. And that's where Jello is going, that's where *The Miami Herald* is going, that obscenity ought to be legal.

MR. BIAFRA: What I am really worried about is that more and more things are going to be declared obscene, a domino effect, if you will.

MR. THOMPSON: Oh, come on.

KINSLEY: But, Jello—

MR. BIAFRA: All right. Let me make my point here.

BUCHANAN: Sure.

MR. BIAFRA: I myself do not write songs that are sexist or prodrug or proviolent. I've done the opposite. And yet I was busted two years ago on one of the Dead Kennedys albums. The charges were thrown out. But that didn't matter to the prosecutor. He just wanted to see us go through the motions of losing a lot of money, having to raise it publicly since we didn't have any, go through the near nervous breakdown that having a trial hanging over your head can cause. So, what they're really trying to stamp out is not necessarily four-letter words. No one can do that. But the emotional and political content behind those words.

KINSLEY: Okay.

MR. BIAFRA: Rap artists in particular are targeted because they are telling it like it is or how they feel it is. Not everybody wants to hear Lee Atwater sing the blues. We want to know what's really going on.

BUCHANAN: Okay, Jello. We'll be back with more of rock music, four-letter words, Jello Biafra, and James Madison.

[Commercial break]

BUCHANAN: Welcome back. We're discussing the filthy lyrics of some rock musicians, specifically the work of 2 Live Crew. That's a black

group which managed the mathematically difficult task of cramming six hundred dirty, sexy, obscene, or filthy words into one album. And they've titled it *As Nasty as They Wanna Be.* A Florida judge ruled the record obscene and a Fort Lauderdale record-store owner who defied him and continued selling the album was hauled in today all the while invoking the First Amendment.

Here to discuss the merits of the case and the merits of these records are Jack Thompson, here in Washington, who's an attorney and antipornography activist from a Miami suburb. And he initiated the protest down there in South Florida that's causing some stir nationally tonight. Out in Chicago, we've been talking with Jello Biafra. He's a rock musician, formerly a guitarist and songwriter with a punk rock band that was known as, quote, the Dead Kennedys, unquote. And now, we have, from Miami, Bruce Rogow—I think I've got that right—attorney for 2 Live Crew. He's a First Amendment law professor at Nova University in Fort Lauderdale.

Bruce Rogow, I hope you got your fee up front because we— Michael and I have looked over this album, and we can't—some of the—we can't even find a line in some of these songs that we can read on the air. It is obviously filthy and obscene. And the judge says it has no merit. Now, isn't—tell us what kind of merit this has that we should suspend or throw out the obscenity laws in order to have 2 Live Crew's stuff being played on the airwaves and bought in the stores.

BRUCE ROGOW, Attorney for 2 Live Crew: Pat, the testimony in this case was unrebutted. Serious music critics said that there was serious artistic value to the record. We were surprised that the judge ruled against that. In fact, Mr. Thompson was surprised. He wrote a letter to the judge, saying that the sheriff had taken a dive in the case and the sheriff was about to lose. So, I think—

BUCHANAN: Mr. Rogow, would you read—I mean, I guess we wouldn't let you do it. But would you sit on national television and read, say, one third of some of the—some of the—what we would call the more obscene songs, would you read those over the air?

MR. ROGOW: Pat, I wouldn't sit on national television and read Oscar Hijuelos's *Mambo Kings Play Songs of Love,* which won a Pulitzer

Prize. Have you read that book? Have you seen the descriptions there of sex? They're fantastic. So, that's not the test—

BUCHANAN: Well—

MR. ROGOW: That's not the test.

BUCHANAN: When you got something—you got something, excuse me, Bruce, that *The Washington Post*, which is a fairly progressive, as they say, paper, would not print in it, we wouldn't say it over the air, a judge rules it's obscene, Michael Kinsley, who's very liberal in these matters, says it's filthy and obscene—

KINSLEY: Hey, I don't like the way I'm being invoked here.

BUCHANAN: Well, I mean, I don't know how any reasonable—

MR. ROGOW: Michael didn't say it's obscene—

BUCHANAN:—person can say otherwise.

KINSLEY: I did not say it was obscene.

BUCHANAN: And as a factual matter, the guy—the judge ruled and then the guy broke the law.

MR. ROGOW: Well, you're—the guy who broke the law is a different matter. We're talking about the judge's ruling that 2 Live Crew's album was obscene under the Miller v. California test. That's going to be taken up on appeal. But that's not the point here tonight. You're confusing things, Pat, when you say that because it won't be printed in *The Washington Post* that therefore it's obscene. That's not the test. That's not the legal test. There are a lot of things that *The Washington Post* won't print that are protected by the First Amendment.

KINSLEY: Yeah. Your column, for example.

BUCHANAN: Community standards.

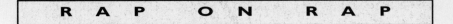

KINSLEY: Jack—Jack, 1.7 million people found some merit in this album, they went out and bought it. I don't know what merit they found in it, but I don't care. They went out and bought it. They found merit in it. Why this hang-up over—you don't find merit in it—

MR. THOMPSON: No.

KINSLEY: What's—who cares what you think?

MR. THOMPSON: Let me point out that Luther Campbell, who's the evil prince behind this album who owns Skyywalker Records, and he can't use Skyywalker anymore because Lucasfilm got an injunction against his theft of that name, said that the album is obscene. In fact, he promised that his next album, which will be released on July Fourth coming up, *Banned in the U.S.A.*, as it's titled, will be even, quote, "more obscene." And Luther Campbell has also said on—

KINSLEY: Is Luther Campbell a lawyer?

MR. THOMPSON: Well, Luther Campbell is—Luther Campbell is no dummy. And he's also said, however, that this stuff is so harmful to children that he will not allow his own daughter to listen to it. And yet he sits there having received millions of dollars from the sale of this album to children—

MR. BIAFRA: Jack, if I could—

MR. THOMPSON:—which is—Michael, which is racketeering activity—

MR. BIAFRA: How can you prove that it was children who bought those albums?

MR. THOMPSON: Because Luther—hey, Bruce, you know—

BUCHANAN: It's not Bruce. It's Jello. Go ahead.

MR. THOMPSON: Jello, you don't know, then, that Luther Campbell admitted on January thirteenth on WNWS radio that at least thirty percent of them—

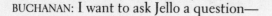

BUCHANAN: I want to ask Jello a question—

MR. THOMPSON: At least thirty percent of the sales of this album have been to children.

KINSLEY: Jello, let me ask—

MR. BIAFRA: You mean, like ten-year-olds or seventeen-year-olds?

KINSLEY: Yeah—

MR. THOMPSON: People under eighteen.

KINSLEY: Jello, let me ask you a question. This is Mike Kinsley. You know, I'm with you on this because I believe in the First Amendment. But I don't understand why people like you take this line about children. Obviously children should not have access to this. And parents, when you say, "Parents should be—it's up to parents to make sure their children don't get it." In a society like ours parents need help. And it would be a lot easier to make the case that you and I both want to make that grown-ups should have access to anything they wanted if the record industry and recording artists were willing to be more honest and more frank—

BUCHANAN: Why are you making it so—

KINSLEY: —that it's so easy to buy for children.

MR. BIAFRA: Okay.

KINSLEY: —to make it harder to buy for children?

MR. THOMPSON: Michael, Michael, do you know that—

MR. BIAFRA: This—can I reply to that?

BUCHANAN: Let him go. Let's hear from Jello.

KINSLEY: Let's hear from Jello.

BUCHANAN: Yeah, go ahead, Jello.

MR. BIAFRA: I do not want to be reduced to having to decide whether or not my lyrics will offend one parent anywhere and therefore I can't say it. I do not want any music that I listen to to be reduced to the level of Mr. Rogers just in case a child might hear it.

MR. THOMPSON: Let me—let me point out—

MR. BIAFRA: They're claiming child protection here when what they're actually trying to do is put the blindfold on adults.

MR. ROGOW: That's true.

MR. THOMPSON: Let me—let me point out something that's very important here. Bruce Rogow, who's a member of the ACLU and in concert with the ACLU, filed this lawsuit to have this album deemed either obscene or not obscene. They were the plaintiffs. So, they're the ones who initiated this thing and they got shot right between the eyes between a Jimmy Carter–appointed judge who found that the constitutional standards of obscenity when applied to this album means that the album is obscene. You guys did it to yourselves.

MR. ROGOW: Can I—

BUCHANAN: Bruce Rogow, go ahead and respond. Then, we've got to break. Go ahead, Bruce.

MR. ROGOW: All right. Let me—first of all, we filed the lawsuit because the sheriff had banned the album. He'd already repressed the First Amendment and we won on that point. And secondly, this album has always been stickered—long before the recording industry did it, Luther Campbell, 2 Live Crew's been sensitive about children. And so, what you're saying is completely wrong. This deals with adults. Adults cannot buy this record. This is contraband just like cocaine now in South Florida and that's ridiculous.

KINSLEY: Okay. Okay, Bruce. We have to take another—

MR. BIAFRA: I think what—

KINSLEY: No. Excuse me. Excuse me, Jello. We have to take a break. When we come back, I'm going to ask Jack whether he's not the best thing that ever happened to 2 Live Crew.

[Commercial break]

KINSLEY: Jack, in the old days, which I think you want to bring back, book publishers used to put on their books "Banned in Boston," which meant that they were sure that they were going to sell copies because people knew it must be something to read. You've achieved the very same effect with 2 Live Crew. Banned in South Florida. People all over the country are rushing out to buy this thing thanks to you. You're the best thing that ever happened to them.

MR. THOMPSON: Well, when I came on the scene armed with the lyrics transcribed by Focus on the Family, children as young as seven years of age were buying it throughout the state. They can't get it now. It's very difficult for adults to get it in the state of Florida. I'm glad Mr. Rogow used the analogy of cocaine. We've got a society engaged supposedly in a drug war now. And the government of our country has given a certain amount of visibility to the Medellín Cartel. I've had to give visibility to this—these bunch of racketeers and obscenity—

KINSLEY: You don't understand any difference between drugs and—and a communication, no matter how much you don't like it?

MR. THOMPSON: Well, apparently you don't understand the similarity.

KINSLEY: You don't understand it?

MR. THOMPSON: There are eight-year-old children who have had to have psychiatric counseling because of the content of 2 Live Crew's—

KINSLEY: They—they—

MR. THOMPSON: Well, that being—

MR. BIAFRA: To take 2 Live Crew away from the rest of us because of that is like taking the Bible away from everybody because of Mark Chapman. It's irrational. And what frightens me is when people like Jack Thompson and Focus on the Family and Tipper Gore and Jesse Helms are allowed to decide for the rest of us what is obscene.

BUCHANAN: All right. But, Jello, they're not—

MR. THOMPSON: Let me say—

BUCHANAN: Hold it. The Florida legislature and the Florida judges—you don't understand these things are done democratically. Jesse Helms doesn't—

MR. BIAFRA: Who's putting the money behind them, sir?

BUCHANAN: But when you pass laws, Jello, whether you like them or not, you've got to obey them, don't you?

MR. THOMPSON: You know, Pat—

MR. BIAFRA: It depends on whether or not it's a good law or a bad law. Just because a lot of people thought Hitler was right at the time does not mean he was right.

KINSLEY: Jack—Jack, you understand as Pat does not understand that the Constitution and the Bill of Rights protects individual freedoms against the majority when they pass the law.

MR. THOMPSON: It doesn't protect obscenity and you know that.

BUCHANAN: Mr. Rogow—

MR. BIAFRA: But, you know, just because—

BUCHANAN: Mr. Rogow, Pat Buchanan here.

MR. BIAFRA: I think Focus on the Family is obscene because they lie to people and rip them off.

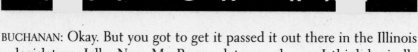

BUCHANAN: Okay. But you got to get it passed it out there in the Illinois legislature, Jello. Now, Mr. Rogow, let me ask you. I think basically this is going to be ruled obscene right up to the Supreme Court. How do you think it's going to come out?

MR. ROGOW: I think we're going to win the case. I think Justice Scalia is concerned about any attempt to make things obscene. There's a Catholic justice, a very conservative justice, who recognizes this is a futile task. You were right, Michael, what—what Jack Thompson has done has been to put 2 Live Crew on the map. And now, everybody wants the forbidden fruit. If he wanted this thing to go away, he should have said nothing and like many things it would have passed. But he's made 2 Live Crew a martyr to the First Amendment. And they're going to sell all of their records for the next five years.

MR. BIAFRA: I would argue that being labeled obscene sells records. After I was found—

KINSLEY: Okay.

MR. BIAFRA: —innocent of the same crime, a lot of stores wouldn't distribute my records.

KINSLEY: Sorry, sorry.

MR. THOMPSON: Sounds like—

MR. BIAFRA: In Ohio—

KINSLEY: None of you—

MR. BIAFRA: —they put everything with my name on it—

KINSLEY: None of you have the First Amendment right including you, Jello. We're out of time. Thanks a lot. Thanks a lot, Jello Biafra. Thank you, Bruce Rogow down in Florida. And thank you, Jack Thompson here.

MR. THOMPSON: Thank you.

KINSLEY: Pat Buchanan and I will exercise our First Amendment right in a moment.

[Commercial break]

BUCHANAN: Tomorrow night Jesse Jackson joins the Capital Gang to talk about the cocaine trial of Marion Barry, Jesse Helms's new black challenger, and the survival prospects of the National Endowment for the Arts. Join Jesse and the gang right here on CNN at seven P.M. Eastern.

KINSLEY: Pat, you know, I think a lot of what you read and listen to has a very unwholesome effect on you and through you on America. But I don't want to control it 'cause I made a deal that this country's all about. I don't control what goes in your head. You don't control what goes into my head.

BUCHANAN: Michael, just as there's garbage that pollutes the Potomac River, there's garbage polluting our culture. We need an Environmental Protection Agency to clean it up. And this thing is going to be the first candidate.

KINSLEY: Do you believe in the First Amendment?

BUCHANAN: I believe the First Amendment isn't any more absolute than the Second Amendment.

KINSLEY: From the left, I'm Mike Kinsley. Good night for *Crossfire*.

BUCHANAN: From the right, Pat Buchanan. Join us tomorrow night for another—join us Monday night for the next edition of *Crossfire*.

(June 8, 1990)

Black Culture Still Getting a Bum Rap

by Ice Cube

Four hundred years ago, when black slaves were brought to America, Africans who spoke the same language were separated from each other. What we're seeing today, with this insane campaign to intimidate rappers and rap music, is just another form of separating people that speak a common language. Too bad Nelson Mandela arrived here just in time to see this.

Chuck D of Public Enemy has called rap the black network we never had, and I believe it's true. Rap is the number-one-selling form of music today. Rap has brought black kids a new sense of pride. Rap has brought black kids and white kids closer together. Thanks to rap, white kids are gaining a better understanding and a new respect for black culture. Rap has done nothing but bring people together. So, what's the problem?

It's the people who don't understand the music or the culture that are creating problems. 2 Live Crew has been around since the mid-eighties, but as long as black kids were buying their records, nobody said a thing about obscenity. As soon as white kids in the suburbs started buying them, and MTV started playing them, now suddenly we've got a controversy. That hypocrisy makes me mad.

2 Live Crew sings about sex, a natural part of life. Advertisers use it every day. What's next? *Playboy* magazine? How about *Muscle and Fitness* magazine? It has a girl in a bikini on the cover: Let's bust her.

You can't slap the right hand without slapping the left. Andrew Dice Clay is offensive to some, but not to all. Same with 2 Live Crew. If Clay were black, would they go after him? How about Eddie Murphy, or is he too powerful? And how much you want to bet that not more than a mile away from the record store raided for selling 2 Live Crew albums, there's an X-rated movie theater or bookstore? Of course, I don't think anything or anyone should be censored. But what we're seeing today isn't only censorship, but also clear discrimination.

Three weeks ago in this newspaper I told Robert Hilburn that rap is the most positive thing for black kids because it gives information and talks about society, about black history. But none of that matters to the police. Rappers are an easy target because basically we're out there alone trying to defend ourselves. We never had much support from the music or radio industries. What if 2 Live Crew were on a major label like CBS, instead of a small black-owned independent label? What would've happened if the courts interfered with the record sales of major companies? I know if someone tried to take Bruce Springsteen or Guns N' Roses off the shelves, the whole music business would have united to fight.

As for me, I've been fighting my whole life. This is just one more obstacle, one more example of society trying to hold us back and steal the soul. No two rappers are alike in that we all have different ways of get-

ting our points of view across, different ways of helping young people get it together. But we're all together in soul. The title track on my new album, *AmeriKKKa's Most Wanted*, has a few lines that go

As long as I was robbin' my own kind
The policeman paid me no mind
Then I started robbin' the white folks
Now I'm in the pen with soap on a rope.

Different subject, same message.

This siege is not just a problem for rappers; it's a problem for the whole country. If they succeed in banning 2 Live Crew, they'll go after other rappers, and later other kinds of musicians or artists that someone happens to find "offensive." They've opened the door with 2 Live Crew. I'd like to see it shut right back in their damn faces.

(June 25, 1990)

2 Live Crew, Decoded

by Henry Louis Gates, Jr.

The rap group 2 Live Crew and their controversial hit recording *As Nasty as They Wanna Be* may well earn a signal place in the history of First Amendment rights. But just as important is how these lyrics will be interpreted and by whom.

For centuries African Americans have been forced to develop coded ways of communicating to protect them from danger. Allegories and double meanings, words redefined to mean their opposites (*bad* meaning "good," for instance), even neologisms (*bodacious*) have enabled blacks to share messages only the initiated understood.

Many blacks were amused by the transcripts of Marion Barry's sting operation, which reveal that he used the traditional black expression about one's "nose being opened." This referred to a love affair and not, as Mr. Barry's prosecutors have suggested, to the inhalation of drugs. Understanding this phrase could very well spell the difference (for the mayor) between prison and freedom. 2 Live Crew is engaged in heavy-handed parody, turning the stereotypes of black and white American culture on their heads. These young artists are acting out, to lively dance music, a parodic exaggeration of the age-old stereotypes of the oversexed black female and male. Their exuberant use of hyperbole (phantasmagoric sexual organs, for example) undermines—for anyone fluent in black cultural codes—a too literal-minded hearing of the lyrics.

This is the street tradition called "signifying" or "playing the dozens," which has generally been risqué, and where the best signifier or "rapper" is the one who invents the most extravagant images, the biggest lies, as the culture says. (H. "Rap" Brown earned his nickname in just this way.) In the face of racist stereotypes about black sexuality, you can do one of two things: you can disavow them or explode them with exaggeration. 2 Live Crew, like many "hip-hop" groups, is engaged in sexual carnivalesque. Parody reigns supreme, from a takeoff of standard blues to a spoof of the black power movement; their off-color nursery rhymes are part of a venerable Western tradition. The group even satirizes the culture of commerce when it appropriates popular advertising slogans ("Tastes great!" "Less filling!") and puts them in a bawdy context. 2 Live Crew must be interpreted within the context of black culture generally and of signifying specifically. Their novelty, and that of other adventuresome rap groups, is that their defiant rejection of euphemism now voices for the mainstream what before existed largely in the "race record" market—where the records of Redd Foxx and Rudy Ray Moore once were forced to reside.

Rock songs have always been about sex but have used elaborate subterfuges to convey that fact. 2 Live Crew uses Anglo-Saxon words and is self-conscious about it: a parody of a white voice in one song refers to "private personal parts," as a coy counterpart to the group's bluntness.

Much more troubling than its so-called obscenity is the group's overt sexism. Their sexism is so flagrant, however, that it almost cancels itself out in a hyperbolic war between the sexes. In this it recalls the intersexual jousting in Zora Neale Hurston's novels. Still, many of us look toward the emergence of more female rappers to redress sexual stereotypes. And we must not allow ourselves to sentimentalize street culture: the appreciation of verbal virtuosity does not lessen one's obligation to critique bigotry in all of its pernicious forms.

Is 2 Live Crew more "obscene" than, say, the comic Andrew Dice Clay? Clearly, this rap group is seen as more threatening than others that are just as sexually explicit. Can this be completely unrelated to the specter of the young black male as a figure of sexual and social disruption, the very stereotypes 2 Live Crew seems determined to undermine?

This question—and the very large question of obscenity and the First Amendment—cannot even be addressed until those who would answer them become literate in the vernacular traditions of African-Americans. To do less is to censor through the equivalent of intellectual prior restraint—and censorship is to art what lynching is to justice.

(June 19, 1990)

Lewd Music

by Barbara Grizzuti Harrison

It's ironic: In all the furor over 2 Live Crew's record album *As Nasty as They Wanna Be*— ruled obscene by Federal Judge José Gonzalez in Fort Lauderdale, Florida—those who took a hard-line, reflexive First Amendment approach were unable or unwilling to bolster their arguments with quotations. Apparently, they judged the lyrics too filthy, too patently offensive, to be allowed to see the light of day. None of the journalists, music critics, or television commentators who blathered on about "free speech" exercised *their* freedom of speech to enlighten readers and viewers as to what, specifically, all the uproar was about. What the mainstream media were saying, in effect, was: *We* wouldn't stoop to airing this trash, but anybody depraved enough to have an appetite for it should be allowed to have it.

The New York Times tells me that "it is not easy to imagine that jurors would detect anything sexually arousing in this album's vile references to sex, insults to women, and dirty nursery rhymes." The more likely reaction: "anger, boredom, or perhaps a giggle or groan of disgust." Yet this album sold 1.7 million copies *before* all the publicity. One point seven million people—how many of them do you wanna bet were male?—didn't buy *As Nasty as They Wanna Be* to be angered, bored, or disgusted.

Furthermore, the *Times*'s editorialist doesn't seem to understand— what do you wanna bet *he* is male?—that some men *need* to insult women before they are turned on, that men who rape are inspired, not by lust, but by fantasies of power—fantasies that these lyrics fuel.

Three criteria must be met to satisfy the Supreme Court's 1973 definition of obscenity: Material must be patently offensive to community standards; an average person must find that it appeals primarily to prurient interest; and it must lack serious artistic, political, or scientific value.

One dictionary definition of *prurient* is "having an uneasy or morbid desire or curiosity"; another is "given to the indulgence of lewd ideas." Well? As a woman who has experienced sexual violence, I know that these lyrics are tantamount to crying *Fire!* in a crowded theater—which does not qualify as constitutionally protected speech.

The *Times* tells me that "officials should hesitate before striking down, directly or indirectly, a cultural phenomenon they do not fully understand." By this they mean that the members of 2 Live Crew are black; rap music is a black cultural phenomenon; and criticism of these lyrics is inspired by racism. I have heard black men make these charges, including 2 Live Crew's leader and producer, Luther Campbell; I have not heard a single black woman make these charges, and I'm not likely to. (Of course, a black woman might argue that the white "comedian"

Andrew Dice Clay is equally obscene—a complaint in which I'd be glad to join her.)

It is patronizing for *The New York Times* to define black culture; it is condescending. It is stupid and insensitive to women for *Times* music critic Jon Pareles to say that "2 Live Crew's raps are proudly artificial." There's nothing artificial about teenage pregnancy or rape. It's loopy to say that they are "wildly exaggerated" and "grossly funny" unless you're convinced that rape is a wildly exaggerated and grossly funny sex act.

I am not arguing, necessarily, that these lyrics *cause* rape—although one could make a case for their doing so. I am arguing that they *celebrate* rape. And that, I think, is obscene.

(October 1990)

Grand Juries

by Anna Quindlen

Stupid prosecutor's trick of the
month—and the competition is
fierce for this one—goes to the
assistant state attorney in the
2 Live Crew case who said one
of the jurors, a seventy-six-year-
old retired professor, was
trouble from Day One. "She
was a sociologist, and I don't

like sociologists," Pedro Dijols said. "They try to reason things out too much."

Now there's an indictment if I ever heard one. You let people go reasoning things out, next thing you know they'll be using logic. And before you know it the place will be overrun with common sense and then where will we be?

In the jury room, that's where.

I confess: Like everyone else I thought the Mapplethorpe jury was going to convict, and that the 2 Live Crew panel would do the same. I pictured them as children, listening to a prosecutor saying: "This is obscene. Why? Because I say so."

I thought one panel would see photographs of things they never imagined took place and didn't want to look at, and respond "guilty." I thought the other would hear nasty, misogynous violent rap lyrics, and ignore the fact that rock and roll mirrors society, and often the dregs of society at that.

Which only goes to show that I had forgotten the blessed jury system, the only thing in America that still sometimes works.

"I wouldn't want my case decided by twelve people too stupid to get out of jury duty," lawyers sometimes say, cracking wise, underestimating their most important audience. Defense attorneys in the Mapplethorpe case were dismayed that the jury pool consisted largely of people who had no interest in museum-going. The prosecutor was so arrogant in his apparent belief that saying they were dirty pictures made it so, that his only real witness was a censorship maven who had written some tunes for Captain Kangaroo.

In Miami things were little better. The lawyers for 2 Live Crew flavored their case with suggestions that unless you were young, black, and male, you might never understand what the group was trying to do in its music. The prosecutors presented a performance tape of the band so badly recorded that it could have been Michael Jackson, *The Mikado*, or a transmission from the Times Square subway station.

And then along came the saving graces. A group of strangers come together as a jury, and for some reason that probably has to do with a distillation of civic responsibility, self-importance, and the kind of dedication you can bring to putting together a really difficult jigsaw puzzle in a summer house on a rainy Sunday, they take their mission seriously. Given what lawyers and judges hand them—and that's a big given—they try to do the right thing.

Some people are still angry that the jury didn't slam Marion Barry,

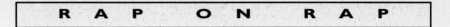

the mayor of Washington. And some people are still upset that jurors were able to find reasonable doubt in the McMartin preschool case. Those cases, and others like them, remind me of looking at photographs of a particularly horrible murder in the offices of the police crime-scene unit. "You have no idea who did this?" I said to a sergeant. "Oh, we know who did it," he said. "We just don't have a case."

In Miami the jury foreman was philosophical about the fact that the jurors were less bigoted than the leader of 2 Live Crew, who had written them off as too white, too straight, too old. "He stereotyped us, just as certain people were stereotyping him because of his performance," said the foreman, elevating good sense to an art form.

And in Ohio a warehouse manager on the Mapplethorpe jury said: "It's like Picasso. Picasso, from what everybody tells me, was an artist. It's not my cup of tea, I don't understand it, but if people say it's art then I have to go along with it." People have used that quote to attack the jurors, but I see it as a commentary on our obscenity standards, which are as murky as the bottom of a kid's fish tank. What the juror was saying is what I say every time I see a Wagnerian opera: sometimes artistic merit is hard for the layman to fathom. Or, in plain language, there's no accounting for taste.

They sat and they listened to discussions of composition and parody and prurient interest. Then they went into a little room and looked at the prosecution case, the defense case, the judge's charge, and the law, and they went to work. In a country where making a tough decision has receded into the distant mists of our historical past, that is no small accomplishment. "You take away one freedom," one of the 2 Live Crew jurors reportedly said during deliberations, "and pretty soon they're all gone." Put that on a button and I'll wear it.

(October 25, 1990)

Today They're Trying to Censor Rap, Tomorrow . . .

by Luther Campbell

The First Amendment states that "Congress shall make no law . . . abridging the freedom of speech. . . ." This same clause has been incorporated into the Fourteenth Amendment so that the very same restrictions apply to the states as well.

In other words, the government has no power to restrict expression because of its message, its ideas, its subject matter, or its content. So what's the problem? I write a few songs that are purely for adult entertainment and the whole world is after me.

Either there's a double standard regarding rap music and other entertainment or the Salem witch-hunt has returned, and I have been labeled the head warlock.

Today's society is based on sex—just look at how many strip bars and how much pornographic literature is available. Why condemn me—a black artist and entrepreneur—for my particular brand of adult entertainment?

There's a new breed of sheriff turning the music industry upside down. A few right-wing individuals have appointed themselves the judge and jury for what's right and wrong.

It's amazing to me, how during interviews those right-wing individuals neglect to point out that clean versions of all my records are geared toward minors and that I voluntarily sticker all of my adult material.

I hope that these people who are pointing fingers are really standing up for the First Amendment and are not using the American flag to hide behind racist motives. I own and operate one of the largest independent recording companies around, and that could be why I was singled out. People need to realize that I'm not in stores with guns to customers' heads forcing them to buy my albums. It's freedom of choice, and that's what America is supposed to be about.

America, the home of the free, and our just legal system, which is supposed to be the finest in the world, helped show the world how organized our judicial system really is. After a week of selecting an unbiased jury and another week of spending taxpayers' money (on a crime that has the same punishment as stealing a hubcap), we were victorious, but at what cost?

It seems to me that our priorities are all in the wrong order. We have an outrageous amount of people sleeping in the streets and without anything to eat, but we find rappers more important.

Our environment is slowly being pulled apart, and we put people in jail for a bunch of words. Kids can't read or write, but that's not enough. We don't want them to think for themselves either. Sometimes I wonder what the starving people in Ethiopia would think about the money we've wasted on taking this to court.

Right now, I don't think we're setting a good example for our future leaders. How can anyone say that an adult can't go into a store and buy

what he or she wants? How can anyone say that an adult can't under-stand what the 2 Live Crew is all about? If anyone can't see that the 2 Live Crew is a comedy group, then I feel sorry for them. We have placed warning stickers on our albums and put out two versions of each album—an adult and a G version—in order to satisfy the public. And as far as I know, we're the only band that does that.

Our victory should be sweeter. Charles Freeman, the Broward County, Florida, record-store owner convicted for selling *As Nasty as They Wanna Be* to an adult, should also be celebrating. Freeman only sold *As Nasty as They Wanna Be* to adults. We did our part, and he did his. I do not believe that his conviction is representative of Broward County.

Every day we get calls from people throughout Florida wanting to know what they can do to help. And we tell them the best thing they can do is vote.

A number of the staff members of Luke Records have been depu-tized to register voters and have made efforts to go to local malls, sports events, flea markets, nightclubs, and many other places to encourage young adults to register and vote. Our staff has registered more than forty thousand in Dade and Broward counties alone this year.

And for anyone who says that rap is not black culture, all I have to say is that I'm a black man who has lived in one of the roughest black areas in Miami—Liberty City—and this is my culture. This is a part of what I grew up with. Every day there was some guy trying to outboast another, and the only things off limits were mothers and the deceased. 2 Live Crew's music—and lyrics—is nothing but a group of fellas brag-ging.

The best thing to come out of this entire fiasco was that the music industry united and stood up for one another. Ads ran in major newspa-pers and on music networks asking people to prevent censorship. We were heard as a collective musical voice because we know that today they're trying to censor rap and tomorrow it could be classical music or theater or . . .

(November 5, 1990)

A Different Story If It Were "Exec Killer"

by Mike Royko

A Chicago cop showed me the protest letter he was sending to some big executive at Warner Bros. Records, which is part of the huge Time Warner company.

It's the same letter that is being sent by thousands

of Chicago cops. Variations are being sent by police in other parts of the country.

We, as members of the Chicago Police Department and members of their families, are appalled and offended that you and your company are willing to promote the Ice-T song called "Cop Killer."

We are urging you to remove this song from the record stores and the media. Until such time, we intend to boycott any and all products, movies, and amusement parks, such as your Six Flags, that are owned and operated by Time Warner.

With all the turmoil in the world today this song promotes more civil unrest.

If you continue to promote this song, rest assured that you will be held liable and accountable for officers that are killed as a result of subjects using this song as a plea in their defense.

When I finished reading it, he said: "What do you think?"

What do I think? I think that a police boycott will have little impact on Time Warner. I doubt if it will persuade many people to cancel plans to go to Six Flags, see the new *Batman Returns* movie, or drop their subscription to *Time* magazine.

Teenagers, the biggest customers for pop music, won't deprive themselves of their favorite hearing abuse.

And the boycott most definitely won't convince any of the Time Warner executives that putting out the "Cop Killer" record was an error in judgment. The record is selling. It's making money.

That's the only judgment that counts.

On the other hand, why not try a boycott? If I were a cop, I would. In fact, I could support the boycott strictly as a music lover, the rap song is that bad.

I have to admit that I consider all rap to be just about the most brain-dead pop music we've ever had. The same dull thump-thump beat, the same mumble-mouth lyrics. It almost makes the classic "How Much Is That Doggy in the Window?" seem profound.

And this particular song has to be about as bad as anything ever put on a record or disc.

Here are some of the lyrics, with a few partial deletions of the obscenities:

> I got my black shirt on
> I got my black gloves on
> I got my ski mask on . . .
> I got my twelve-gauge sawed off.
> I got my headlights turned off.
> I'm about to bust some shots off.
> I'm about to dust some cops off.
>
> (Chorus)
>
> Cop killer, I know your family's grievin'
> Cop killer, but tonight we get even . . .
> My adrenaline's pumpin'.
> I got my stereo bumpin'.
> I'm about to kill me somethin'.
> A pig stopped me for nuthin'!
>
> (Chorus)
>
> Die, die, die, pig, die!
> (Bleep) the police!

There's more. The last line is repeated about a dozen times.

But you get the idea. These rappers really don't like cops.

Naturally, Time Warner and some socially aware critics are defending the song on the grounds that it is a social statement, expressing the despair and frustration of society's abused underclass.

Nah. It's not a social statement. It's crap.

Of course, that doesn't mean it should be banned. If we banned all crap, our TV sets would be blank about ninety percent of the time, most movie houses would close, and our radios would go dead.

The entertainment industry's single biggest product is crap. It's just a question of personal preference as to the form it takes.

So, instead of mealy-mouthing about how the song is a social statement, a cry of dissent, a plea to be understood, and that attempts to ban it are a threat to free press and free speech for all Americans, Time

Warner ought to be truthful. It could issue a statement saying something like

We have received many complaints from policemen, their families, and others about the song "Cop Killer." We are threatened with a boycott.

These people don't understand. True, this song is crap. But what do you expect? We are in the crap business.

When the rap group came to us with this song, we said: "Boy, is this crap. It should really sell." And we were right. Hey, if Mozart had written stuff like this, instead of just talking dirty at parties, he wouldn't have died without a pfennig.

Naturally, we are sympathetic to the feelings of policemen.

If someone put out a record encouraging people to kill executives at Time Warner, I'm sure our wives and children would be alarmed and I would be hysterical. We'd probably sue. But then, we are a big, powerful media corporation and you ain't, so tough tootsies, coppers.

In conclusion, we will resist all efforts to impede free expression and our right to life, liberty, the pursuit of happiness, and the marketing of any crap that will sell.

God bless America.

Now, call security and tell them not to let any cops in the lobby.

(June 23, 1992)

The Controversy

by Ice-T

So what happened? The record
is out. My fans didn't consider
Body Count a controversial
record. They listened to "Cop
Killer" and smiled and understood it. My fans got a direct
line on me, and they know that
if I'm controversial, they are
too. You just don't hear them

because they don't have a platform like I do. They're not on *Arsenio* or CNN.

The album debuted at 32 on Billboard's Top 50 albums—not bad for the first hard-core rap-to-rock crossover. Body Count toured with Lollapalooza in the summer of '91. In twenty-one cities, 430,000 predominantly white kids waved their fists in the air and screamed "Cop Killer" along with us. Nothing happened. In the winter of 1991–1992 Body Count headlined its own tour. We hit seventy cities, performed "Cop Killer" to wild fans at about eighty shows. Nothing happened.

Then the first verdict comes in. After looking at Rodney King writhe around on asphalt for about a year, with people watching the cops go free, the shit hits the fan. Cops are now being found guilty of brutality all over the United States.

For the first time in a long time, people outside of the ghettos were looking at the cops as the actual savages and criminals that some of them really are. But honest cops were being prejudged and hurt behind this sweat. This is just how it went down.

People were glaring at the cops. The cops. The cops. The cops. The cops. "The cops started the riots. The cops killed my brother. Fuck the cops. . . ."

Out of nowhere a cop in Houston, Texas, discovers "Cop Killer," and the record must have scared the shit out of him. "Oh shit," he figured. "They're rioting in L.A. And now, here's a record telling people to go kill the cops. Oh, my God, even more frightening, it's a rock record and it's backed by Bugs Bunny's company!"

Through rock 'n' roll I injected black rage into white kids. I have no doubt the cops were just as angry we formed a South Central rock group as they were about the song.

They said, "This muthafucka's not even doing rap. But let's call it rap in the press to make it even more incendiary." Rap immediately conjures up scary images of Black Ghetto. If they'd said it was a rock record, people might have said, "Well, okay, rock, I grew up on Fleetwood Mac. Maybe I might like it."

No, the cops knew they didn't need any sympathizers. "We need a word that conjured up niggers—rap, yeah, black rapper. You never liked that shit."

"Rapper Ice-T" created an immediate response. Rednecks quickly lined up to hate.

My message connected to that corporation was scary as shit. I was being powered by a big business—not a business run by the Japanese, they wouldn't target that, but specifically a white-owned, white-run, all-American apple-pie business.

To make matters worse for the original cop, *Body Count* was probably in the record collection of his kid. I cannot imagine that cop going into a record store and buying that album. At the very least, whoever hipped him to the record had a kid who owned it.

The police group was aptly called the Fraternal Organization of Cops. We found out this "Fraternal" gang is connected in with the Masons, and I wouldn't be surprised if some of the members were connected in with the Ku Klux Klan.

So, the Fraternal Organization of Cops *decides* that this record is going to be the cause of police getting killed and somebody else—possibly Ollie North, one of America's archvillains—came to them and said it's also a good way to take the heat off the cops. They decided to go after Warner Bros. and run a big boycott. Bill Clinton—probably in an attempt to create sympathy before announcing the Gores on his ticket—Dan Quayle, and George Bush compound this propaganda campaign by coming to the "aid" of the police and attacking me.

What did it all add up to? They managed to camouflage the issue of police brutality with me. They said, "Look how terrible Ice-T is! Look how terrible Warner Bros. is! America, can you believe Warner Bros. has a record out like this?"

Immediately, everybody in this country gets mad at me and says I'm terrible. And predictably, America totally forgets about the cops who are on the street hurting people.

All of a sudden I become headline news every night. They split America down the middle and the people who came in to aid me marched in defense of the First Amendment.

This isn't where I needed help. I didn't need anybody to come and say I had the right to say it. I needed people with credibility to step up and say, "Ice-T not only has the right to say it, but also fuck the police! Fuck the police! Who the fuck are the muthafuckin' police that they can control you like this? We're not apologizing to you cops for what YOU'VE been doing. It's time for people to get angry along with the guy who wrote 'Cop Killer.' And some of you muthafuckin' cops might end up dead!"

No one had the courage to come out and make statements like these. Everybody just said, "Oh, Ice-T and Body Count, you have the right to say it. We love you guys, really."

I tried to make it painfully clear. I said that if police were a totally legitimate organization, I might even be a cop. I never said I agreed with crime, but I am saying that when you guys stepped over the boundaries and decided you can pass judgment, then fuck you. Fuck you.

Everybody knows a lot of cops are on the job to get over inferiority complexes they've harbored since childhood. Now as police they've got a chance to go out and whip on people. They use that badge as a shield to get out their anger. When red lights start flashing in your rearview mirror, you don't say, "All right, a cop. I'm safe now." No, instead, you're fucking scared. If you're me, you know not only can they arrest you but they might just kill you right there or throw you into a judicial system that's not equipped to treat you fairly.

Where I come from, cops never did come get your cat out of a tree. They came to collect people. If you don't believe this, you live in a state of denial. When you're sitting on a jury in Simi Valley, you believe in the myth of the American way. "The police were right. You can't lie and be a cop, can you?"

People are so mind-fucked by the myth that no matter what they see on TV or hear on the news, they refuse to believe cops are corrupt. They certainly don't believe the testimony of a black man. But if Clint Eastwood is doing the narrating, well then, that's a whole different story.

During the exact same time my record was being condemned, the film *Unforgiven* was winning critical praise across the country. What's *Unforgiven* about? A cop killer. Eastwood takes justice into his own hands after his buddy, a black man, is unjustly murdered by a corrupt cop.

What's "Cop Killer" about? A black youth takes justice into his own hands after his buddies are unjustly murdered by corrupt cops. Just like Eastwood I'm saying, *"Fuck the police,* for my dead homeys," but my story is real. I know firsthand how bad the street is. America is simply not ready to hear it from me.

Now that this whole thing has blown up, I'm supposed to feel bad. I don't give a fuck about the police's problems, if I offend them or I cause them to be mad at records. They are not above scrutiny. They're not above ridicule. So now, they're mad at me. Do you think it's possible for the police to treat me worse than they've always treated me? Fuck them.

This rock 'n' roll record by "Rapper Ice-T," who was waving the Time Warner flag behind him, really fucked with them. Believe me, if I could give them one night of inconvenience for the four hundred years they done fucked over my people, I was happy to do it.

Even though there were people who understood this and really were on my side, they didn't have a platform to voice their opinions. The people who did have a platform were way off backing me on the First Amendment.

That's not where all the anger should have been directed. The anger should have been generated back at the police. It was a wide-open opportunity for America to redeem itself and say, "You know what? Y'all muthafuckas better get your shit together, because y'all muthafuckas are out of pocket. I can see why a kid might want to kill you."

Okay? That's what needed to be said. Not, "Ice-T has free speech." That's bullshit. Because people jumped on the wrong issue they were able to drive this thing totally through Warner Bros.

After the cops called this embargo against Warner Bros., they moved into criminal activity. They sent death threats to Warner Bros. They actually sent two bombs to the label. Real bombs. These came from either the police or police sympathizers. It doesn't really make a difference: If a cop sends a bomb, he is a criminal. But if these people are so down with justice, yet they would send a bomb, they're criminals too.

It's irrelevant whether it was the police or a police sympathizer. They're supposed to be down with the law, so why are they committing a crime?

There is no way I can prove that the bombs came from police, but they did make death threats. They made death threats to the president of Warner Bros., Lenny Waronker: "Do you know where your kids are?" Somebody went to my fifteen-year-old daughter's high school and pulled her out of class and asked her questions about me. I mean, real tacky shit.

These are the people who are supposed to be upholding justice. In effect, I had reached out and scared the guards of the system, and the system—which is made up of people who think everything is fine in this country—use the guards to protect them. When I scared their guards, the guards ran to the people and said:

"Are you gonna let him threaten us?"

"Oh, no, no, no," they cried.

"If you let him threaten us, we won't protect you anymore. Don't you want us to protect you?"

It irritated me that none of the attacks were really aimed at me. I was watching the TV and it's all Warner Bros., Warner Bros., Warner Bros., Warner Bros. You can read any paper and you'll never find anybody who said, "Where does Ice-T get the anger to make the record?"

The cops never accused me of faking the anger. They knew it was real. They were just saying, "Why would you, Warner Bros., put it on record?"

Ultimately, the guards of the system said to Time Warner, "We understand why you're mad, Ice-T. But why would the big white corporation—who's a member of the same country club as us, whose kids go to spring break with our kids, who supports the same politicians that we do—be associated with those niggers?"

And that question just rings on in my head.

"How can you be associated with that rage? We're not mad at Ice-T for making the record; we know why Ice-T would make that record. But why would you give him a platform, allowing him to reach the masses with that anger? I thought we were friends. You can't do that. Not if you want to be in business with us.

"Matter of fact, we may not like another record. As long as you put out records and you want to be in business with us, we're gonna have to approve it."

Warner Bros. responded that they could not afford to have the cops controlling the company, and they decided to back me. They didn't back me because they cared about me. Warner Bros. is an information company, and they cannot be told what they can or cannot do. What happens if they don't like another Ice-T record? What happens if they don't like a movie Warner puts out? They were totally paranoid of paying off for the hostages, paying the extortionist.

Meanwhile, I get to the point where I am getting tired of seeing myself on the news every night. The media even got personal with me. I was tired of this shit. It wasn't worth it because nobody who had a voice was backing me on the real reason.

Ironically, thirty-five thousand black police officers said they would not join in with any boycott of Ice-T or Time Warner because they knew I was saying the truth. Since July hundreds of cops have come up to me saying, "Ice, I know what that record is about, I'm not dumb."

I've signed more autographs this year for cops than I have in my life. "Cop Killer" totally divided the police stations. I've had cops come to me and say, "Ice, I feel like killing some of these guys I work with." Others said, "We ain't all bad." That meant a lot to me. Even the thought that they would think I'm worthy of being spoken to was cool. It was like they care that I care.

I understand a lot of cops out there are trying to do the right thing. And in a way, those cops are on the same mission I am. So it's not like they shouldn't care. I respect that.

But the other ones, fuck 'em.

As the controversy raged on, I knew I had to make a move to deal with it. I didn't want anything to happen to someone at Warner Bros., because I knew everybody up there didn't agree with my record. In addition, it wasn't for them to fight my battle.

I didn't have any fear about something happening to somebody on the street, 'cause that's not my job. I've been putting music out on the street for years. If cops were all out there doing an honest job, people wouldn't hate them so intensely. I was more worried about some lunatic hurting somebody at Warner Bros. or even about one of those cops going out and killing a cop and trying to pin it on me.

Nobody came to me and asked me to pull the record—definitely not, no matter what muthafuckas want to say. The guys in my group didn't even know I was gonna do it. I called a meeting with Body Count and said, "This record is out of control. They are going over the top with it and ain't nobody really down with it but us. Our fans who wanted the record have already bought the album, it's gold. All the new people who are buying the record are just snooping assholes. That's not why we want to sell records. So let's pull the muthafuckin' record. The cops are arguing that we're doing it for money. So let's pull it and then tell them to shut the fuck up."

Now it's gone. Now what? In other words: Come on out and say that you just don't like Ice-T. Just come on out and say it. It had become a chess game, and they shut up.

Stories about brutal police officers were starting to crop up in the press. Newspapers began running articles about new police-brutality charges. The area my stories had been taking up was now being replaced with reality.

The cops had really created fiction. "Ooh, look what this record is gonna do. This record is gonna make people kill us. This is a dangerous issue." It never was. They concocted a brilliant fictional monster: a record. And they scared the life out of people with it.

The minute I pulled it, cops killed a kid in Texas who was thirty feet

away from 'em. Cops killed a kid in Detroit. People are marching: "Ice-T was right." It flips now.

During this period I also faced a backlash. After I pulled "Cop Killer," people started jumping off and saying I shouldn't have pulled the record. They said it was a sign of weakness.

I didn't give a fuck. Ice Cube told reporters on MTV, "I'm not qualified to tell Ice-T what to do." Cube's basically saying, "I got respect for Ice." And Chuck D made the best comment to MTV's Kurt Loder out of everybody. He said, "Those who aren't in the war should never comment on the battle." All these people who condemned me weren't in the war.

It's so easy to pass judgment when you don't know what the fuck's going on. The people who were on the inside told me I'd made the right move. Because in a war—and make no mistake, this is a war—sometimes you have to retreat and return with superior firepower.

Even though Warner Bros. had my back, they only had my back on that issue. I didn't really feel like I had my feet placed strongly enough to hold on. So what good is holding on to that record, if I can't come back out with a record bigger and crazier than that?

I knew Warner Bros. felt they could get over the "Cop Killer" incident, but there would be no reply to "Cop Killer" on my next album.

I knew where I stood. I decided I had to retreat and come back correct. I just looked around and I said, "All you muthafuckas ain't shit. Fuck you. I'm in this controversy by myself."

The next heated element of the controversy was predictable: Did Warner Bros. ask me to pull the record? The answer to that is, no. Warner Bros. has defended artistic freedom since the beginning. Warner Bros. is the number-one-hated label by the Parents Music Resource Center. They've been fighting Tipper Gore for years. They've put out everyone from Sam Kinison to Slayer, from Andrew Dice Clay to Prince and Madonna. They never shied away from controversial music. They put out every one of my records without censoring them. Dig this, they put out "Cop Killer."

But they got hit with the Establishment's vibes. The cops very wisely moved on Time Warner, which is the parent company of Warner Records and twenty times bigger than the label. So they put a whole bunch of people who had no concept of art into the game by hitting their bank accounts.

Time Warner was not only attacked from the outside, they were attacked from within. The politicians and the cops managed to get

Charlton Heston and people among Time Warner's shareholders to side with them. Tactical infiltration, pure and simple. It wasn't just a bunch of cops crying to the shareholders, "We don't agree."

Time Warner had people on the inside, who had never listened to my music and who had no understanding of where I was coming from, saying, "Look at what we're selling. This is our money being threatened, and I don't agree with it." Heston, who disputed my lyrics at the shareholders' meeting in '92, is probably a hired gun, hired to smear me and the company. They probably hired him. And believe me, that muthafucka probably got paid off. But then again, he's such a right-winger he probably didn't need to get paid.

I had a meeting with Lenny Waronker, and he said he felt Heston did a terrible thing at the shareholders' meeting. Lenny told me directly that Heston's attack on my music was like saying "Fuck you" in the face of all the Warner Bros. record executives. He said Heston's attack on the creative process was wrong—pure and simple.

Who the fuck is Charlton Heston, anyway? Who is he?

Lenny told me his entire career has been based around making music and putting ideas out there, and Heston comes out of nowhere and puts down his whole career.

It was some real ill shit. I know I'm fucked if I want to say something about it on the next record. Warners wouldn't come out and say I couldn't attack Heston or the cops, but you knew they were thinking it. They had Warner Bros. by the balls. The cops had won. Warner Bros. said the controversy cost them in the area of $150 million. I don't know if they ever regained that money. The police groups pulled a lot of their pension-fund money out of Time Warner stock, and they caused people to panic.

In the meantime, we go out on tour and I run into these new boycotts out on the road. These cops are threatening the club owners, saying they'll shut them down if they let us play.

People were shocked: "Goddamn, didn't they want you to pull the record? You pulled the record and now they're still fucking with you." So we came up with the conclusion that their animosity and their vendetta against me will now be for the rest of my life. They feel I threatened their life, so it's on. Fuck it. If you want to play like that, cool. I never apologized to the police, and I refuse to apologize. All I am to these muthafuckas is defiant, and that defiance bothers them more than anything else.

The only concession I'll make is to the honest cops who misunder-

stood the record and took it as a blatant attack on all police officers, which it is not. It's directed at your criminal partner, who you have to deal with. It's his record.

I ran into plenty of "criminal partners" on the road. Club owners repeatedly came up to me and said, "I never knew the cops were this criminal. I never knew it, man. Damn, the techniques they use to threaten me with . . ."

Some club owners stayed down because they got angry, others caved in. Although the tour had no violence, no problems, we had one show canceled in Pittsburgh because the cops threatened the owner. I can't get mad at the owner, because I understand this is my mission and I'm serious about it. But I can't expect other people to be as serious as I am.

I wish everybody was down. If everybody was as focused as me, then they'd really be in trouble. We'd have really solid attitudes about shit; the shit would move. We would have shut this case up once and for all. But at this moment I'm not dealing with those types of soldiers out there.

When this tour wrapped, I knew that.

When we finished my next album, *Home Invasion*, for a November 15, 1992, release, Warner Bros. was biting its nails. Warner had the album reviewed by a "crisis attorney," an attorney who assesses potential problems, the same attorney who reviewed *The Last Temptation of Christ*.

This was the first work I'd put out since the "Cop Killer" drama. So he listens to the record and finds a few places where the album, he decides, will cause problems. References to cops here and there, which I didn't give a fuck about.

I knew they were going to ask me to change the lyrics—something they had not done before—so before they could tell me to change them, I gave them my idea. "You guys look worried. I ain't trying to get y'all in trouble. But I ain't trying to change my record neither. So why don't we ask ourselves why they're after us? Are they after you? Are they after me? Or is it some political shit, the timing of the record's release? Let's wait till after the presidential election." Now I'm playing record executive here. "Let things cool down. We have Ice Cube's album coming out, we've got Dre's album coming out, Paris. You've got all the other toxic material coming out. Let's let them hit and see what happens."

Warner Bros. was off the hook, breathing easy.

So we wait and nothing happens.

Now the new release date is February 14. And I decide to put more songs on the album in the time I'm waiting. You can't let rap get stale, so each time it rolled back a month, I'd put a new song on it.

Now, the date's here and everything is cool. They haven't decided to change any of the words. We got beyond that. But they did come at me with one song that worried them: "Ricochet." The song starts out:

You go on and on and you don't stop.
You got sticky sneakers from the blood of a shot cop.

I explained to them that the record was *already* out. "Ricochet" was the title song to a movie I'd been in, with Denzel Washington and John Lithgow.

"They wouldn't fuck with that," I told them.

"They might," they said.

The Warners people weren't angry at me or my music; it was simply a paranoid reaction on their part. They had become slaves to the "chilling effect." They'd say, "We're not crazy. But there are crazy people out there who are gonna fuck with us."

I decided that "Ricochet" was already out as a sound-track single, and it had sold well. It was already an old song. Fine, I'll drop it, and I'll create new songs rather than fight over an old record that's already been out.

I'm working with them. I'm Mr. Calm. But there's always a point where you push it too far.

Although they had already approved *Home Invasion*'s cover art, we got a phone call a week before the album was scheduled to drop: "You can't have that album cover."

I was still on the road, and I'm pissed. I love the album cover. But fuck it. At this point I want my record to come out.

I told them to put the album out with a black cover. It'll be *The Black Album*. Fuck it. Just get it out there. I don't give a fuck.

But when I got back to L.A., I realized fully for the first time that Warner Bros. cannot afford to be in the business of black rage. They can be in the business of white rage, but black rage is much more sensitive. The angry black person is liable to say anything. The angry black person might just want to kill everybody. You just don't know. So, they can't be in the business of black anger while being in the business of black control, which is another part of the system.

So, we wrote them a letter asking to get out of my contract. As much as they felt I had become a liability to them, they in effect had become a liability to me. In my attempts to keep them out of trouble, my integrity had come under fire. My entire career is based on integrity. And I didn't want to be their token "free speech" employee. I didn't want them to be able to say, "We're a free speech haven because we've got Ice-T, and he's radical," while they turn around and tell me what I can and cannot say. I'm not a puppet.

They gave me a release.

(1994)

From "This Bridge Called My Pussy"

by Andrew Ross

To begin with the obvious, the least queer people to occupy the pages of *Sex* are Vanilla Ice and Big Daddy Kane. The sequences in which they appear are abject studies in heterosexual discomfort. Ice, the hypester from hell, so desperately wants to be seen there but can't generate any heat. He seems to be the one person who doesn't know he's only been invited along for his kitsch value as a has-been who really never was in the first place. By contrast Kane, the strong, silent ladies' man, would clearly rather be somewhere else. Neither seems to know where to put his hands; the only safe place is between the lady's legs.

Not that Madonna could care less. Sexual diversity, after all, is her semiencyclopedic aim—all access, straights included somewhere—and so the end justifies the means, even if it never justifies her love of access. Perhaps it might have made a difference if she had chosen, say, a bubbly manchild like Marky Mark, or a lecherous prankster like Sir Mix-A-Lot, but the joke would still have been on them. And why not? It's hard to argue with a world where straight masculinity's most powerful genre is that of farce, which mixes self-ridicule with good sportsmanship, rather than tragedy, which involves the daily (social) death of others. Apart from the rape scene in the school gym, where the unlikely assailants are nipple-ringed refugees from central casting at the Vault (a camp echo of the lesbian slave sequence, where torturers hold a knife to her crotch), Madonna's *Sex* is a world which the unqueer, unlike the undead, do not haunt with menace, and where picaresque adventures in the flesh trade are conducted with safe passage across a landscape lavished with neon proclaiming THIS IS DANGEROUS. TRY IT, and, more subliminally, GOODS NONRETURNABLE. It's a playground that might be an obstacle course if you're not in the mood for a lesson ("things can go really wrong"), but if you are, then you might think it's the sentimental education of someone else's lifetime; the mind fuck of the century, the sassiest way yet of going down on history. Smells Like Queer Spirit. (Which Madonna could seriously bottle and market, if only Warner were in the perfume business).

It's all the more important to recall, then, that Ice and Kane are rappers—this is no coincidence—and, as such, they are *Sex*'s dubious ambassadors from another theater of the cultural wars, where queerness is a big-time liability and not a raidable asset for the Time Warner–Madonna Complex. In the theater called rap, especially hardcore, hands are what you put your life in, so you'd better know what to do with them, or else keep 'em to yourself. "Smooth—not what I am/Rough—'cause I'm a man," sing the dire straights. "No Vaseline" goes the chorus line. Gotsa to be hard. Or Boom Bye Bye, in the words of Buju Banton's battyboy bashing anthem of Jamaican dancehall, gangsta rap's fellow traveler in the killing fields of homophobia. This is

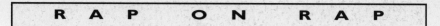

the other leading edge of popular culture, not the one that teaches the Big Gender Fuck, but the one which preaches Big Fucking Gender. Of course, it's conventional by now to say that both are striking a pose— the hand that squeezes the trigger in the Hip-hop Nation and the clamp that squeezes the nipple in the Queer Nation. It's conventional to say that both are harmless, fantasmatic representations, with no effectivity in the real world . . . blah, blah, blah. It's even conventional to say that the utopian conventions of Madonna's "It makes no difference if you're black or you're white/If you're a boy or a girl" are as conventional as the dystopian conventions of Ice-T's spoken intro to "Body Count":

You know sometimes I sit at home you know and I watch TV, and I wonder what it would be like to live someplace like, you know, *The Cosby Show* or *Ozzie and Harriet*, where cops come and got your cat out of the tree, and all your friends died of old age. But, you see, I live in South Central Los Angeles, and, unfortunately, shit ain't like that. It's real fucked up.

Remember, however, that, in both cases, we are still talking about culture created around places where death is a familiar visitor—the bodybag legacies, respectively, of the drive-by or the killercop, and the AIDS hospice bed or the queerbasher. Whether utopian or dystopian, these are stories about wishing that the daily world were propelled by the power of possibility, and not by the channeling of the death drive by the powers that be. But the difference between them, as everyone ought to know, lies in the divergent careers of Ice-T and Madonna at Time Warner. In 1992 the rapper's decision to "voluntarily" withdraw "Cop Killer" from the *Body Count* CD set the standard for widespread music industry censorship, at the same time as it caved in to police and right-wing pressure groups. Madonna's decision to suck toes and bite asses in public set a new standard for celebrity exhibitionism, at the same time as it profitably exploited outrage from the moralistas. Time Warner executives, in the meantime, kept their noses clean. To begin with, they turned the *Body Count* affair into a free speech platform for the corporation. Co-CEO Gerald Levin publicly proclaimed that the censorship of "Cop Killer" "would be a signal to all artists and journalists that if they wish to be heard, they must tailor their minds and souls to the reigning orthodoxies." As the pressure built, from the White House down, there was every indication that Warner began discreetly to put the rapper's back to the wall while publicly maintaining an anti-censorship stance. No one who smelled the post-L.A. fear of white America in May and June of 1992 would fully believe Ice-T's claim that he had not been coerced into his decision. By contrast, Warner welcomed *Sex* in November as the messianic harbinger of a nirvanic phase of development within the culture industries. In the words of Warner Books president Laurence Kirshbaum, *Sex* was a "review-proof" publication, pushing this Warner product into the realm of the guaranteed sell, beyond all critical influence, beyond the vagaries of reception. Free at last, the Industry Transcendent. Or, alternately, the hand that gave us Madonna was the hand that eventually took away *Body Count* in February 1993 when Ice-T was finally released from his Warner contract for "creative differences."

Even though Madonna is not actually gay, and "Cop Killer" was being aired circa the tragedy of South-Central L.A., there was an overriding pattern here, for which the differing treatment of each product was quite symptomatic. Madonna, for example, was able to mobilize key sectors of the FBI in a sting that tracked down some prepublication prints stolen from Lexington Labs: "Thanks," she cites in *Sex*'s acknowledgments, "to Gavin De Becker and the FBI for rescuing photographs that would make J. Edgar Hoover roll over." (Given the recent revelations about photographs of Hoover himself, this is a rich comment.) In the meantime the sons of J. Edgar were probably routinely wiretapping Ice-T and his posse. Whenever Ice-T performs in public, he summons up the ghosts of Malcolm and Martin by openly predicting, for his audience, the day of his own martyrdom while offering some conclusive wisdom: Never bow down before a badge, and take care, there are criminals in uniforms out there on the streets.

However apparent the double standard, I don't want to suggest that the different careers of Madonna and Ice-T at Warner can *entirely* be ascribed to discriminatory differences in the way in which sex and race are treated within the culture industries. Madonna has had her own run-ins with the forces of censorship, and the public demonizing of any gangsta rapper can hardly be considered a career setback. Besides, in 1992, the outlawing of Ice-T, however self-generated, took place against the backdrop of the much discussed commodification of Malcolm X. Madonna's queer-positive book appeared against the backdrop of an emergent wave of antigay sentiment. Don't be confused. These are the contradictory outcomes of pursuing a politics of race and a politics of sex in a consumer culture. . . .

━━━ ▭

This strikes me as a rather important moment in the history of popular culture, and well worth the discussion. In particular, one of the concerns of this essay is to understand why the affinity-style loyalties that are currently associated with the name of Madonna only extend into certain communities, and are considered a liability in others. Unlike most white performers, Madonna has never had to rely upon siphoning off credibility from the central reservoirs of African-American music and culture. There's little evidence that she, unlike most white performers, has ever thought that she was black. The throaty slow rapping she slurs through on parts of the *Erotica* album sounds more like a cross between a druggy phone sex monologue and a film noir voiceover than any conventional rip-off of rap rhymes. Rather, she has drawn sporadically from the margins of gay black experience and from whitegirl fantasies about the ethical grace of Latino masculinity. Much criticized as exercises in subcultural tourism, these are cultural bridges nonetheless; avenues where white female sexuality can hitch a ride in relative safety. Who knows, finally, what straight men (of whatever color) who see her as a sexual object think about her version of Pussy Power—an autocracy that demands attention to sexual diversity. No doubt it captures their attention, and perhaps it questions their disrespect, and there's even a chance that it forms a queer bridge over the panicky intersection that passes for heterosexuality these days.

But when it comes to the tribal identification demanded by *their* peers, Madonna's musical persona enjoys little loyalty. Thrash, power metal, and hard-core rap govern the field. The black dick, in particular, commands allegiance from audiences that the white pussy cannot. In Tijuana, in January 1993, I saw Ice-T sing with Body Count. It was not a particularly memorable concert (Ice-T was hoarse, and he didn't seem to realize that he was in Mexico), except for Ice-T's virtuoso presentation of "Evil Dick" in which he paid a semiparodic tribute to the adolescent male religion of jacking off, by careening around the stage and fucking the floor while furiously stroking an imaginary outsized penis. This awkward frenzy of masturbation is the staple erotic rhythm of whiteboy thrash and hard-core music, and Ice-T's theatrical take on the ritual was a calculated component of the crossover experiment of Body Count. But, in the ultimate fuck-you, he also reminded his audience of the semiofficial cultural status of the black penis as public enemy number one, one of the longest-running fantasies of the North American nation state. Nothing so plucky could have been attempted on the hard-core hip-hop stage. It was only by vaulting over the barriers of musical apartheid that the rapper could perform this burlesque of masculinity that brought the house down. In her own not unrelated way, Madonna has taken the gambit of sexuality onto a different stage, hurdling a different set of barriers.

What Ice-T does with his evil dick in thrash, what Madonna does with her pussy with nine lives in erotica, these are the public spectacles of our times, charged with the legacy of what Elvis did with his hips in 1956. The formations of race, sexuality, and gender that were fused together in the torso movements of a Southern whiteboy almost forty years ago have spun apart, separately and, as always, unequally, in the intervening decades. It is not necessary, but it may be useful to see Madonna's ascendancy alongside the rise to prominence of hard-core rapper masculinity. In many ways they are part of the same cultural moment, even though the dialogue between them is probably not the first thing most folks would stop to consider.

There is nothing arbitrary about the line of demarcation that separates Madonna's domain from that of Ice-T. It is as historically powerful as anything in our culture right now. No doubt it can be aligned with larger patterns of institutional racism, sexism, and homophobia in society and the music industry, but it cannot be easily transcended by a direct attack on these structural prejudices. Musical culture, in particular, has all sorts of genres and conventions for mediating the prejudices; it even has conventions for converting prejudices into convictions of taste, precisely those convictions through which fan loyalty is won and maintained. The most skilled interpreters of the rules, like Madonna herself, will always disappoint us since we always expect too much of them. Asking Madonna to justify your love may be more useful, in the long run, than scolding her for "not doing enough." For one thing, you'll get more attention. And according to the rules of fanthink, you may even get lucky.

(1993)

Larry King Live

SISTER SOULJAH, **Rap Artist: I reserve the right to fight against racism. I have not ordered anyone to kill anyone!**

GOV. BILL CLINTON, **Democratic Presidential Candidate: Was it right or was it wrong to say that there are no good white people? Was it right or was it** wrong to say that, instead of black-on-black crime, blacks should take a week to kill white people? I think it was wrong. It is not a good idea.

ANNOUNCER: Welcome to *Larry King Live*. Tonight: Bill Clinton says her words and her art are destructive. She says whites can't understand. The exchange made headlines. Now, rap artist Sister Souljah explains. Plus, a controversial suggestion for unhappy wives: Have an affair. Now, here's Larry King.

LARRY KING: Good evening on this Friday night from Washington— another edition of *Larry King Live*. A couple of quick notes: Next week, the author of the hottest book in the world, Andrew Morton, will be with us. He's written that biography about Princess Di. Also next week, the attorney general of the United States, William Barr.

A young black rap artist from New York is suddenly in the center of our national debate over racism. Until this week, much of white America probably hadn't heard of Sister Souljah. This is her work, and if it makes white people uncomfortable, that is part of the point.

SISTER SOULJAH: I am African first. I am black first. I want what's good for me and my people first. And if my survival means your total destruction—then so be it!

KING: Then came Bill Clinton. While L.A. riot victim Reginald Denny lay near death, Sister Souljah was telling *The Washington Post*, "I mean, if black people kill black people every day, why not have a week and kill white people?"

At the Rainbow Coalition last weekend, Clinton followed Sister Souljah to the stage and condemned those remarks. Jesse Jackson suggested that Clinton should apologize. He has not. The political fallout—enormous. Clinton's critics say that he's losing black support. Jackson critics say that Jackson should not be defending incendiary remarks. What about Sister Souljah? She says she's been misquoted and misunderstood.

Sister Souljah, the woman in the middle, joins us from our studios in New York.

Sister, before we talk about the controversy, just a little

about you. Why did you choose rap music as a form of entertaining expression?

SISTER SOULJAH: I think the important thing for people to understand is that in America we have an educational system that does not speak to the needs of African children. And so what hip-hop music has done is served as an alternative communication mechanism and given African children in this country some of the only understanding of African history that they'll ever receive.

KING: How about all the great female black jazz, blues, and rock artists?

SISTER SOULJAH: Well, Mr. King, I'm sure that you don't think that the history of African people is limited to music, or that music can build the esteem, the mind, heart, spirit, and intellect of African children in and of itself.

KING: No, the question, Sister, was why you chose rap music as your form of musical expression?

SISTER SOULJAH: Oh, because, clearly, hip-hop music is what reaches the young population. And in America, African children are in a state of emergency. So the best vehicle to use is the vehicle that they enjoy, which is hip-hop music.

KING: Okay, let's try to put this in perspective. Were you misquoted?

SISTER SOULJAH: Yes, I was definitely misquoted. Not only what—

KING: What did you say, and what did they— They printed what you said about killing whites. You said you didn't say that?

SISTER SOULJAH: What I'm saying is that what you and other people in the media have not done is said what the question that the reporter asked me was, what I said before and after the comment that people are blowing up and magnifying all over the world.

KING: All right, that's what I just asked you now.

SISTER SOULJAH: All right.

KING: What happened?

SISTER SOULJAH: The question was "But even the people themselves who were perpetuating that violence, did they think it was wise? Was that wise, reasoned action?" So the reporter is asking me what the people who did the violence in Los Angeles think.

KING: Right.

SISTER SOULJAH: And I responded to him—

KING: By?

SISTER SOULJAH:—in the voice of the people who did the violence, which is that white people have known that every day in Los Angeles black people are dying from gang violence, but that they did not care. But when it became a question of white people dying and a billion dollars in property being lost, that's when it became a concern. But in the mind of a gang member, if the social and economic system has neglected your development and you have become a casual killer who will kill even your own brother, in your mind-set, why not kill a white person? Because murder will not discriminate by color.

The other thing that I said is that injustice anywhere is a threat to justice everywhere, and that if white America continues to neglect the development of African youth and it turns into an economic and criminal-justice crisis, they will be the victims of that system as well as black people.

KING: When *The Washington Post* printed that, did you then issue any kind of a statement saying that "Here is the way it was asked, here is the way it was answered, and, taken on those terms, you're reading it wrong"?

SISTER SOULJAH: No. Actually, I'm used to newspapers having preconceived notions and preconceived actions. Because the issue of white
supremacy and racism in America is so explosive, what happens is
people don't want to hear what African people are actually saying.
They want to hear what they want to hear, and so they manipulate
the African leadership's words all the time.

KING: Do you think that Governor Clinton before making those remarks
should have called you and asked you if you stated them?

SISTER SOULJAH: I think that Governor Clinton is a dishonest person,
because he said he made those remarks because he was morally
outraged. But interestingly enough, he didn't make the remarks till
five to seven weeks after the article appeared in *The Washington
Post.*

KING: Well, that's because you had spoken at the same coalition he was
speaking at, so it came to mind then.

SISTER SOULJAH: No, I don't think that that's the reason. I think that an
aide in his camp brought him the article and he thought it would be
a strategic political move to show how macho he is, to jump on this
young African woman about her artwork, which, even though she has
the freedom of speech and freedom of expression— And there are so
many things in America to attack if you want to attack racism that it
would seem odd to attack an African woman who is the primary victim of racism.

KING: So you think it was designed to gain attention by saying
it to a group like the Rainbow Coalition, and he knew that that
would get a lot of press and attention and get white votes, as you
read it?

SISTER SOULJAH: I think it was an attack on Reverend Jackson to try to
prove that Reverend Jackson keeps radical company, to try to dis-
tance—

KING: Why would Clinton want to do that to someone who is support-
ing him?

SISTER SOULJAH: Clinton— First of all, Reverend Jackson has not en-
dorsed Mr. Clinton. Second of all—

KING: Well, it's expected that the black vote will go to the Democrats.
Why would he want to harm his own base?

SISTER SOULJAH: Because, as we know, Reverend Jackson is a powerful
contender for the vice-presidential slot, and that—

KING: The contenders—

SISTER SOULJAH: Excuse me. Give me a chance to answer—

KING:—were only in Mr. Clinton's mind, Sister.

SISTER SOULJAH: Give me a chance to answer the question. As we know,
Reverend Jackson is a powerful contender for the vice-presidential
slot, and, as we know, racism and white supremacy exist in full effect
in America. So in order to justify not having Reverend Jackson as the
vice-presidential candidate, even though he has delivered the most
votes to the party, Clinton has to find a justifiable reason. So trying
to prove that Jesse Jackson in some strange way is a racist or is un-
palatable to America is something that he tried to do by using Sister
Souljah, when, clearly, Sister Souljah and her philosophies and
Reverend Jackson and his philosophies are two different things.

KING: All right, what will be, do you think, the political payoff for
Clinton from this?

SISTER SOULJAH: Well, usually, African youth do not vote in the elections
because we receive such poor choices of candidates. And so what I
think Clinton did was awaken a sleeping giant, because I am very
loved by African people in this country and they feel personally attacked by what Clinton did because they believe that it was an in-
tegrityless attack for an agendaless candidate.

KING: So you think these people will then vote for Mr. Bush or Mr.
Perot?

SISTER SOULJAH: I think that African people will form a collective agenda, because a lot of people have been motivated by what has happened. And we will stand to see what will develop from that. But I don't believe that the support will go to Mr. Clinton.

KING: Sister, did you also say to *The Washington Post*—and I want to get this correct—"I don't think that anything we can do to white people would ever equal what they've done to us. I really don't. White people are born guilty, and there is no redeemer."

SISTER SOULJAH: Oh, I absolutely said that.

KING: What do you mean by "born guilty"?

SISTER SOULJAH: What I mean is this: that in America white children are raised to be white supremacists, meaning to believe that they are superior. And as they are raised, they are integrated into a system of power that protects their alleged superiority. We, as African people, have never enslaved and captured European people, taken them from their land, raped their women, changed their culture, suppressed their ability to be educated, and do all of the wicked things that white America has done to African people. Therefore, there is no such thing in my mind as reverse racism—

KING: Okay.

SISTER SOULJAH:—because reverse racism would imply that we had in some way evened the scales. And certainly, as African people, we have not done that.

KING: Do you know any white Americans who resisted that education and went the other way?

SISTER SOULJAH: Resisted what education?

KING: The education to grow up superior.

SISTER SOULJAH: It depends on what you say is "went the other way."

KING: Fought for equal rights, got involved in the civil rights movement, put their life on the lines as young men did in Mississippi and Alabama in the civil rights movement—you don't think whites did that?

SISTER SOULJAH: I think that there are white people who have made ostensible moves toward addressing this system. But I think when we get down to the fundamental issues of power—meaning not the question of whether blacks and whites can go to restaurants together, or whether Africans and Europeans can marry one another, not the ostensible question, but when it comes down to the question of power—white people, European people, in this country have not served us well.

KING: We'll be right back with Sister Souljah. We'll be including your phone calls. This is *Larry King Live* in Washington. Don't go away.

GOV. CLINTON: I know she is a young person, but she has a big influence on a lot of people. And when people say that—if you took the words *white* and *black* and you reversed them, you might think David Duke was giving that speech.

[Commercial break]

KING: Welcome back to *Larry King Live*. Our guest at our studios in New York—Sister Souljah. We'll go to your calls in just a couple of moments.
   Sister, Jesse Jackson has been drawn into this. Jesse Jackson came from Martin Luther King's movement and Jesse Jackson is a proponent of integration, harmony, peace, nonviolence, and groups working together, actively working together—black, white, what-have-you. That is the Rainbow Coalition. Do you share all those viewpoints?

SISTER SOULJAH: No, I do not, but I don't think that that's the point. I think that Reverend Jackson has proven himself in the areas and the philosophies in which he believes, and I think that he has served this country.

2 0 2

KING: Where do you disagree with him?

SISTER SOULJAH: I think the difference between myself and Reverend Jackson is this: He's a much bigger person than I am. I have lost hope and faith in white America—completely. Reverend Jackson tends to keep hope alive. He will go and serve white farmers, Latino people, people of all races. I believe that African people are in such a state of disarray that it must be my total concentration to rebuild the minds, hearts, and spirits of African people.

KING: Toward what goal?

SISTER SOULJAH: Toward the goal of self-sufficiency, independence, the ability—

KING: Segregated?

SISTER SOULJAH: No, I didn't say that. Are you trying to put words in my mouth?

KING: No, I'm asking you what—if you disagree with Jackson, where are you going? And you don't like that he works with whites and Latinos—

SISTER SOULJAH: No, I didn't say that. You sound like the Washington reporter.

KING: I'm trying to figure out—well, but this is on the air. It's not going to be in print, so what you answer is going to be said.

SISTER SOULJAH: Right.

KING: Okay.

SISTER SOULJAH: And what I am answering is exactly what I wanted to say.

KING: You've lost hope?

SISTER SOULJAH: What I'm answering is exactly what I want to say, and what I am saying is this: My goal and objective is to educate African children to be independent so that they can run their own economic structures and determine their destinies; so that African children on the continent of Africa will not be dying en masse from hunger, poverty, and AIDS, as they are now; so that African children in America will not be suffering and devastated, as they are now; so that African Haitian people in Haiti will not be mistreated, as they are now.

I believe that our destiny lies in our ability to be independent, to be strong and powerful, and to speak up against a system which is designed to destroy us throughout this entire world.

KING: Sister, Governor Clinton says he would like to sit down and meet with you. He said it last night on this program. Would you like to sit down and meet with him?

SISTER SOULJAH: I said at my press conference that I am willing to communicate with anyone. I'm very rational, civilized, and intellectual. I'm willing to meet with Mr. Clinton. The problem, however, is that Mr. Clinton has told everybody that he wants to meet me, except me.

KING: Do you condemn out of hand, just by nature, violence?

SISTER SOULJAH: Do I condemn out of hand—what do you mean by that question?

KING: Do you think violence is a bad way to get a goal?

SISTER SOULJAH: I tell you what—

KING: On anybody's part, anywhere.

SISTER SOULJAH: I tell you what, I think that violence, like the violence that America did in Panama, the violence that whites do in South Africa, the violence done in Grenada, the violence against African children in America, is very wicked and very bad, and should be eliminated.

KING: Now, how about violence by, say, black gangs, or Latino gangs, or Italian Americans, or Jewish Americans? When they commit violence, is that okay?

SISTER SOULJAH: I don't believe that it's okay, but I believe that there needs to be an educational system that is African-centered so that African children can be strong-minded; and that, in the absence of that system, we will continue to see violence.

KING: But do you agree killing doesn't solve anything? Is that a fair statement?

SISTER SOULJAH: Oh, I certainly do not advocate killing anyone.

KING: We'll be right back with your calls for Sister Souljah on *Larry King Live*. Don't go away.

[Clip from "The Final Solution: Slavery's Back in Effect," courtesy of Epic Records]

SISTER SOULJAH: See the war—smell the war—hear the war—you'd better feel the war! We're talking total annihilation—wicked and shrewd. The black man will be harder to find than dinosaur food. You should have read the books and understood—that America's no damn good!

VOICES: The reeducation of the Negro—Sister Souljah!

SISTER SOULJAH: I ain't the hero. I warned you!

[Commercial break]

KING: All right, let's go to your calls for Sister Souljah. Columbus, Georgia, hello.

FIRST CALLER: [Columbus, Georgia] Hey, how're you doing?

KING: Hi.

FIRST CALLER: Just two questions, two short ones. The first one is, I'd like to know why she keeps referring to black Americans as Africans. And secondly, I'd like to know why she thinks that white people ought to continue to be responsible for the upbringing of black youth, black inner cities?

KING: All right. Sister?

SISTER SOULJAH: Okay, the first answer is this. I call myself an African person because our people originated in Africa. So when you find African people in Jamaica, in Haiti, in Latin America, in Brazil, in various places in the world, they're still African people, even though they were born in that place. And I am very proud of the fact that I am an African person.

KING: And what about white Americans and educating black Americans?

SISTER SOULJAH: The second question is strange, because I just gave an entire bunch of comments about independence and self-sufficiency.

KING: Yes.

SISTER SOULJAH: And he's asking me why I think white people should raise the children, which is indicative of the fact that he has a problem. I do think, however—

KING: For the benefit of the caller, she was saying the opposite. Right?

SISTER SOULJAH: I was saying the opposite. I do think, however, that as long as African people in this country are taxpayers, that we have impact on the American government and that we should say how dollars are advocated to the upliftment of our people.

KING: Seattle, Washington, for Sister Souljah. Seattle, are you there? [silence] Okay, Seattle, good-bye.
   We go to Washington, D.C. Hello.

SECOND CALLER: [Washington, D.C.] Hello. I'd like to know exactly how Sister Souljah might feel about a comment that was made by a white D.C. disc jockey who made reference to Martin Luther King Day by saying, "We get a day off for Martin Luther King. Why don't we kill a few more of them, and get a week off?"

KING: Now, in fairness, that was many years ago, and he apologized for that many, many times.

SISTER SOULJAH: Well, I can still answer her question.

KING: Sure. Sure, I just wanted to set the record straight.

SISTER SOULJAH: I think that that's indicative of white racism in America. But one thing about white racism in America is, it's very subtle. And every now and then, somebody will pop out and say what they really think. But the thing that kills African people in America is not what white people say, but what they do: their policies, their actions, and how it affects African people domestically and internationally.

KING: Camp Dennison, Ohio, hello.

THIRD CALLER: [Camp Dennison, Ohio] Hi, Larry.

KING: Hi.

THIRD CALLER: Sister, I really appreciate what you're doing, but I'd like to ask you, what do you think is the difference between you and a David Duke? And why don't you take some of that money you spend on your expensive jewels and give it to the African people you're talking about?

SISTER SOULJAH: [laughs] Okay, I'll answer the first part first.

KING: Well, Clinton compared you to Duke, so it's a fair question.

SISTER SOULJAH: Oh, I have no problem with the question. You can ask me anything you want to ask me.

KING: Okay.

SISTER SOULJAH: First of all, David Duke was a member of the KKK—Ku Klux Klan—which is a terrorist organization that advocates, and does perform, the murder of African people and has over a period of 150 years killed African people, burned down our houses, blown up our churches, killed our children, and hung our men from trees. Sister Souljah does not own a gun, has never shot anyone, has never killed anyone, does not have a criminal record, and has never been a member of a terrorist organization that advocates the murder of white people.

The other thing is, in terms of my jewels, I think that's a very paternalistic attitude that you have. And most white people tend to think that African people as individuals should not enjoy any of the benefits of their material accomplishments, even though we have to work twice and three times as hard as white people in order to get it. The other thing—

KING: What—

SISTER SOULJAH: Excuse me—that you should know is that I do support various causes for the upliftment of African children back in my community, in Harlem and in Brooklyn, and that I encourage young people to develop businesses by giving them money and running contests to stimulate the thoughts about entrepreneurship in our community.

KING: One more thing I want to discuss with you—your thoughts on Ice-T. Vice President Quayle today attacked Time Warner, the company that owns the recording company he records for, because of his statements about killing police officers in his rap music. I haven't heard your thoughts on that.

SISTER SOULJAH: My thought is that America refuses to deal with white supremacy and racism, so what they do is run around attacking everybody who's African and outspoken: Ice-T, Public Enemy, Minister Farrakhan—[laughs]—anybody that has an opinion or who's pissed off at the fact that we're beat down, brutalized, and when we go and seek justice in the courts we still cannot get it. So I'm not surprised at their attacking Ice-T.

The other thing I wanted to say is this: that you take a guy like Quayle and you really start to understand racism. Here is a man who has absolutely no intelligence, political savvy, or understanding of the majority of people in the American society. But just simply because he's white and born into a privileged family, he can actually run around and pretend to be the Vice President of this country.

KING: Do you like Ice-T's music?

SISTER SOULJAH: I am not a person that purchases Ice-T's music, but I certainly support his right to express himself.

KING: Thanks very much, Sister Souljah. Thanks for joining us.

SISTER SOULJAH: Thank you very much for having me. I appreciate the opportunity.

KING: My pleasure. Sister Souljah, joining us on *Larry King Live*.

We're going to break and, when we come back, we're going to have a discussion about an extraordinary new book called *The Erotic Silence of the American Wife*. It's a book about infidelity and how infidelity in many cases has helped marriage. We'll also have a debate on it, because the author of another book says that may not be a very good idea. We'll also include your phone calls.

And don't forget, next week, the attorney general of the United States, William Barr, will be with us. This is *Larry King Live* in Washington. Stay right there.

ANNOUNCER: How many unhappy wives find fulfillment in outside flings? A new book says "More than you think."

[Commercial break]

(June 19, 1992)

Yo! A Rapper's Domestic Policy Plan: How Clinton Can Bring Hope to Alienated Black America

by Paris

A lot of people are giving Bill Clinton advice these days. Here's mine.

Although many Americans are joyfully anticipating your inauguration, I see no reason to celebrate yet. In one sense, I'm glad you won. Unlike many of my generation who bemoan the uselessness or corruption of the political process, I rejected the easy pessimism of not voting and cast a ballot for you.

Your campaign, however, placed me and most other blacks in a painful predicament. By claiming you were running against the "special interests" (blacks, labor, and feminists) that have supposedly kept the Democrats out of the White House for the last twelve years, you skillfully undermined honest debate about racial justice. And by dissing Sister Souljah and distancing Jesse Jackson at a single stroke, you confirmed the bitter belief among many of us that even well-intentioned whites are unable to play the game of racial politics above-board.

Here's our dilemma: If we speak up, we're special-interest whiners, but if we keep quiet, we lose self-respect and reinforce our own invisibility. I, for one, cannot remain silent. Your actions were, in my view, calculating and unprincipled, and they angered me—but not enough to make me believe that you could not redeem yourself.

Although I hold a degree in economics, I am a radical rapper by profession, an artist whose outrage pushed me to write and record "Bush Killa," which appears on my album, *Sleeping With the Enemy.* The song has sparked controversy because it imagines the stalking and slaying of the President, that ready-made symbol of politics and policies that have assaulted black America for nearly half my life. I understood that the language in this violent fantasy would be disturbing to many, but what I hoped to call attention to—the real-life economic violence visited upon millions of African-American people every day of their lives—is more disturbing and more real.

I am, nonetheless, at least slightly hopeful about what you can achieve with your presidential power. I like your rhetoric about putting people first, and I can't see you being worse than your predecessor.

As the old saying goes, when America sneezes, black America catches cold. Judging by that standard, we have double pneumonia. The black infant mortality rate is double the figure for whites. The unemployment rate for young black men has reached forty percent, triple that of whites. The number of black children living in poverty now exceeds forty-five percent, while overall 10 million African Americans are officially poor. As you know, there are now more black men in prison (over 600,000) than in college (435,000). Though one out of our four Americans with AIDS is black, George Bush, as Magic Johnson pointed out, dropped the ball on this issue. It is a notorious fact that

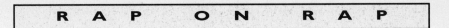

homicide is the number-one cause of death for young black men. It is less often noted that suicide has climbed to become the third leading cause of death for this group. Recognize that there is despair in America. So what is to be done? The first thing is not to fall for the easy right-wing argument that black America has only itself to blame for its problems. African Americans are well aware of the work we must do ourselves to improve our lot. We know from hard experience that we cannot rely on the government to improve our mind-set or morale or to nurture the black family. We need to do these things ourselves.

And we are. In San Francisco, my hometown, the Omega Boys Club is taking hardheads off the street, teaching them about themselves and their heritage, and preparing them to go to black colleges. So far more than two hundred young men—former hustlers, dope dealers, and stickup kids—have gone on to higher education, while maintaining contact with their roots. In your new home city, Washington, the Nation of Islam has nearly eliminated drug dealing at the Mayfair Mansion apartment complex. Too often, though, these success stories are neglected by the pundits either out of ignorance or out of hostility to the message of black pride. Don't confuse black pride with black racism.

You need to know about these heroes of the black community because they are working daily to combat one of our most serious problems: a socialization process that teaches black youth a complete lack of regard for black life, a process that is reinforced by TV, movies, and music. In Arnold Schwarzenegger's *Total Recall* (a popular movie among young blacks), the only black character was a traitor with a Jheri curl and a gold tooth who lived on Mars. Even in outer space we are demonized.

And too many of my fellow rap artists only contribute to the problem. Their words are taken as gospel truth, more than those of parents and teachers, and yet those words reinforce the same stereotypes offered by Hollywood: Get it for yourself regardless of the consequences.

Ironically, that's the same message we get from black conservatives. Their arguments, although sometimes well intentioned, don't make sense for most black people. They demand that black people be less dependent on welfare—a proposition that no one would disagree with—while carefully avoiding discussion of truths that might alienate their corporate patrons. I don't need to tell you that over the last twelve years, the Reagan-Bush administrations raised taxes on the poorest twenty percent of the American people—a group that is disproportionately black—while cutting taxes for the richest one percent, a group that is, safe to say, mostly white. If you think working white people are tired of paying for poor black people on welfare, understand how working black people feel about funding welfare for rich white folks.

In short, we don't need lectures on "values" and "responsibilities" from the conservative forces in Washington responsible for the Iran-Contra, Iraqgate, Department of Housing and Urban Development, and S&L scandals (or from those media liberals who failed to expose them). Nor do we need or want handouts. We simply want a level playing field.

That's why I want to propose a few commonsense solutions to the problems that haunt the majority of black Americans, poor whites, and people of other colors.

First, socialize health care. Universal health care is the mark of a civilized society, one concerned about the total well-being of its citizenry. We currently spend more than thirteen percent of GNP for health care while the number of people who are uninsured stands at 37 million. By comparison, no other industrialized country spends even ten percent of its GNP on health care while providing universal coverage for its citizens. Right now, influential health-care lobbies have protected the profits of a bureaucracy composed of doctors, hospitals, and other institutions that provide health care. This has driven costs totally out of control. Do you have the political will to oppose them, or will the "managed competition" you call for turn out to be yet another health-care fiasco?

Universal health care for Americans might cost an extra $50 billion, but we are already spending $820 billion for those already insured. If we distributed a progressive tax burden over the wealthier half of the American population, we could easily finance universal health care.

Secondly, address the crisis of public education. The inequality of resources between schools in rich neighborhoods and schools in poor ones is a national disgrace. You must pay the highest salaries to the best teachers as an incentive to teach in the inner cities, while funding a national scholarship to recruit people of color to the profession of teaching. Promote a multicultural curriculum to reflect multicultural America and counteract the alienation felt by so many black youth with

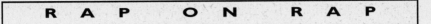

regard to the educational process. Letting kids stay home from school on Martin Luther King Day and talking of Harriet Tubman during Black History Month are the merest tokens of concern and scarcely begin to address the problem. As for older students, no one should be denied a higher education because of its cost. The ability to think critically shouldn't be the sole province of the privileged. Don't write us off.

Finally and most importantly, develop a comprehensive urban plan that addresses unemployment and job creation. Universal employment is a basic and nonnegotiable human right. The shift from a manufacturing to a service economy has meant the evaporation of low-skilled, high-wage jobs for many workers, affecting blacks disproportionately and causing high rates of black unemployment. Revive programs such as the Neighborhood Youth Corps and CETA, programs that provide remedial education and job training whose benefits far outweigh their costs. And don't neglect tax incentives for would-be lenders to minority-owned businesses in the black community. A full-employment policy that retrains workers would at last take advantage of the human capital of the inner cities now being tragically wasted.

All of this would be good business. If you could put back to work— perhaps through a revamped Works Progress Administration—the 8.8 million Americans who are unemployed, you would increase the GNP by 6.1 percent. And that doesn't even count the billions in savings on unemployment and welfare benefits.

The most radical aspect of my suggestions is that they are clearly achievable if you have the will to implement them. I hope you do. What many of us told ourselves during your campaign will now be tested: that you only ignored black people in order to get elected. Now that you're in there, it will take more than appointments of blacks to high places in your administration to do the right thing. Help those poor blacks, whites, and people of color who live in our nation's inner cities and who for too long have been nobody's special interest. Otherwise, the next generation of black youth will be writing their own sequels to "Bush Killa"—and that will be the least of your problems.

(January 3, 1993)

PART 4

Planet Rock

SPIKE LEE'S ALL-STAR B-BOY CAPS

GEORGETOWN HOYA'S—*Black America's Team.* Coach John Thompson, Patrick Ewing, Alonzo Mourning—the team white America hates.

UNLV—"Tark the Shark" hats only showed up once they won the NCAA.

KANSAS CITY ROYALS—Nice design, nice royal blue.

PHILADELPHIA SIXERS—Dr. J's Team, now Barkley; bright, red, big attraction.

OAKLAND RAIDERS—Hat made popular by NWA and Chuck D; a lot of it has to do with the Raiders' rep.

LOS ANGELES LAKERS—What can you say? *Kareem, Magic, Showtime,* and kick the *Celtics'* ass.

NEW YORK METS—The year they won the World Series, '86, was the last time I've worn their hat. Met management was never too keen on black or Hispanic ball players; cater to Long Island and Queens fans.

NEW YORK GIANTS—GREAT LOGO; Lawrence Taylor.

NEW YORK YANKEES—The best known insignia in sports which Steinbrenner has made a joke.

U. OF NORTH CAROLINA TARHEELS—Dean Smith, Michael Jordan, James Worthy; powder blue, basketball tradition

MONTREAL EXPOS—Funny-looking; clown hats.

BROOKLYN DODGERS—Classic.

NEW YORK GIANTS (BASEBALL)—Willie Mays, Denzel Washington wears this one in "Mo' Better Blues."

BROOKLYN DODGERS (WHITE)—My favorite hat! The *classic-classic.*

OAKLAND A's—People liked this hat even before they won the series; great color combination.

LOS ANGELES KINGS—Made popular by NWA; very few African-Americans like hockey, so you know it's something else. . . .

CALIFORNIA ANGELS—The white joint, regular is black. I've always liked the "A" with the halo around it.

NEW YORK KNICKS—This black version is new. My favorite team in all of sports. If I could fire Al Bianchi and take his job we'd be in the NBA Finals in 2 years! The acquisition of Kiki killed the delicate chemistry of the team that may never be fixed.

SYRACUSE ORANGEMEN—Pearl Washington was the one player that really got the Orangemen out there, too bad he was a *bum* in the NBA.

CHICAGO BULLS—One of the most popular hats no matter where you go. You gotta give it up to Air Jordan.

LOS ANGELES DODGERS—Classic.

DETROIT PISTONS—"*The Bad Boys*", *NBA champs, BACK TO BACK*!!! Good. Anybody but the Celtics.

PITTSBURGH PIRATES—Made famous by Chuck D—by him wearing it, it became the PE joint.

BOSTON CELTICS—*Boston sucks.* This guy is an "Uncle Tom."

The Hermeneutics of Rap

by Ann Marlowe

The Public Enemy T-shirt worn by *Terminator 2*'s young hero John Conner aligns him with "resistance" in some vague form, but hardly with an underground. After all, everyone knows who Public Enemy are, or their name wouldn't be in a big-money entertainment

aimed at a nation of millions. The shirt works as a Stones T-shirt might have in 1970, but not as a Sex Pistols T-shirt would have in 1980. It functions like the Guns N' Roses song on the sound track: we're hip, the filmmakers are saying, but accessible. (And we contain multitudes, from Axl to PE's Chuck D.) Yet this shirt is far more richly symbolic than any rock band's would have been. For whites in the audience, it's suggestive of racial tolerance and political concern, but also of toughness, danger, controversy, and difference. Public Enemy's image is *heavier* than any rock group's, and goes farther to signify John Connor's total righteous cool. No matter how multiracial rap's audience, this costume choice suggests, rap isn't part of rock.

Public Enemy themselves don't glory in this difference. "We ride limos too," Chuck D assures us, "Run with the rock stars, still never get accepted as." These lines from PE's 1988 hit "Bring the Noise" reflect a view of rap stars as second-class citizens in the musical firmament. It's worth asking why Chuck D thinks being "accepted as" a rock star, rather than the world-famous rap star he is, would be a worthy goal.

Loosely speaking, rock stars aspire to heroism—their best technicians, in fact, are known as "guitar heroes." And since Achilles, the hero in the West has stood for the aloneness of radical difference. This isolation from the group is the source of his poetic aura, and of his vulnerability. Rock stars are notoriously mortal, and rock was accumulating dead avatars from its infancy; its energy comes from the death drive, or its forestallment. Rappers like Chuck D, on the other hand, aspire less to heroism than to leadership. And despite its roots in a community where violent deaths are legion, and where one in four young men is behind bars, this music has produced few martyrs. It is about surviving, and proud of it—like Ice-T when he sneers, "You should've killed me last year." There's no death-entranced rap equivalent to David Bowie's "Rock 'N' Roll Suicide" or Lou Reed's "Heroin." When rappers mention death, it's usually boastingly, as something that can't happen to them.

However fraudulently, much rock still promises Dionysian release. But the ecstasies of rap lie not in abandon but in the precision of breathtaking verbal fluency. Rap is realistic rather than escapist, challenging rather than comforting. It's street music, and you don't trance out on the street. While rock vocalists are seen to give themselves up to something, rappers strive for control—and lose sexual appeal and charisma. What makes performers sexy isn't their power to master us but their ability to give in to their feelings and be moved, and rappers are rarely allowed the luxury of weakness or sorrow. There's been a tragic consciousness in rap from the beginning, but it's usually been tied to the specific unhappy situation of African Americans (in Grandmaster Flash's "The Message," for example) rather than to the human condition. The Geto Boys' recent hit "Mind Playin' Tricks on Me" is an extraordinary exception, and the group in general is the only one I've seen live that comes close to *terribilità*.

These differences reflect the broader divide between the avant-gardist cultural assumptions of all but the most commercial rock and the more mainstream values of rap. Rap has a willingness to please that's the antithesis of rock's jazz-descended cool. There are gradations, of course, but even hard-core rappers extend more courtesy to their audiences than rock bands. It's hard to imagine Ice-T, Chuck D, or any of the Geto Boys turning his back on the audience for most of his show, or deliberately insulting them—which happens frequently enough in rock. And though there are underground rockers and jazz musicians who like to boast of the difficulty of their playing, of how they won't *really* be understood for twenty years, rappers want to be understood now. In practice, rappers' striving to be "large" amounts to the ordinary writ large, not to radical difference or experimentalism.

Rappers are unique among twentieth-century artists in the candor of their pursuit of material success. At one end of the spectrum, Public Enemy champion sobriety, education, and black capitalism; at the other, the Geto Boys make malt liquor ads and assure us "I Ain't With Being Broke." Even misogyny wears a material face: the main sin women are accused of in rap is gold digging. What's pathetic about much rap materialism is in fact the modesty of its aspiration. L.L. Cool J's "The Do Wop," written when he was eighteen, takes us through a rapper's day, including a mink coat, a BMW—and a visit to a White Castle. The adoring crowd aside, there's nothing in his fantasy beyond the reach of a moderately successful small businessman.

You didn't hear much in the media about materialism in rap until gangster imagery exploded in the late eighties. As rappers told stories of selling drugs and shooting people, bohemian critics reeled in disbelief; gangster metaphors had to be explained away, or condemned. Frank Owen wrote in *Spin* in 1988, "The rappers' gangster imagery is, in the phrase coined by French writer Jean Baudrillard, hyperconformism: the simulation of the mechanism of the very system that excludes them." We should credit rappers with more imagination. Yes, some of the motive behind rap gangsterism is admiration for criminality—the same American fascination that has spawned *noir* novels, journalism, and film, which no one has called hyperconformist. Some is, in the words of David Samuels, "the conscious manipulation of racial stereotypes" for white suburban voyeurs. And as Alan Light has pointed out, "Rappers knew that they could cross over to the pop charts with minimal effort, which made many . . . attempt to prove their commitment to rap's street heritage." But behind the boasts there's also amazement—that they're getting paid to enjoy speech, rather than serving time in an office or bagging groceries for minimum wage. Like criminals they're getting away with something. It's not that gangsterism is admirable per se, but that rapping is as radical an answer to the grimness of work and as breathtaking an escape from the dour structures of adult life.

For some time now the problem with capitalism hasn't been that it doesn't work but that it's no longer fun. Opposition culture has failed to make good on this. Rock musicians are as often as not appalled at the possibility of uniting work and play that they in fact represent; they wear their bad conscience on their sleeve, from the ambivalences of the Byrds' "So You Want to Be a Rock 'N' Roll Star" on. Yes, the business of rock is joyful excess, but excess looks more and more like business as usual. The business of rap is just business, yet it still looks like fun. Rap is postmodern not only in form—its samples extending the "cut-up" and the appropriationist collage to music—but in its culture, where art looks more and more like business even as it looks more and more like play.

Rap doesn't exactly join work and play, but it blurs the division considerably, not only in the pleasure taken in making the music and living the life, but in the delight in speech underlying the whole art. On first hearing, the sheer fluency of some rappers suggests the ecstasy of the child's first immersion in speech, repeating strings of words over and over for the thrill of it. Rap's suggestion of a union of work and play, art and business, recalls the worlds both of pro sports and of criminal activity, and rap's poses shadow and are shadowed by the sports team and the gang. With its cult of the posse, its identification with the neighborhood, and its call-and-response dynamic, rap is the music of the group, not the lonely hero. Its world functions in many ways like the world of sports: although each team has its star or stars, the fan identifies with the team rather than with the individual player. (All those team caps are no coincidence.)

Like gangs and teams, rappers have been given to trademark clothing, jewelry, and logos. Their now-waning taste for gold chains and designer names has often been tagged by middle-class whites as vulgar, and pathetically enthralled with the most bankrupt aspects of capitalism. Owen offers a deeper interpretation: "Rather than simply aping the life-styles of the rich and famous, homeboys are recoding the trappings of affluence, caricaturing mainstream consumption." Making broad signs of identity is also a logical response to the way white society has cartooned blacks. Rap's symbol system is often a form of mirroring: if society thrusts on you a stereotypical yet inescapable identity, put on a crude and exhibitionistic mask. The exaggerated looks in rap culture reflect both blacks' and whites' obsession with blacks' appearance—i.e., with the color of their skin. (The young Oakland rapper Del tha Funkeé Homosapien's "Dark Skin Girls" is remarkable because many male rappers take the opposite preference for granted.) Rap's symbolic defiance is essentially reactive, and many of its visual identifications are a return of the repressed. Rappers themselves have noted that gold chains are, after all, chains.

Rap's imagery isn't so much poetic as suggestive, obeying the language of dreams, of psychoanalysis, or of Surrealism. Sometimes rap's politics seem surreal, too, in their wrongheadedness, or in the way they simultaneously cut through and regurgitate the dead tissue of the past. Like the Geto Boys at Madison Square Garden in January, first asking for the black power salute, then sampling from the "Star-Spangled Banner"—and this as the intro to the anti–Gulf War song "Fuck a War." Like Choice, a woman rapper from Houston, restoring, or ignoring, four hundred years of American history as she belts out what's just an aside in "Payback": "The South is in the goddamn house!" This is what the Civil War was fought for. What's crucial to these moments isn't, finally, that the artists in question are black, but that they're American, born to covet both limos and street credibility, to valorize work and criminality at once, to hope against all merely reasonable expectation for lives that are adventures. It remains to be seen whether rap has been using capitalism or is being used by it, but it also remains to be seen whether the rest of us are capable of taking up the pleasures, and astonishments, it offers us.

(March 1992)

Rap Moves to Television's Beat

by Jon Pareles

Ask most pundits about rap music, and they'll describe it as rude, jumbled noise. A few others may consider it million-selling postmodernism in audible form—songs as mix-and-match collages that treat the history of recorded music as a scrapheap of usable rubble and, often, trade narrative and logic for a patchwork of bragging, story-telling, speechifying, and free-form rhymes.

But rap, which as the nineties begin is both the most startlingly original and fastest-growing genre in popular music, didn't come out of some art-historical think tank. Instead, it is music shaped by the most pervasive instrument of American popular culture—commercial television. In its structure and its content rap is the music of the television age, and the first truly popular music to adapt the fast, fractured rhythms, the bizarre juxtapositions, and the ceaseless self-promotion that are as much a part of television as logos and laugh tracks. Where television shatters chronology and logic, rap shows us how to dance on the shards.

It had to happen, sooner or later, that popular music would reflect the ubiquity of television—and it's true to American musical history that a black subculture picked up the new rhythms first. Bebop and rhythm-and-blues reflected the individualism of post–World War II America; 1960s soul mirrored rising expectations while free jazz expressed barrier-breaking rebellion. Rap has found the musical metaphor for a time in which everyone has tuned in to the tube—in 1990, the Television Advertising Bureau estimates, there will be two television sets for every houschold in Amcrica, and 98.2 percent of households will have television—and the unfolding video spectacle is often mistaken for reality.

But unlike so many viewers, rap musicians aren't passive couch potatoes. Just as jazz musicians transformed mainstream popular music—turning mawkish pop standards into virtuosic, subtle, multileveled, passionate improvisations—rappers are turning television's rhythms to their own ends. Some of those ends are as inane as most television programming, or as depressing as the adolescent-male misogyny and homophobia that taint too many rap records, or comic, bawdy, political, rude. Recently more and more rappers, notably KRS-One and Boogie Down Productions, recognizing their own impact, have turned to positive, socially responsible messages.

Marvin Young, aka Young M.C., boasts, "I'm rough like Hunter, clever like MacGyver" and raps, "If I'm not on tour, I'm at home watching cable." Ice-T, a Los Angeles rapper who has been criticized for his violent tales of gang warfare, actually follows the same strategy as television's police shows, providing titillating close-ups of shootings and beatings, then finishing off with crime-does-not-pay messages. In a rap responding to his critics he says, "It's entertainment, like *Terminator* on TV." (He must have seen the movie on the small screen.)

Television isn't just entertainment, of course; it's entertainment as bait for advertising. And rappers are no more immune to advertising than the rest of the population. Many rappers present themselves as status-conscious, conspicuous consumers, reeling off brand names like Adidas and Gucci and Porsche. Until recently (when politically conscious rappers pointed out how much of the world's gold comes from South Africa) many rappers flaunted outsize gold chains.

Network television spends a considerable part of its time advertising itself—tonight's newscast, tomorrow's prime time, next week's special. By the time next week's *Roseanne* has appeared, the promo spots have probably occupied more time than the half hour the program takes to air. Rappers have married such copious, video-age self-promotion to older African and American boasting traditions, so that there's hardly a rap song without at least a line of chest-thumping. Even in songs with other subject matter, rappers' advertisements for themselves freely break through, not bothering with transitions, until it seems as if the other subjects are interrupting the ego trip. Rappers, like television's hosts and newscasters, are personalities above all.

Rappers have latched on to television's rhythms, but they haven't accepted television's version of mainstream culture. With every recycled funk bass line and James Brown scream, they insist on the durability and richness of a black street culture that's still invisible on most television programming, although the popularity of *Yo! MTV Raps* shows how easily rap can use its television savvy on the screen itself. Rap may end up devaluing its materials—as television too often does—or transforming them into something brilliant and unexpected. Either way, rap already has the ears of a generation for which television has made all of the difference.

A television viewer sees the same snippets again and again—as previews from a drama and minutes later in the drama itself, in out-of-context bits to promote the next week's sitcoms, in endlessly repeated commercials. Those prerecorded, chopped up, repeated snippets echo in the music behind rappers: bits of old records, scratched on turntables or sampled through digital processors, atomized and then put together in new arrangements where rhythm is paramount and non sequiturs are perpetual. A few words from an elder—from James Brown or Curtis Mayfield or Richard Pryor—can sum up a chorus or provide a transition, just like television's pretaped cameos.

Beyond that, rap's music usually ignores the carefully plotted drama, the slow-building tension and release, of older-style popular music. The only way to understand "The Adventures of Grandmaster Flash on the Wheels of Steel," a ground-breaking 1981 single by the disk jockey Grandmaster Flash with his turntables, was to let go of any lingering linear notions of continuity.

Most rap arrangements are simultaneously jumpy and droning; they're full of interjections and sudden changes, but they don't develop from a beginning to an end—a few elements keep coming back. And while the funk syncopations and densely layered sounds of rap look back to African music, the jolts and interruptions—and the sense that a song could be cut off at any moment—link rap's music to the ongoing video collage of everyday television.

Television's fragmentation also extends to rappers' words. While some rap songs are straightforward tall tales or ballads without tunes (including most of the rap hits that reach pop radio stations, like Tone-Loc's "Wild Thing" and D.J. Jazzy Jeff and the Fresh Prince's "Parents Just Don't Understand") and others recall sermons or jazz musicians' variations on a theme, many others are assemblages that ricochet from topic to topic, from boasting to narrative to commentary to musical cues to nonsense rhymes. Defying the standard pop songwriting methods that insist on a single narrowly defined topic, raps flaunt their tangents and interruptions and bursts of lingual dexterity.

Public Enemy's Carlton (Chuck D) Ridenhour is probably the rapper who zaps between channels fastest. His "Bring the Noise" opens:

Bass! How low can you go?
Death row. What a brother knows.
Once again, back is the incredible
the rhyme animal
the incredible D, Public Enemy No. 1
Five-O said, "Freeze!" and I got numb
Can I tell 'em that I never really had a gun?
But it's the wax that Terminator X spun
Now they got me in a cell 'cause my records, they sell.

The lyric cross-cuts boasts about Chuck D and the disk jockey Terminator X with glimpses of a prison setting. It's a montage in cryptic telegraphic bursts. (Sometimes Public Enemy jump-cuts too fast for

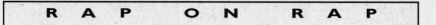

comfort. Its new single, "Welcome to the Terrordome," has drawn charges that one couplet—"Crucifixion ain't no fiction. So-called chosen, frozen./Apologies made to whoever pleases. Still, they got me like Jesus"—accuses Jews, the "so-called chosen" people, of deicide and of persecuting Chuck D. The group now asserts that "they" refers to all of the group's critics.) Rap concerts are equally fractured. Songs are rarely the same as their album counterparts; halfway through they're likely to be switched off in favor of call-and-response with the crowd or a leap to a different song. Unlike most pop and rock—and unlike radio programming—rap no longer takes for granted that even a three-minute span of time, the length of a short pop song, is an inviolable unity.

While popular music has never been the most erudite of the arts, rap presents a universe that's almost entirely electronic, derived from television, movies, and records; rappers compare themselves constantly to pop-culture figures from Rambo and Mike Tyson (two favorites) to Don Ho, and in their references the classics come from cable reruns, video stores, and golden-oldies bins, not the library. Rap's prolix, specific verbiage, more than most rock's carefully turned romantic platitudes, is the feedback of an all-electronic culture.

Some rappers refer directly to the TV influence. De La Soul and MC Lyte open albums with imitations of game shows; on his album *No One Can Do It Better*, the D.O.C. (who has the current No. 1 rap single) includes what he calls a "commercial," rapped by others, while he rests up between songs.

While individual rappers have earned praise and scorn, the power of the music goes beyond its innovators and imitators. Rap is on the way to becoming a global style, turning up in salsa and Haitian music, in British rock, and even in Italian pop.

The prospect of multilingual monotone boasting may not be entirely appetizing (especially if rap doesn't outgrow its most primitive prejudices), and rap will probably never please a generation that expects songs to include memorable tunes. But at its best rap fights television's incursions with television's own pace and effects.

When rap made its way from dance-club disk jockeys to hit singles in the late 1970s, most of the music business expected it to be a short-lived fad. Instead, rap gathered momentum through the 1980s and there's no reason to think that its popularity has peaked. Across pop music, melody is becoming less important than rhythm, noise, texture, and attitude; the naked self-aggrandizement of rappers may have been the purest expression of the Me-First Decade. Rap now defines rock's

generation gap; a younger generation loves it, an older one plugs its ears.

Yo! MTV Raps, seen daily on MTV (at four P.M.) and twice on Saturdays (ten A.M. and P.M.), consistently draws the cable channel's largest audiences, proving that rap appeals to fans a long way from its early strongholds in black urban neighborhoods. While commercial radio stations are leery of anything but an occasional comic rap novelty, leading rappers like L.L. Cool J, Young M.C., De La Soul, Public Enemy, and Rob Base and DJ E-Z Rock become million-sellers with or without frequent radio exposure. The music is heard on college radio stations, in clubs, from car tape players, and at thousands of private parties; while it grates on outsiders and parents (which can be part of its purpose), it is the chosen soundtrack for millions of fans.

Yet no one should have been surprised by the rap explosion. If rap is rock and soul music through a television wringer, then in hindsight its growth makes sense. Rap reached a generation weaned on *Sesame Street*, acculturated by television's discontinuities and sound bites. (It's probably no accident that the rap term for stealing other people's ideas is "biting" their style.) During the 1980s, while television tightened its hold on all kinds of public discourse, its impact also spread to music. The formula for a pop hit is to put a veneer of novelty on a familiar format, and what's more familiar than television?

Television has changed the way viewers perceive reality, packing more disparate information into shorter spans of time and changing the rhythm of lives that now twitch to the expectation of a punch line before the next commercial.

To say that rap reflects television doesn't discount its deep roots in black culture; the networks didn't invent rap, ghetto disk jockeys did. Rap comes out of the storytelling and braggadocio of the blues, the cadences of gospel preachers and comedians, the percussive improvisations of jazz drummers and tap dancers. It also looks to Jamaican "toasting" (improvising rhymes over records), to troubadour traditions of social comment and historical remembrance that stretch back to West African griots, and to a game called "the dozens," a ritualized exchange of cleverly phrased insults. And of course, rap wouldn't exist without the 1960s and 1970s funk records—especially James Brown songs—that supply beats, bass lines, and interjections for innumerable rap recordings.

Rap rephrases that culture in video-age terms, yet it holds on to black cultural history with every sample of an old record, as when Big

Daddy Kane borrows both the title and the chorus of "Ain't No Stoppin' Us Now," the one hit by McFadden and Whitehead; unlike television, it doesn't take place exclusively in the present tense. Rap's continual transformation of its sources, however, has been conditioned by television in ways large and small.

Consider the structure of an evening of television—news broadcast, game show, sitcom, cop show. The news may be the most fragmentary programming, juxtaposing cool newscasters with footage of disasters, triumphs, and sports highlights, jumping from grim to cheerful tidings, all studded with commercials. The other shows have some dramatic thread, but their continuity is also fractured, interrupted with mechanical regularity for commercials, network promotions, late-news previews (themselves interrupted by commercials), voice-overs pushing the next show. Zapping between channels, remote-control in hand, can shred any remaining coherence.

As rap reveals and revels in the changes television has made in our perception of time and logic, it suggests that we are not entirely at the mercy of our electronics. Rappers' raw egotism signals that they have survived all the dislocations and discontinuities of the video era not as part of a faceless mass but as swaggering, fast-talking, self-made myths.

(January 14, 1990)

Fresh Princeton

by Glenn O'Brien

Back in the day, hip-hop style was inspired by what they wore in the joint: work jackets and big, baggy beltless pants down around the ass with drawers riding high. Now it's pleated khaki trousers, striped button-down shirts, and jackets with a coat-of-arms crest. Yo, wuzzup?

Is the Attica look out and the Nautica look in? Is the Harvard Square look the dopest of the dope?

These days white boys be slouching in Carhartt overalls and L.A. Kings caps like they're straight outta Compton, while homeboys stroll around dressed like Dobie Gillis in oxford shirts and chinos like they're straight outta Princeton. A fashion inversion is going on, but that's to be expected. This is the melting pot. So let's melt.

If you're a white kid from Westchester it's exotic to dress like Ice Cube; if you're a black kid from Bed-Stuy it's exotic to dress like David Letterman. After all, fashion has always been about finding the grain and going against it. Maybe black fashion got worn by too many whites. Hey, you see blond dudes in 8-ball jackets and Raiders hats at hockey games. So if white guys are wearing your look, who you gonna call? Ralph Lauren is unquestionably dope. Tommy Hilfiger is indubitably phat. Calvin Klein is in the house. The Gap is dap. Banana Republic has flavor.

Actually all of this was prophesied long ago on a twelve-inch single entitled "Preppy Rap—Do the Alligator" by Chatsworth and Burt. Dig it:

My name is Chatsworth
And mine is Burt
And we're here to say a word
About the people of the hour
Who raise their hands for preppy power
Those hands are clean, no sign of dirt
And the alligator on my shirt
Is another indication son
That the revolution has just begun
No common folk could grace our crowd
Our club's elite, no jeans allowed

The neopreppy thing is about elitism. It's about stuff that is expensive. *Recognizably* expensive. It's about conspicuous consumption. So when hip-hop impresario number one Russell Simmons recently launched Phat Farm, his own clothing line, it owed a lot more to Ralph and Tommy than to Stüssy or Spike's Joint. This is not the first time that a white look has been appropriated by black youth: It happened a few years ago when the homeboys adopted the look of New

England outdoorsmen, making a cult of Timberland boots and Pendleton shirts.

Appropriation is the essence of hip-hop. It all started with appropriated music, taking parts of existing records and making them your own. So now smart-dressing urbanite rappers like D-Nice, Ali of A Tribe Called Quest, and Bosco of Downtown Science have discovered the scientific freshness of traditional casual clothing. A button-down shirt here, baggy madras shorts there. Polo shirts with triple-XL jeans and Adidas or Pumas—they're all ingredients in the mix.

Mike Tyson, former heavyweight champion of the world from Brooklyn, has favored the preppy look for some time. Tyson always looked intimidating, but in his button-down shirts he looked freshly, intriguingly intimidating. Of course now Mike has gone Muslim, but that may make him preppier than ever. Look at Louis Farrakhan in his neat suits, white shirts, and bow ties. Look at Denzel as Malcolm X. The Black Muslims were among the first advocates of the preppy aesthetic—because it stood for achievement and countered the glitz of drug-dealer money. The neat look means business. But it ain't wimpy.

Monica Lynch, president of the hip-hop label Tommy Boy and a keen fashion observer, has observed the homey-preppy trend with interest. "I remember seeing a photo of Tommy Hilfiger with Grand Poobah Maxwell, formerly of Brand Nubians, an avowed Five Percenter who isn't exactly looking to give the white man any respect. A lot of the appeal is that people will look at it and say, 'It's exclusive. It costs more. He must be a better man for it.'"

Fab 5 Freddy, MTV star, director, author, and wearer of fly vines, explains: "It's all about appropriating the status symbols of the rich and reinventing them. But it's not about being anything else than what you are. The whole Ralph Lauren thing started with a certain area of Brooklyn in the late eighties where it became the style to wear Polo. Homeboys would go into stores twenty, thirty, forty deep and snatch all the Polo. It was a big fad on the streets. They all had names like Zeke Lo and Mike Lo."

Fashion is a language and hip-hop culture is constantly reinventing the language. Hip-hop shuffles the elements of preppy style like a deck of cards, breaking the codes and coming up with new ways to wear the old uniform. An untucked looseness and a baggy nonchalance are another way of living extra-large. Stylin' and profilin' in a dialectical synthesis of Ivy League and Afrolistic is all about personal style. And true personal style is always classical and universal.

That's the philosophy of Russell Simmons's Phat Farm collection. "It's obvious, not trendy. Run-DMC wore baggy khaki suits in 1982 before they made a record. The shit L.L. Cool J was wearing when we signed him at sixteen is the shit he can wear today," Simmons explains. "Nobody likes to look at a shirt and know what year it was made."

(November 1993)

Fear of a Hip-hop Syllabus

by Robert Walser,
Robin D. G. Kelley,
Michael Eric Dyson

Classes about rock started appearing, oddly enough, around the same time that professors young enough to enjoy the music started getting tenure. Some are worthwhile; many have become yawners with titles like the Signifying Rebel: Modalities of Sexual

Aggression from Morrison to Madonna. To get a fresher look at some fresh music, consider a course in hip-hop. We've asked hip professors (really) to list the required-listening titles that would be on their syllabuses. Listen up.

ROBERT WALSER
ASSISTANT PROFESSOR OF MUSIC
DARTMOUTH COLLEGE

Hip Hop Greats: Classic Raps (1990). A compilation of influential early rapping that also documents hip-hop's musical growth out of funk and disco.

MC Lyte, *Lyte as a Rock* (1987). The language games of someone who is tired of patriarchy come to you directly from the planet of Brooklyn, N.Y.

Public Enemy, *Fear of a Black Planet* (1990). When I only get to teach one hip-hop album, I teach this one. Framed by dynamic, noisy grooves, Chuck D's unsurpassed rhythmic virtuosity enacts survival in a conflicted, polyphonic, technological world.

Sir Mix-a-Lot, *Mack Daddy* (1992). Through the ages, male lust has resulted in a great deal of impressive art. In that tradition, rapper-scratcher-producer Sir Mix-a-Lot excels at everything.

ROBIN D. G. KELLEY
ASSOCIATE PROFESSOR OF HISTORY
AND AFRO-AMERICAN STUDIES
UNIVERSITY OF MICHIGAN

Hip Hop Greats: Classic Raps (1990). There really are no albums by a single artist that capture early hip-hop. This one has many of the pioneering jams: Sugar Hill Gang, "Rapper's Delight"; Grandmaster Flash and Melle Mel, "White Lines"; Sequence, "Funk You Up," one of the first all-female groups; UTFO's "Roxanne, Roxanne"; the nearly forgotten Fat Boys' "Fat Boys"; and Run-DMC's "It's Like That."

Eric B & Rakim, *Paid in Full* (1987). Rakim's rhyme style is kinda slow, smooth, with rhymes flowing into the next stanza. Eric B's amazing mixture of scratching and funk-R&B samples added to the revolutionary intervention of this group. Together they changed hip-hop forever.

Salt-N-Pepa, *Hot, Cool & Vicious* (1987). This album opened up in-

credible space for women rappers. Salt-N-Pepa were unique for simultaneously challenging sexism and expressing their sexuality.

Public Enemy, *It Takes a Nation of Millions to Hold Us Back* (1988). The Bomb Squad brilliantly uses "noise" to create the most vibrant, dissonant, exciting music produced in hip-hop up to that date.

De La Soul, *3 Feet High and Rising* (1989). It's cultural hybridity at its best, challenging the hegemony of hard-core hip-hop. De La Soul challenges listeners with way-out metaphors and an almost mystical use of language.

MICHAEL ERIC DYSON
ASSISTANT PROFESSOR OF AMERICAN
CIVILIZATION AND AFRO-AMERICAN STUDIES
BROWN UNIVERSITY

Run-DMC, *Raising Hell* (1986). Broke music industry's racist barriers and jump-started rap's mainstream success.

Public Enemy, *It Takes a Nation of Millions to Hold Us Back* (1988). The primal scream of black-nationalist sentiment compressed into rhetorical rebellion against white racism and black bourgeois opposition to black juvenile culture. Five years later, *It Takes a Nation of Millions* retains its ability to instruct about rap's postmodern premises.

N.W.A., *Straight Outta Compton* (1989). The announcement and apotheosis of West Coast gangsta rap, it underscores the prescient power of the genre's best social criticism.

Queen Latifah, *All Hail the Queen* (1989). Expressing forceful and flavorful feminist philosophy.

Naughty by Nature, *Naughty by Nature* (1991). Hip-hop history in a nutshell with its def(t) blending of catchy anthems, swaggering braggadocio, infectious rhythms, dope beats, and social criticism.

(September 30, 1993)

Cracking Ice

by Chris Santella

"My rap music . . . tells a story. You can write a book on each of my thoughts."

—Vanilla Ice, *Newsweek*, December 3, 1990

In the first stanza of his work "Ice Ice Baby," Vanilla Ice reaches deep into the American canon for Melville's archetypal image of evil, the great white whale: "Something grabs ahold of me tightly / Then I flow like a harpoon daily and nightly." A lesser poet might equate himself with the harpoonist or perhaps even the whale. Mr. Ice's allusion is genius. His narrator *is* the

harpoon, a pen if you will, flowing over the stark, blank parchment of America. Will "Ice Ice Baby" be the *Wasteland* of our era? Only time will tell. As the narrator indulges in cannibalism ("I'm cooking MCs like a pound of bacon"), toys with ritualistic voodoo ("I'm killing your brain like a poisonous mushroom"), and penultimately flees his persecutors ("I'm trying to get away before the jackers jack") he is ever conscious of his responsibility as poet. Mr. Ice stresses: "Anything less than the best is a felony." Sloppy verse is indeed a culpable offense.

In the final stanza, scholars get an introspective glimpse at the man behind the voice: "'Cause my style's like a chemical spill / Feasible rhymes that you can vision and feel." Mr. Ice creates a bridge between the elemental world and man's relentless pursuit of technology in the name of progress. The result? A metaphoric yet tangible toxic wasteland. One is forced to acknowledge the grandeur and enormity of Mr. Ice's achievement—this victory of form over function. It is indeed a "hell of a concept."

(July 1991)

The Rap on Rap: The "Black Music" That Isn't Either

by David Samuels

This summer Soundscan, a computerized scanning system, changed *Billboard* magazine's method of counting record sales in the United States. Replacing a haphazard system that relied on big-city record stores, Soundscan measured the number of records sold nationally by scanning the bar codes at chain-store cash registers. Within weeks the number of computed record sales leapt, as demographics shifted from minority-focused urban centers to white, suburban, middle-class malls. So it was that America awoke on June 22, 1991, to find that its favorite record was not *Out of Time*, by aging college-boy rockers R.E.M., but *Niggaz4life*, a musical celebration of gang rape and other violence by N.W.A., or Niggas With Attitude, a rap group from the Los Angeles ghetto of Compton whose records had never before risen above No. 27 on the Billboard charts.

From *Niggaz4life* to *Boyz N the Hood,* young black men committing acts of violence were available this summer in a wide variety of entertainment formats. Of these none is more popular than rap. And none has received quite the level of critical attention and concern. Writers on the left have long viewed rap as the heartbeat of urban America, its authors, in Arthur Kempton's words, "the preeminent young dramaturgists in the clamorous theater of the street." On the right this assumption has been shared, but greeted with predictable disdain.

Neither side of the debate has been prepared, however, to confront what the entertainment industry's receipts from this summer prove beyond doubt: although rap is still proportionally more popular among blacks, its primary audience is white and lives in the suburbs. And the history of rap's degeneration from insurgent black street music to mainstream pop points to another dispiriting conclusion: the more rappers were packaged as violent black criminals, the bigger their white audiences became.

If the racial makeup of rap's audience has been largely misunderstood, so have the origins of its authors. Since the early 1980s a tightly knit group of mostly young, middle-class, black New Yorkers, in close concert with white record producers, executives, and publicists, has been making rap music for an audience that industry executives concede is primarily composed of white suburban males. Building upon a form pioneered by lower-class black artists in New York between 1975 and 1983, despite an effective boycott of the music by both black and white radio that continues to this day, they created the most influential pop music of the 1980s. Rap's appeal to whites rested in its evocation of an age-old image of blackness: a foreign, sexually charged, and criminal underworld against which the norms of white society are defined, and, by extension, through which they may be defied. It was the truth of this latter proposition that rap would test in its journey into the mainstream.

"Hip-hop," the music behind the lyrics, which are "rapped," is a form of sonic bricolage with roots in "toasting," a style of making music by speaking over records. (For simplicity I'll use the term *rap* interchangeably with *hip-hop* throughout this article.) Toasting first took hold in Jamaica in the mid-1960s, a response, legend has it, to the limited availability of expensive Western instruments and the concurrent proliferation of cheap R&B instrumental singles on Memphis-based labels such as Stax-Volt. Cool DJ Herc, a Jamaican who settled in the South Bronx, is widely credited with having brought toasting to New York City. Rap spread quickly through New York's poor black neighborhoods in the mid- and late 1970s. Jams were held in local playgrounds, parks, and community centers in the South and North Bronx, Brooklyn, and Harlem.

Although much is made of rap as a kind of urban streetgeist, early rap had a more basic function: dance music. Bill Stephney, considered by many to be the smartest man in the rap business, recalls the first time he heard hip-hop: "The point wasn't rapping, it was rhythm, DJs cutting records left and right, taking the big drum break from Led Zeppelin's 'When the Levee Breaks,' mixing it together with 'Ring My Bell,' then with a Bob James Mardi Gras jazz record and some James Brown. You'd have two thousand kids in any community center in New York, moving back and forth, back and forth, like some kind of tribal war dance, you might say. It was the rapper's role to match this intensity rhythmically. No one knew what he was saying. He was just rocking the mike."

Rap quickly spread from New York to Philadelphia, Chicago, Boston, and other cities with substantial black populations. Its popularity was sustained by the ease with which it could be made. The music on early rap records sounded like the black music of the day: funk or, more often, disco. Performers were unsophisticated about image and presentation, tending toward gold lamé jumpsuits and Jheri curls, a second-rate appropriation of the stylings of funk musicians like George Clinton and Bootsy Collins.

The first rap record to make it big was "Rapper's Delight," released in 1979 by the Sugar Hill Gang, an ad hoc all-star team drawn from three New York groups on Sylvia and Joey Robinson's Sugar Hill label. Thanks to Sylvia Robinson's soul music and background, the first thirty seconds of "Rapper's Delight" were indistinguishable from the disco records of the day: light guitars, high-hat drumming, and hand-claps over a deep funk bass line. What followed will be immediately familiar to anyone who was young in New York City that summer:

I said, hip-hop, de-hibby, de-hibby-dibby,
Hip-hip-hop you don't stop.
Rock it out, Baby Bubba, to the boogie de-bang-bang.
Boogie to the boogie to be.
Now what you hear is not a test,
I'm rapping to the beat . . .
I said, "By the way, baby, what's your name?"
She said, "I go by the name Lois Lane
And you can be my boyfriend, you surely can
Just let me quit my boyfriend, he's called Superman."
I said, "He's a fairy, I do suppose
Flying through the air in pantyhose . . .
You need a man who's got finesse
And his whole name across his chest."

Like disco music and jumpsuits, the social commentaries of early rappers like Grandmaster Flash and Melle Mel were for the most part transparent attempts to sell records to whites by any means necessary. Songs like "White Lines" (with its antidrug theme) and "The Message" (about ghetto life) had the desired effect, drawing fulsome praise from white rock critics, raised on the protest ballads of Bob Dylan and Phil Ochs. The reaction on the street was somewhat less favorable. "The Message" is a case in point. "People hated that record," recalls Russell Simmons, president of Def Jam Records. "I remember the Junebug, a famous DJ of the time, was playing it up at the Fever, and Ronnie DJ put a pistol to his head and said, 'Take that record off and break it or I'll blow your fucking head off.' The whole club stopped until he broke that record and put it in the garbage.

It was not until 1984 that rap broke through to a mass white audience. The first group to do so was Run-DMC, with the release of its debut album, *Run-DMC*, and with *King of Rock* one year later. These albums blazed the trail that rap would travel into the musical mainstream. Bill Adler, a former rock critic and rap's best-known publicist, explains: "They were the first group that came onstage as if they had just come off the street corner. But unlike the first generation of rappers they were solidly middle class. Both of Run's parents were college educated. DMC was a good Catholic schoolkid, a mama's boy. Neither of them was deprived and neither of them ever ran with a gang, but onstage they became the biggest, baddest, streetest guys in the world." When Run-DMC covered the Aerosmith classic "Walk This Way," the resulting video made it onto MTV, and the record went gold.

Rap's new mass audience was in large part the brainchild of Rick Rubin, a Jewish punk rocker from suburban Long Island who produced the music behind many of rap's biggest acts. Like many New Yorkers his age, Rick grew up listening to *Mr. Magic's Rap Attack*, a rap radio show on WHBI. In 1983, at the age of nineteen, Rubin founded Def Jam Records in his NYU dorm room. (Simmons bought part of Def Jam in 1984 and took full control of the company in 1989.) Rubin's next group, the Beastie Boys, was a white punk rock band whose transformation into a rap group pointed rap's way into the future. The Beasties' first album, *Licensed to Ill*, backed by airplay of its anthemic frat-party single "You've Got to Fight for Your Right to Party," became the first rap record to sell a million copies.

The appearance of white groups in a black musical form has historically prefigured the mainstreaming of the form, the growth of the white audience, and the resulting dominance of white performers. With rap, however, this process took an unexpected turn: white demand indeed began to determine the direction of the genre, but what it wanted was music more defiantly black. The result was Public Enemy, produced and marketed by Rubin, the next group significantly to broaden rap's appeal to young whites.

Public Enemy's now familiar mélange of polemic and dance music was formed not on inner-city streets but in the suburban Long Island towns in which the group's members grew up. The children of successful black middle-class professionals, they gave voice to the feeling that, despite progress toward equality, blacks still did not quite belong in white America. They complained of unequal treatment by the police, of never quite overcoming the color of their skin: "We were suburban college kids doing what we were supposed to do, but we were always made to feel like something else," explains Stephney, the group's executive producer.

Public Enemy's abrasive and highly politicized style made it a fast favorite of the white avant-garde, much like the English punk rock band the Clash ten years before. Public Enemy's music, produced by the Shocklee brothers Hank and Keith, was faster, harder, and more abrasive than the rap of the day, music that moved behind the vocals like a full-scale band. But the root of Public Enemy's success was a highly charged theater of race in which white listeners became guilty eaves-

droppers on the putative private conversation of the inner city. Chuck D denounced his enemies (the media, some radio stations), proclaimed himself "Public Enemy Number One," and praised Louis Farrakhan in stentorian tones, flanked onstage by black-clad security guards from the Nation of Islam, the S1Ws, led by Chuck's political mentor, Professor Griff. Flavor Flav, Chuck's homeboy sidekick, parodied street style: oversize sunglasses, baseball cap cocked to one side, a clock the size of a silver plate draped around his neck, going off on wild verbal riffs that often meant nothing at all.

The closer rap moved to the white mainstream, the more it became like rock 'n' roll, a celebration of posturing over rhythm. The back catalogs of artists like James Brown and George Clinton were relentlessly plundered for catchy hooks, then overlaid with dance beats and social commentary. Public Enemy's single "Fight the Power" was the biggest college hit of 1989:

Elvis was a hero to most
But he never meant shit to me, you see
Straight-up racist that sucker was simple and plain
Motherfuck him and John Wayne
'Cause I'm black and I'm proud
I'm ready and hyped, plus I'm amped
Most of my heroes don't appear on no stamps
Sample a look back, you look and find
Nothing but rednecks for four hundred years if you check.

After the release of "Fight the Power," Professor Griff made a series of anti-Semitic remarks in an interview with *The Washington Times*. Griff was subsequently asked to leave the group, for what Chuck D termed errors in judgment. Although these errors were lambasted in editorials across the country, they do not seem to have affected Public Enemy's credibility with its young white fans.

Public Enemy's theatrical black nationalism and sophisticated noise ushered in what is fast coming to be seen as rap's golden age, a heady mix of art, music, and politics. Between 1988 and 1989 a host of innovative acts broke into the mainstream. KRS-One, now a regular on the Ivy League lecture circuit, grew up poor, living on the streets of the South Bronx until he met a New York City social worker, Scott La Rock, later murdered in a drive-by shooting. Together they formed BDP,

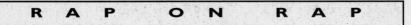

Boogie Down Productions, recording for the Jive label on RCA. Although songs like "My Philosophy" and "Love's Gonna Get 'Cha (Material Love)" were clever and self-critical, BDP's roots remained firmly planted in the guns-and-posturing of the mainstream rap ghetto.

The ease with which rap can create such aural cartoons, says Hank Shocklee, lies at the very heart of its appeal as entertainment: "Whites have always liked black music," he explains. "That part is hardly new. The difference with rap was that the imagery of black artists, for the first time, reached the level of black music. The sheer number of words in a rap song allows for the creation of full characters impossible in R&B. Rappers become like superheroes. Captain America or the Fantastic Four."

By 1988 the conscious manipulation of racial stereotypes had become rap's leading edge, a trend best exemplified by the rise to stardom of Schoolly D, a Philadelphia rapper on the Jive label who sold more than half a million records with little mainstream notice. It was not that the media had never heard of Schoolly D: white critics and fans, for the first time, were simply at a loss for words. His voice, fierce and deeply textured, could alone frighten listeners. He used it as a rhythmic device that made no concessions to pop-song form, talking evenly about smoking crack and using women for sex, proclaiming his blackness, accusing other rappers of not being black enough. What Schoolly D meant by blackness was abundantly clear. Schoolly D was a misogynist and a thug. If listening to Public Enemy was like eavesdropping on a conversation, Schoolly D was like getting mugged. This, afficionados agreed, was what they had been waiting for: a rapper from whom you would flee in abject terror if you saw him walking toward you late at night.

It remained for N.W.A., a more conventional group of rappers from Los Angeles, to adapt Schoolly D's stylistic advance for the mass white market with its first album-length release, *Straight Outta Compton*, in 1989. The much-quoted rap from that album, "Fuck tha Police," was the target of an FBI warning to police departments across the country, and a constant presence at certain college parties, white and black:

Fuck the police coming straight out the underground
A young nigger got it bad cause I'm brown
And not the other color. Some police think
They have the authority to kill the minority. . . .

A young nigger on the warpath
And when I'm finished, it's gonna be a bloodbath
Of cops, dying in L.A.
Yo, Dre, I've got something to say: Fuck the police.

Other songs spoke of trading oral sex for crack and shooting strangers for fun. After the release of *Straight Outta Compton*, N.W.A.'s lead rapper and chief lyricist, Ice Cube, left the group. Billing himself as "the nigger you love to hate," Ice Cube released a solo album, *AmeriKKKa's Most Wanted*, which gleefully pushed the limits of rap's ability to give offense. One verse ran:

I'm thinking to myself, *Why did I bang her?*
Now I'm in the closet, looking for the hanger.

But what made *AmeriKKKa's Most Wanted* so shocking to so many record buyers was the title track's violation of rap's most ironclad taboo—black-on-white violence:

Word, yo, but who the fuck is heard:
It's time you take a trip to the suburbs.
Let 'em see a nigger invasion
Point blank, on a Caucasian.
Cock the hammer and crack a smile:
"Take me to your house, pal. . . ."

Ice Cube took his act to the big screen this summer in *Boyz N the Hood*, drawing rave reviews for his portrayal of a young black drug dealer whose life of crime leads him to an untimely end. The crime-doesn't-pay message, an inheritance from the grade-B gangster film, is the stock-in-trade of another L.A. rapper-turned-actor, Ice-T of *New Jack City* fame, a favorite of socially conscious rock critics. Tacking unhappy endings on to glorifications of drug dealing and gang warfare, Ice-T offers all the thrills of the form while alleviating any guilt listeners may have felt about consuming drive-by shootings along with their popcorn.

It was in this spirit that *Yo! MTV Raps* debuted in 1989 as the first national broadcast forum for rap music. The videos were often poorly produced, but the music and visual presence of stars like KRS-One,

L.L. Cool J, and Chuck D proved enormously compelling, rocketing *Yo!* to the top of the MTV ratings. On weekends, bands were interviewed and videos introduced by Fab 5 Freddie; hip young white professionals watched his shows to keep up with urban black slang and fashion. Younger viewers rushed home from school on weekdays to catch ex–Beastie Boys DJ Dr. Dre, a sweatsuit-clad mountain of a man, well over three hundred pounds, and Ed Lover, who evolved a unique brand of homeboy Laurel and Hardy mixed with occasional social comment.

With *Yo! MTV Raps*, rap became for the first time the music of choice in the white suburbs of middle America. From the beginning, says Doug Herzog, MTV's vice-president for programming, the show's audience was primarily white, male, suburban, and between the ages of sixteen and twenty-four, a demographic profile that *Yo!*'s success helped set in stone. For its daytime audience, MTV spawned an ethnic rainbow of well-scrubbed pop rappers from M.C. Hammer to Vanilla Ice to Gerardo, a Hispanic actor turned rap star. For *Yo!* itself, rap became more overtly politicized as it expanded its audience. Sound bites from the speeches of Malcolm X and Martin Luther King became de rigueur introduction to formulaic assaults on white America mixed with hymns to gang violence and crude sexual caricature.

Holding such polyglot records together is what *Village Voice* critic Nelson George has labeled "ghettocentrism," a style-driven cult of blackness defined by crude stereotypes. PR releases, like a recent one for Los Angeles rapper DJ Quik, take special care to mention artists' police records, often enhanced to provide extra street credibility. When Def Jam star Slick Rick was arrested for attempted homicide, Def Jam incorporated the arrest into its publicity campaign for Rick's new album, bartering exclusive rights to the story to *Vanity Fair* in exchange for the promise of a lengthy profile. Muslim groups such as Brand Nubian proclaim their hatred for white devils, especially those who plot to poison black babies. That Brand Nubian believes the things said on its records is unlikely: the group seems to get along quite well with its white Jewish publicist, Beth Jacobson of Electra Records. Antiwhite, and, in this case, anti-Semitic, rhymes are a shorthand way of defining one's opposition to the mainstream. Racism is reduced to fashion, by the rappers who use it and by the white audiences to whom such images appeal. What's significant here are not so much the intentions of artist and audience as a dynamic in which anti-Semitic slurs and black criminality correspond to "authenticity," and "authenticity" sells records.

The selling of this kind of authenticity to a young white audience is the stock-in-trade of *The Source*, a full-color monthly magazine devoted exclusively to rap music, founded by Jon Shecter while still an undergraduate at Harvard. Shecter is what is known in the rap business as a Young Black Teenager. He wears a Brooklyn Dodgers baseball cap, like Spike Lee, and a *Source* T-shirt. As editor of *The Source*, Shecter has become a necessary quote for stories about rap in *Time* and other national magazines.

An upper-middle-class white, Shecter has come in for his share of criticism, the most recent of which appeared as a diatribe by the sometime critic and tinpot racist Harry Allen in a black community newspaper, *The City Sun*, which pointed out that Shecter is Jewish. "There's no place for me to say anything," Shecter responds. "Given what I'm doing, my viewpoint has to be that whatever comes of the black community, the hip-hop community which is the black community, is the right thing. I know my place. The only way in which criticism can be raised is on a personal level, because the way that things are set up, with the white-controlled media, prevents sincere back-and-forth discussion from taking place." The latest venture in hip-hop marketing, a magazine planned by Time Warner, will also be edited by a young white, Jonathan van Meter, a former Condé Nast editor.

In part because of young whites like Shecter and van Meter, rap's influence on the street continues to decline. "You put out a record by Big Daddy Kane," Rubin says, "and then put out the same record by a pop performer like Janet Jackson. Not only will the Janet Jackson record sell ten times more copies, it will also be the cool record to play in clubs." Stephney agrees: "Kids in my neighborhood pump dance-hall reggae on their systems all night long, because that's where the rhythm is. . . . People complain about how white kids stole black culture. The truth of the matter is that no one can steal a culture." Whatever its continuing significance in the realm of racial politics, rap's hour as innovative popular music has come and gone. Rap forfeited whatever claim it may have had to particularity by acquiring a mainstream white audience whose tastes increasingly determined the nature of the form. What whites wanted was not music, but black music, which as a result stopped really being either.

White fascination with rap sprang from a particular kind of cultural tourism pioneered by the Jazz Age novelist Carl Van Vechten. Van Vechten's 1926 best seller *Nigger Heaven* imagined a masculine, criminal, yet friendly black ghetto world that functioned, for Van Vechten

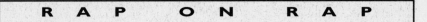

and for his readers, as a refuge from white middle-class boredom. In *Really the Blues* the white jazzman Mezz Mezzrow went one step further, claiming that his own life among black people in Harlem had physically transformed him into a member of the Negro race, whose unique sensibility he had now come to share. By inverting the moral values attached to contemporary racial stereotypes, Van Vechten and Mezzrow at once appealed to and sought to undermine the prevailing racial order. Both men, it should be stressed, conducted their tours in person.

The moral inversion of racist stereotypes as entertainment has lost whatever transformative power it may arguably have had fifty years ago. MC Serch of 3rd Bass, a white rap traditionalist, with short-cropped hair and thick-rimmed Buddy Holly glasses, formed his style in the uptown hip-hop clubs like the L.Q. in the early 1980s. "Ten or eleven years ago," he remarks, "when I was wearing my permanent-press Lee's with a beige campus shirt and matching Adidas sneakers, kids I went to school with were calling me a 'wigger,' 'black wanna-be,' all kinds of racist names. Now those same kids are driving Jeeps with MCM leather interiors and pumping Public Enemy."

The ways in which rap has been consumed and popularized speak not of cross-cultural understanding, musical or otherwise, but of a voyeurism and tolerance of racism in which black and white are both complicit. "Both the rappers and their white fans affect and commodify their own visions of street culture," argues Henry Louis Gates, Jr., of Harvard University, "like buying Navajo blankets at a reservation roadstop. A lot of what you see in rap is the guilt of the black middle class about its economic success, its inability to put forth a culture of its own. Instead they do the worst possible thing, falling back on fantasies of street life. In turn, white college students with impeccable gender credentials buy nasty sex lyrics under the cover of getting at some kind of authentic black experience."

Gates goes on to make the more worrying point: "What is potentially very dangerous about this is the feeling that by buying records they have made some kind of valid social commitment." Where the assimilation of black street culture by whites once required a degree of human contact between the races, the street is now available at the flick of a cable channel—to black and white middle class alike. "People want to consume and they want to consume easy," Hank Shocklee says. "If you're a suburban white kid and you want to find out what life is like for a black city teenager, you buy a record by N.W.A. It's like going to

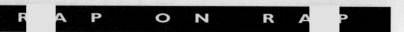
an amusement park and getting on a roller-coaster ride—records are safe, they're controlled fear, and you always have the choice of turning it off. That's why nobody ever takes a train up to 125th Street and gets out and starts walking around. Because then you're not in control anymore: it's a whole other ball game." This kind of consumption—of racist stereotypes, of brutality toward women, or even of uplifting tributes to Dr. Martin Luther King—is of a particularly corrupting kind. The values it instills find their ultimate expression in the ease with which we watch young black men killing each other: in movies, on records, and on the streets of cities and towns across the country.

(November 11, 1991)

Rapman

from *Spin*

Now you can sound exactly like all your favorite rap DJs in the privacy of your own home! Well, okay, maybe not *exactly* like them, but at least close—for a lot cheaper than the price of a truckload of equipment. Casio's Rapman keyboard combines twenty-five sound

effects—from sitars to sirens—with thirty rhythms from rap to rock, and features a scratch simulator, percussion pads, and a microphone with effects that will take your voice from Pee Wee to Satan and back. Rapman's in the house.

(December 1991)

A Newcomer Abroad, Rap Speaks Up

by James Bernard

From small clubs in Moscow to the *favelas* of Rio de Janeiro to MTV in Tokyo, rap has begun to elbow its way onto the world's stage. This is not to suggest that hip-hop's insistent beats and unruly lyrics have attained a global influence approaching their impact in the United

States, where rap is at the epicenter of pop music. But increasingly, rappers in other countries are using their music to reflect on and grapple with their local realities, adding their own flavor to an American art form.

Why is a music so closely identified with the rebelliousness of young American blacks catching on far from its homeland? Rap's rising popularity may have to do with the reasons it has been villified in this country. Rap is abrasive, loud, often crude, and disrespectful of melody and traditional pop-song structures, say its critics. But such irreverence lends it an aura of danger and exhilaration, which speaks to the restlessness inherent in youth. How well this defiant spirit translates outside an American context, where rap and race are inextricably bound, is another question.

Rap's emphasis on rhythm rather than melody makes it easy to export. It is catchy, visceral, danceable. Where pop songs offer solace from an increasingly perplexing world, rap engages it. Its beats are upfront and impolite, not content to be mere background music. Rap embraces chaos as art: complex drumbeats stagger and stutter, punctuated by dissonant samples using everything from James Brown to obscure jazz to television commercials, the mix held together by a steady stream of intricate wordplay. The music's sound and pace seem to cut through the din that is a by-product of an information age. For young people, rap's immediacy provides a bunker against feeling overwhelmed or lost in a world undergoing rapid change.

The promise of rock was that anyone could learn the basic chords and make music; rap is even more democratic. It's not hard to imagine an aspiring hip-hop artist rigging up two turntables and a microphone in a Prague park, just as the deejay Afrika Bambaataa did in the South Bronx fifteen years ago. Even today, with sophisticated samplers and synthesizers, a few hundred dollars can buy enough equipment to produce high-quality homemade tapes. Too Short, one of the best-selling rappers of all time, got his start by selling homemade tapes. For five dollars he would incorporate the purchaser's name in a rhyme, produce the music in his bedroom, and deliver the tape in a matter of hours.

Rap is about being a witness: talking about what one sees, feels, and experiences. It's one thing to discuss single parenthood in detached, clinical terms. It's quite another to offer a powerful, intimate portrait of a mother struggling to raise her daughters on a tight budget, which Yo-Yo does on the song "Mama Don't Take No Mess." The Australian rap-

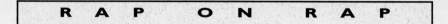

pers Sound Unlimited Posse pick up on the idea of bearing witness. On the song "Paradise Lost" they grapple with the shame associated with their country's mistreatment of the Aborigines. The Brazilian rapper Ademir Lemos warns about the "fishnets," the youth gangs that terrorize the streets of Rio.

> **Hanging out, just waiting for the bus**
> **And when it finally comes, we all gasp**
> **Packed to the roof; can it get any worse?**
> **Hide your cash, your watch, and your jewels**
> **Looks just right for a fishnet.**

Q-Tip, the leader of the American group A Tribe Called Quest, likes to say that his favorite rap albums sound like his best friends talking to him on the phone. It's such intimacy that makes hip-hop compelling, and gives it great potential for cross-cultural communication. Chuck D of Public Enemy has described rap as the CNN of young black Americans. Rap has become the means by which teenagers who have never traveled outside their Los Angeles neighborhood learn about their peers in New York or Houston, how they live, and the struggles they face. The possibilities are endless. What lessons could a young Berliner learn from a Zairean rapping about village life?

Much of rap's appeal overseas derives from its being perceived as protest music, be it Japanese rappers condemning greed or their Mexican counterparts issuing a call to action. Their music is popular, but does it have consequence? Ice Cube's "Black Korea" vented tensions between Korean merchants and their black neighbors; critics even said it contributed to the rioting in Los Angeles in April. Because the music addresses racial injustice and urban poverty, hip-hop touches a nerve in the American psyche. It remains to be seen whether rappers abroad can summon the power to unleash such passion.

Also present in homegrown rap is an element of boastful self-awareness that might not find resonance in other cultures. The question of identity has long been a troublesome one for blacks in the United States, where a lack of economic opportunity and positive images have stifled self-esteem. But in music blacks have found a haven for self-expression. Gospel offers praise to a higher being and rhythm-and-blues exalts lovers, but rap is a celebration of self. In contrast to the blues, rap has little patience for the preoccupation with one's shortcomings. When rappers grab microphones, they put themselves at the heart of a

narrative and exaggerate their own abilities and accomplishments. The members of N.W.A. cast themselves as powerful street gangsters, outlaw supermen; Queen Latifah is, well, a queen. While such braggadocio reinforces young blacks' sense of self, it might not play the same in cultures where issues of identity are taken for granted. For a young Muscovite to imitate an Ice Cube or a DJ Quik without their emotional urgency can appear hollow, or merely rude.

But clearly, something is happening here: the exportation of hip-hop culture is under way. Understandably, it seems to have gained its firmest foothold in Western countries, where access to America's popular culture is relatively easy. And therein lies the challenge. Is it the destiny of foreign rappers to emulate American originals, or will a truly international rap community emerge? The answer may come when an L.L. Cool J feels compelled to dis a Russian rapper.

(August 23, 1992)

Def Jám

from *Time*

Sometimes it's hard to tell which name is a rap singer and which is a city in the former Yugoslavia:

Ali Dee	Bor
Dre Dog	Gacko
Dres	Gruz
Kilo	Jimbolia
Kam	Rab
Mad Flava	Ruma
Madrok	Skofja Loka
Treach	Stip
Tarik	Stupni Do
Taji	Subotica

(Rappers are in the left column)

(November 15, 1993)

Suggestions for Further Reading

Following is the best of the material that, for reasons of length or redundancy, or because permission was unavailable, I wasn't able to include in *Rap on Rap*. As in the rest of the book, the emphasis here is on the recent. Artist profiles and interviews, and record reviews that don't have a larger point to make (unlike, say, Joan Morgan's "The Nigga Ya Hate to Love," ostensibly a review of an Ice Cube album but really a meditation on hip-hop misogyny) have been excluded.

2 Live Crew Comics No. 1. Seattle, WA: Eros Comix, 1991.

Allen, Harry. "Hip-Hop Madness." *Essence*, April 1989, p. 78.

Alter, Jonathan. "Let's Stop Crying Wolf on Censorship." *Newsweek*, November 29, 1993, p. 67.

Baye, Betty Winston. "Clinton Needs Lesson in Black Culture." Louisville *Courier-Journal*, June 26, 1992.

Beadle, Jeremy J. *Will Pop Eat Itself? Pop Music in the Soundbite Era*. London: Faber and Faber, 1993.

Bernard, James. "Negative Reviews." *The Source*, November 1994, p. 8.

Blumenfeld, Laura. "Black Like Who? Why White Teens Find Hip-Hop Cool." *The Washington Post*, July 20, 1992, p. C5.

Boseman, Keith. "Kriss Kross in a Men's World" *Chicago Citizen*, October 11, 1993.

Chideya, Farai. "Hip-Hop's Black Eye." *Spin*, August 1993.

Christgau, Robert. "Jesus, Jews, and the Jackass Theory." *The Village Voice*, January 16, 1990, p. 83.

Cooper, Martha, and Henry Chalfant. *Subway Art*. New York: Holt, Rinehart & Winston, 1984.

Cosgrove, Stuart. "Wild Thing." *New Statesman and Society*, July 7, 1989, p. 46.

Costello, Mark, and David Foster Wallace. *Signifying Rappers: Rap and Race in the Urban Present*. New York: Ecco Press, 1989.

Dawsey, Darrell. "Hip-Hop Not Above Scrutiny." *The Detroit News*, May 15, 1993.

Dennis, Reginald C. "25 Old School Turning Points." *The Source*, November 1993, p. 54.

Dent, Gina, ed. *Black Popular Culture*. Seattle: Bay Press, 1992.

DiPrima, Dominique. "Beat the Rap." *Mother Jones*, September/October 1990, p. 32.

Dupler, Steven. "Metalheads Rock to Rap as Crossover Idiom Grows." *Billboard*, July 15, 1989, p. 1.

Dyson, Michael Eric. "Bum Rap." *The New York Times*, February 3, 1994, p. A21.

Ehrenreich, Barbara. ". . . Or Is It Creative Freedom?" *Time*, July 20, 1992, p. 89.

George, Nelson. *Buppies, B-Boys, Baps & Bohos*. New York: HarperCollins, 1992.

———. "Hyper as a Heart Attack." *The Village Voice*, August 25, 1987, p. 71.

George, Nelson, et al., eds. *Fresh: Hip Hop Don't Stop*. New York: Random House, 1985.

Glueck, Grace. "On Canvas, Yes, But Still Eyesores." *The New York Times*, December 25, 1983, Section 2, p. 20.

Goldberg, Danny. "A Song Is Just a Song." *Los Angeles Times*, February 7, 1990, p. B7.

Golden, Tim. "Raiders Chic: A Style, and Sinister Overtones." *The New York Times*, February 4, 1991.

Hartman, Susan. "It's Not Rap, Give a Clap, Call It 'Cheers'." *The New York Times*, August 11, 1988, p. C1.

Hedberg, Kathy. "A Mean, Violent Streak Runs Through Rap Music." Lewiston *Morning Tribune*, June 16, 1990, p. 12A.

Hess, Elizabeth. "Graffiti R.I.P." *The Village Voice*, December 22, 1987, p. 37.

"Hiphop Nation" [special section]. *The Village Voice*, January 19, 1988, p. 23.

Hitchens, Christopher. "Minority Report." *The Nation*, July 30/August 6, 1990, p. 120.

Howard, Susan. "Long Island's Sound." *Newsday Magazine*, April 22, 1990, p. 8.

"Jive Turkeys Revisited." *The New Republic*, March 19, 1990, p. 10.

Kristof, Nicholas D. "China: At the Boundaries of the Permissible." *The New York Times*, August 23, 1992, Section 2, p. 22.

Kuehl, Sheila James. "Ice-T Critics Miss the Rapper's Real Target." *Los Angeles Times*, July 27, 1992, p. F3.

Leland, John. "Rap and Race." *Newsweek*, June 29, 1992, p. 46.

Marcus, Greil. "Real Life Rock Top Ten: 2. Public Enemy." *The Village Voice*, October 17, 1989.

Marlowe, Ann. "Niggaz With Problems: N.W.A. Pull a Ho Move." *L.A. Weekly*, July 12–July 18, 1991, p. 59.

Marsh, Dave. "Hip Hop Gets a Bad Name." *Newsday*, June 19, 1990, p. 50.

Marsh, Dave and Phyllis Pollack. "Wanted for Attitude." *The Village Voice*, October 10, 1989, p. 33.

Maslin, Janet. "Making a Movie Take the Rap for the Violence It Attracts." *The New York Times*, January 22, 1992, p. C13.

Mills, David. "The Rap On 2 Live Crew." *The Washington Post*, June 17, 1990, p. G1.

———. "Five Percent Revolution: The Radical Manifesto of Muslim Rap." *The Washington Post*, January 6, 1991, "Sunday Show" section, p. 1.

Morales, Robert and Kyle Baker. "Old School Retirement Home: Where Every Day Is 'Back in the Day.' " *Vibe*, May 1994.

Neely, Kim. "Rockers Sound Off." *Rolling Stone*, August 9, 1990, p. 27.

Nelson, Havelock and Michael A. Gonzales. *Bring the Noise: A Guide to Rap Music and Hip Hop Culture*. New York: Crown, 1991.

Olson, Dale. "Diseuse Dietrich's Art Lives On in Modern Rap Music." *Daily Variety*, August 17, 1992.

Poulson-Bryant, Scott. "Dreaming America: Notes of a New Jack." *Spin*, May 1992, p. 72.

"Rap 'n' Roll." *Vanity Fair,* July 1993.

Reynolds, Simon. "Nasty Boys." *Melody Maker,* July 19, 1986, p. 26.

Rockwell, John. "France: Felicitous Rhymes, and Local Roots." *The New York Times,* August 23, 1992, Section 2, p. 23.

Rodriguez, Luis J. "Rappin' in the 'Hood: Rebel Radio." *The Nation,* August 12, 1991, p. 192.

Rohan, Brian. "Rapping Republicans in the U.K." *Irish Voice,* October 6, 1992, p. 37.

Ross, Sean. " 'No Rap' Slogan Rings Loud & Clear." *Billboard,* October 13, 1990, p. 12.

Rubin, Rick. "Rap Violence: Authorities Puzzled." *The Village Voice,* August 19, 1986, p. 70.

Samuels, David. "Yo! MTV Unwrapped." *Spin,* September 1991, p. 44.

Shocked, Michelle and Bart Bull. "L.A. Riots: Cartoons vs. Reality." *Billboard,* June 20, 1992, p. 1.

Simmons, Doug. "Gangsta Was the Case." *The Village Voice,* March 8, 1994, p. 63.

Smith, Danyel. "Dreaming America." *Spin,* November 1992.

Smith, R.J. "Public Enemy Quits?" *The Village Voice,* July 4, 1989, p .89.

Soocher, Stan. "As Sampling Suits Proliferate, Legal Guidelines Are Emerging." *The New York Law Journal,* May 1, 1992, p. 5.

Staples, Brent. "High on the Five." *The New York Times Magazine,* December 18, 1988, p. 18.

Stewart, Susan. "Rap Music May Offend, But It's Just Doing Its Job." *The Atlanta Journal and Constitution,* September 29, 1992, p. C1.

Stuart, Dan. "The Rap Against Rap at Black Radio." *Billboard,* December 24, 1988, p. R-8.

Tate, Greg. "Above and Beyond Rap's Decibels." *The New York Times,* March 6, 1994, Section 2, p. 1.

———. *Flyboy in the Buttermilk.* New York: Fireside, 1992.

Thompson, Robert Farris. "Hip-Hop 101." *Rolling Stone,* March 27, 1986, p. 95.

Toop, David. *Rap Attack 2.* Boston: Consortium Press, 1992.

Tucker, Bruce. "Tommy Boy Can CD Future." *Fast Company,* November 1993, p. 53.

Walser, Robert. "Clamor and Community: Rhythm, Rhyme, and Rhetoric in the Music of Public Enemy." *Ethnomusicology,* forthcoming.

Watrous, Peter. "It's Official: Rap Music Is in the Mainstream." *The New York Times*, May 16, 1988, p. C11.

"Who Stole the Soul? Whites As Hip-Hop Music Commentators." The San Francisco *Sun-Reporter*, December 16, 1992.

Acknowledgments

Grateful acknowledgment is made for the following:

Excerpt from *Yo, Hungry Wolf! A Nursery Rap* by David Vozar. Copyright © 1993 by David Vozar. Used by permission of Bantam Doubleday Dell Books for Young Readers.

Excerpt from *MC Squared #3* by Roland Laird, Jr., et al. © Posro Komics, Edison, New Jersey.

"What Is Hip-hop?" by Greg Tate. Used by permission of *Vibe* magazine and the author.

"Hip-hop History." Reprinted by permission of *The Source*.

"Word from the Motherland" by Khephra Burns. Used by permission of *Essence* and the author.

"The Rap on Hip-hop" by William Safire. Copyright © 1992 by The New York Times Company. Reprinted by permission.